The Sociology
of Housework

Also by Ann Oakley:

Woman's Work: The Housewife Past and Present

The Sociology of Housework

ANN OAKLEY

PANTHEON BOOKS
A Division of Random House, New York

Library of Congress Cataloging in Publication Data

Oakley, Ann.
    The Sociology of Housework.

    Includes bibliographical references and index.
    1. Women—Great Britain—Social conditions.
2. Feminism. 3. Home economics. I. Title.
HQ1597.015 1975 301.41′2 75-4668
ISBN 0-394-49774-0
ISBN 0-394-73088-7 pbk.

Manufactured in the United States of America

4689753

Contents

Note on Tables and Tests of Significance

A chi-square test of significance has been carried out on many of the tables which appear in the following pages. For 2 x 3 tables, the precise value of x^2 was calculated, and the probability level for that value taken from R. A. Fisher and F. Yates *Statistical Tables for Biological, Agricultural and Medical Research* London: Oliver and Boyd (1963). With the exception of a small number of tables on which it was thought helpful to work out the exact level of significance, the value of x^2 was not calculated for 2 x 2 tables, but was derived from D. J. Finney, R. Latscha, B. M. Bennett and P. Hsu *Tables for Testing Significance in a 2 x 2 Contingency Table* Cambridge: University Press (1963). In tables where no value of x^2 is given, the probability level comes from this source.

Percentages are given in the tables without decimal points, and are rounded up.

Preface and Acknowledgements

The major part of this book is based on a research study of women's attitudes to housework, and uses material obtained in a series of interviews with London housewives. The study was undertaken for a doctoral dissertation at the University of London.

When I first wrote up the research material in book form, it was part of a larger work on the position of women as housewives. This work acquired quite unwieldy proportions and consequently was split into two books. Chapters on the organization of work and family life in non-industrialized cultures, the historical evolution of the housewife role, the general situation of women in modern industrial society, and ideological aspects of women's domesticity, are now published in a separate volume (Ann Oakley, *Woman's Work,* Pantheon, 1974). Readers might like to consult this for background and contextual reading.

In a sense, I had in mind two audiences while writing *The Sociology of Housework.* One audience is composed of sociologists; the other of people who have a general interest in the housewife's situation, but no particular knowledge of sociology. For this latter group, I have tried to make the material as intelligible and as straightforward as possible. Nevertheless, non-sociological readers may find it easier to omit Chapters 1 and 2 (which deal with sexism in sociology and methodological aspects of the study respectively) and proceed straight to Chapter 3. A word should also be said about the relevance of the study to audiences outside Britain. Although the sample on which the research is based is a British one, the housewife's situation is not fundamentally different in other modern industrialized societies.

ix

Thus American readers, for example, will find themselves familiar with many aspects of the scene described in the following chapters. The discussion of the bias against women in sociology which occupies Chapter 1, but is thematic to the whole book, is, of course, not limited to any one country.

In carrying out the research and writing the book I have depended on help and advice from numerous sources. I am grateful to the Social Science Research Council, which provided financial aid in the form of a postgraduate studentship. I would like to thank George W. Brown of Bedford College for help, advice and encouragement throughout; Anna Davin, Juliet Mitchell and Jan and Ray Pahl for reading various drafts of the manuscript; Tessa Blackstone for reading Chapter 1; David Martin (of Martin Robertson) and Jane Routh for their valuable criticism and help with the final stages of the book's production; and Robin Oakley, for every possible kind of help from the beginning to the end. None of these people does, of course, bear any particular responsibility for the end product. I should also like to take this opportunity of thanking friends who have helped with my own domestic work and with the care of my children over the past four years. Last, but by no means least, I owe a large debt of gratitude to the housewives who generously allowed me to interview them.

The Sociology
of Housework

1 The Invisible Woman: Sexism in Sociology

Who really gives a damn about reading studies, particularly feminist studies, about women, their dilemmas, their problems, their attempts at solution? [1]

A growing body of literature is currently drawing attention to the disadvantaged position of women in society today. Despite legal changes, smaller families and improved educational and employment opportunities over the last century or so, marked inequalities remain between the social and economic roles of men and women. The revival of organized feminism, in the form of the women's liberation movement, has attached a powerful polemic to these differences. It seems that the situation we are witnessing is neither the effect of a biological underpinning of sex roles,[2] nor can it simply be seen as the persistence of institutional inequalities. Discrimination against women is still, of course, to be found in law, and it is codified in other institutional practices determining sex-differentiated rights and opportunities;[3] but a more fundamental source of discrimination lies in the realm of social attitudes and beliefs. The reality of women's situation is daily constructed out of these attitudes: women are, in part, the way they are because of the way they are thought to be.

Thus one finds discrimination against women not only in society at large, but in the academic domain. This is particularly true of sociology, the 'science' that studies social reality. The counterpart to discrimination against women in society is sexism in sociology. In much sociology women as a social group are invisible or inadequately represented: they take the insubstantial form of ghosts, shadows or stereotyped characters. This issue of

1

sexism has a direct relevance to the main topic of this book: a survey of housewives and their attitudes to housework which I carried out in London in 1971. The conventional sociological approach to housework could be termed 'sexist': it has treated housework merely as an aspect of the feminine role in the family – as a part of women's role in marriage, or as a dimension of child-rearing – not as a work role. The study of housework as *work* is a topic entirely missing from sociology. My survey departs from sociological tradition and takes a new approach to women's domestic situation by looking at housework as a job and seeing it as work, analogous to any other kind of work in modern society. The discrepancy between this approach and the implicit assumption of much sociological writing on women derives from the basically sexist orientation of the discipline to date. In this introductory chapter I therefore want to connect the two themes of the sociological neglect of housework, and the wider issue of the bias against women in sociology as a whole.

Sociology is sexist because it is male-oriented. By 'male-oriented' I mean that it exhibits a focus on, or a direction towards, the interests and activities of men in a gender-differentiated society. The social situations of men and women today are structurally and ideologically discrepant, and the dominant value-system of modern industrialized societies assigns greater importance and prestige to masculine than to feminine roles.[4] This bias is reflected within sociology, which tends to adopt the values of the wider society.[5] Attempts at 'objectivity' – a major premise of the sociological method – may reduce many obvious biases, but they do not seem to have affected the deeply ingrained bias of sexism.

The question of sexism raises the question of feminism. Is not feminism just as much of a bias as sexism? To answer this question it must be noted that in sociology (and elsewhere) a feminist perspective appears to be polemical because it runs counter to the accepted male-oriented viewpoint – a viewpoint which is rarely explicitly articulated. The word 'feminist', like the words 'sexist', 'male-biased', or 'male chauvinist', carries heavy polemical implications. Although these are highly political words, we use them because they are the only available ones: conceptually the area of gender-differentiation in sociology is very poorly developed. For these reasons feminist values stand out like a sore thumb. Conventional male-oriented values are buried in the very foundations of sociology and have to be dug up to be seen (but not believed). Wright Mills talks of 'biases' rather than 'orientations' or 'perspectives', but his point stands:

> My biases are of course no more or less biases than those I am going to examine. Let those who do not care for mine use their rejections of them to make their own as explicit and as acknowledged as I am going to try to make mine.[6]

Essentially feminism is a perspective rather than a particular set of prescriptive values. A feminist perspective consists of keeping in the forefront of one's mind the life-styles, activities and interests of more than half of humanity – women. Many different arguments or blueprints for a sexually egalitarian society can be, and have been, constructed on this basis. Institutional sex equality,[7] the overthrow of the capitalist system,[8] the abolition of the family, and the revamping of our entire ideology pertaining to gender roles,[9] have been variously identified as prerequisites for women's 'liberation'. These are all different strands of thought, but their common focus is on making visible the invisible: bringing women 'out from under' into the twin spheres of social reality and cultural belief-systems.

This chapter is not a systematic analysis of the areas of women's invisibility in sociology; rather, it is an attempt to suggest some of the areas and ways in which it is manifested, some of the reasons why it occurs, and why, from the point of view of sociology (and women) it matters.

1 MANIFESTATIONS

The concealment of women runs right through sociology. It extends from the classification of subject-areas and the definition of concepts through the topics and methods of empirical research to the construction of models and theory generally.

The broad subject-divisions current in modern sociology appear, at first sight, to be eminently logical and non-sexist. Social stratification, political institutions, religion, education, deviance, the sociology of industry and work, the family and marriage, and so on: these are, surely, just descriptions of different areas of human social life. To examine whether or not this is so one needs to ask three questions. First, to what extent are the experiences of women *actually* represented in the study of these life-areas; secondly, how does this representation compare with the empirical role of women in social life; and, lastly, do the subject categorizations *themselves* make sense from the perspective of women's particular situation? These represent different criteria of visibility. The position of women as subjects in sociology may give a distorted impression of social reality. Or the experiences and social importance of women may be particularly misrepresented through the need to fit them into predefined male-oriented sociological categories. This last criterion is more problematic than the other two. Male-orientation may so colour the organization of sociology as a discipline that the invisibility of women is a structural weakness, rather than simply a superficial flaw. The male focus, incorporated into the definition of subject-areas, reduces women to a side-issue from the start. For example, a major preoccupation of sociologists has been with the cohesive effect of directive institutions through which power is exercised – the law, political systems, etc. These are male-dominated arenas; women have historically been tangential to them. The more sociology is concerned with such areas, the less it is, by definition, likely to include women within its frame of reference. The appropriate analogy for the structural weakness of sociology in this respect is the social reality sociologists study: sexism is not merely a question of institutional discrimination against women, but the schema of underlying values is also implicated.

Taking the major subject-areas of sociology, such as those listed above, it should in theory be possible to chart the areas in which women are most invisible. The procedure would be to identify discrepancies between the extent to which women are studied in each subject-area, and their actual role in the sphere of social life that the subject-category represents. For example, in the case of housework the omission of this topic from both family sociology and the sociology of work clearly conveys a distorted impression of women's situation. No account is taken of the importance of housework to women, either in terms of the simple amount of time women spend on domestic-care activities, or in terms of the personal meaning of housework to women (which may, of course, vary with different social locations). Using such a critical procedure, two indices could be constructed: an index of women's *sociological visibility* and an index of their *social presence*. Lack of correspondence between the two indices would suggest a failure of sociology to take into account women's experience. It might also point to more appropriate ways of re-classifying subject areas so that the perspectives of both genders are represented. The value of taking this kind of critical stance to the subject-classifications of sociology can be illustrated by taking a brief look at five areas: deviance, social stratification, power, the family and marriage, and industry and work.

(a) Deviance

Patterns of deviance in women are 'lonely, uncharted seas'[10] of human behaviour. Very little of the empirical data collected by sociologists relates to women and, of that which does, a main focus concerns sexual offences. Theories of deviance may include some passing reference to women, but interpretations of female behaviour are uncomfortably subsumed under the umbrella of explanations geared to the model of masculine behaviour.[11] Even where there is some attempt to account for female/male differences in deviant behaviour, the explanation may simply resort to the simplistic notion that sex roles are generally differentiated.[12] One reason why women are under-represented in this area is undoubtedly that the sociology of deviance has, until recently, concentrated specifically on *criminal* behaviour. Since far fewer females than males commit crimes, this preoccupation has been one main source of sexism.

There is no doubt that women *are* less deviant than men, according to various criteria such as official crime statistics, suicide figures, data on vagrancy, and so on. Eight or nine men are convicted of crimes for every single female.[13] Male suicides generally exceed female suicides (although the ratio is reversed for attempted suicide).[14] Some of this lower deviance in women may be an artifact of the definition or administration of the law. There are some crimes for which women cannot be convicted (e.g. homosexuality, rape); courts may deal more leniently with females, and a proportion of female crime may remain undetected because the police are less sensitive to it. Nevertheless, even allowing for these factors, women are almost certainly more conformist than men.

Cultural notions of feminine behaviour probably act to conceal deviance in women. The Wolfenden Committee, reporting on prostitution in Britain, recommended measures to reduce its social visibility (although allowing the phenomenon itself to persist). This 'sweeping under the carpet' syndrome as applied to female deviance reflects the congruency of the sociologist's values with those of the wider society.

But the invisibility of women in the sociology of deviance is not simply a mirror of reality. Women's social presence in this area, as shown by crime statistics, is far greater than their sociological visibility would suggest. For example, in 1970 there were 15,623 occasions on which British women aged between seventeen and twenty were found guilty in court. Over the decade from 1960 to 1970 the rate of all offences committed by females in this age group doubled, while the comparable male rate increased by less than a half.[15] These facts highlight the substantial and increasing importance of female deviance. Moreover there is a well-established pattern of gender-differentiated criminal behaviour. Female shoplifting offences exceed those of men, but women commit only a small percentage of sexual crimes and crimes of violence.[16] The female offender is characteristically older than her male counterpart. Females are less likely to be juvenile delinquents, and sexual promiscuity is the female adolescent behaviour-pattern which is most liable to merit the attention of the authorities. The feminine pattern of crime has the uniformity and degree of constancy which usually attracts the attention of sociologists, yet despite the fact that the sex difference far outweighs any other variable associated with criminal behaviour,

No one seems to have any idea why; but hardly anyone seems to have thought it worth while to try to find out . . . While there have been a few studies of women offenders, investigators have generally looked upon the difference between masculine and feminine criminality merely as a reason for eliminating female subjects from their researches on the ground that they provide insufficient material. Whether this insufficiency reflects a genuine difference in feminine propensity to crime, or merely the superior skill with which female lawbreakers elude detection, and how this difference is related to factors in the training and education of girls which they do not share with their brothers – these questions remain unanswered and indeed unasked.[17]

The situation is a little better today than it was when Barbara Wootton wrote these words fifteen years ago in *Social Science and Social Pathology*. Shoplifting,[18] undetected female crime [19] and the social interior of women's prisons [20] are no longer completely uncharted territories; we know more about the career of the prostitute [21] and about the characteristics of delinquency in girls.[22] However there has still been no systematic attempt to relate female deviancy to women's situation.[23] The 'sexual' interpretation looms large but is inadequate in explaining the large category of female crime which consists of property offences. Since sociologists of deviance are interested in why people become deviant and/or perpetrate criminal acts, it is obviously important to locate the deviant, whether male or female, squarely within the social context in which he or she becomes deviant. This in turn requires a thorough knowledge of the customary socialization and life-styles of non-deviant males and females. But the old and peculiar theory that female delinquency is less 'versatile' than male delinquency is still used to dismiss it.[24] (If female delinquency is less versatile than the male variety, it is also more specialized, but this habit of describing sex differences in terms of women being deficient in masculine characteristics rather than vice versa is common.)

Aside from the question of their own delinquency/criminality, there is the important question of women's influence over masculine patterns of criminal and delinquent behaviour. To what extent do girls act as brakes on, or motivators of, delinquent behaviour in masculine adolescent gang-culture, for example? This question has not been taken up in any serious way. Girls may form a small part of the whole complex of gang behaviour, but the evidence presented in favour of such an interpretation is often very thin. David Downes in *The Delinquent Solution* refers to a study of Chicago gangs carried out thirty years previously for support on this point.[25] He also asserts, although giving no evidence for the claim, that 'the delinquent's girl is a force for conforming behaviour, as opposed to acting as provocateur for delinquent activity'.[26] This is fairly representative of the treatment of the sex difference in the deviancy literature. No study looks systematically either at the role of girls vis-à-vis masculine delinquency, or at the possible importance of girls' groups in female deviancy. Recent research on adolescent girls in South Wales [27] indicates that patterns of social relationships in girls do differ from those of boys; in particular, the 'best friend' phenomenon seems more important. As this researcher points out, the backdrop to women's invisibility in the deviancy literature is the lack of attention paid to girls in sociological studies of adolescence. Quite simply, a sociology of adolescent boys exists, while a sociology of adolescent girls does not.

A major way in which women *are* represented in the study of deviance is through the theory of 'feminine identification', which is a common one in explanations of delinquency and criminality. [28] The relative absence of the husband-father from modern family life supposedly leads boys to over-identify with their mothers, so that in adolescence 'compulsive masculinity' develops as a protest against femininity. Women also appear as 'invisible deviants' supposedly 'causing' delinquency through going out to work. [29] Such theories at least attempt to cope with the reality of the female presence, even if they do not do so accurately.

Finally, does the traditional definition of deviance make sense from a female perspective? Perhaps the rejection of marriage and the espousal of a profession represents a 'deviant career' for women, or perhaps the phenomenon of the obsessive, houseproud housewife could be usefully seen as a form of gender role-related deviance. [30] The male-orientation of the deviancy literature is almost certain to have precluded the study of certain patterns of behaviour which constitute deviant ways of behaving for the female half of the population. If the contention of Pollak [31] and others is correct that the roles of women reduce the public display of deviance, then it is indeed in such 'private' areas that one would expect female forms of deviance to be located.

(b) Social Stratification

In social stratification theory and its application in research a number of assumptions made about the role of women serve to guarantee their invisibility. [32] These assumptions make up a set of inter-related hypotheses about the processes and criteria of

class membership. They are theoretically testable, but in practice remain untested. Three main ones are:
1 the family is the unit of stratification;
2 the social position of the family is determined by the status of the man in it;
3 only in rare circumstances is the social position of women not determined by that of the men to whom they are attached by marriage or family of origin.

The first of these is the lynchpin of the argument. One can offer three principle objections to it, which constitute general criticisms of stratification theory, but relate specifically to the issue of whether women's situation is adequately represented in the theory (or its practice in research). Firstly, not everybody lives in a family. In the US Census data for 1970, more than one in ten of the adult population is an 'unattached individual';[33] in the British Census data for 1966, about one in twelve of the population do not live in families.[34] A second objection is that stratification theory rests on the assumption of a 'normal' unit of male, female and child/children in which the father is the bread-winner. How normal is this? American estimates put the number of family households headed by a female, or by a male who is unemployed or in part-time work only, at two out of five.[35] Fifty-eight per cent of all British households are not of the nuclear family type according to 1966 data, and one in twenty of all households is a single-parent family.[36] Clearly, therefore, there are large numbers of people whose life-styles do not connect with the dictum that 'the family is the unit of stratification'.

Thirdly, while members of the same family are held to share identical degrees of status, privilege, power and wealth, simply by virtue of their common membership of this unit, differences of role, position and status within the family are not themselves considered to be criteria of stratification. This implies (a) that females have no resources of their own, and (b) that the family is an entirely symmetrical status structure. Both these implications are false. Apart from the question of wealth, married women have personal resources of education and sometimes occupational training: many are also employed during their marriages and are in receipt of income and status from this source. The assumption that women's own resources become inoperative on marriage means that abrupt alterations to the class structure are liable to occur every time someone gets married. An occupationally based class categorization of married women would put many in a different class from their husbands. For example, the British 1971 Sample Census data give the following picture:

Table 1.1 Married couples with both partners economically active, by social class of husband and wife

Husband's social class	Percentage of wives whose social class is different from husbands
I	93.8
II	66.2
III non-manual	48.7
III manual	87.8
IV	63.5
V	77.6

(Adapted from 1971 Census, one per cent sample, Summary Tables, Great Britain, Table 36.)

The implication of such substantial discrepancies cannot simply be ignored.

On the status dimension, husband-wife equality cannot merely be assumed either. Haavio-Mannila set out to test the assumption that wives share the same status ranking as their husbands.[37] Some of her findings are set out in Table 1.2 below; this compares the ranks of men and women employed in certain occupations with the ranks assigned by a sample of respondents to the wives of men in these occupations. The data suggest that gender role is influential. Women are generally ranked lower than men, and wives lowest of all. The conclusion that women participate unequally in their husbands' status is congruent with empirical data on the social, economic and legal treatment of married women. For example, 'reflected' status is insufficient qualification for married women entering into hire-purchase agreements on their own; there is discrimination here, as in the area of credit generally. Married women are treated as dependents by the income tax system, whatever their actual economic resources and social situation.[38]

Table 1.2   Mean ranks of male and female representatives of modern occupational groups, and wives of men in these groups. Ranks ordered on an 18-point scale.

	Male	Female	Wife
2.4 Male architect	1		
2.8 Male psychologist	2		
3.7 Female architect		1	
4.2 Female psychologist		2	
6.6 Male advertising agency secretary	3		
7.2 Female advertising agency secretary		3	
8.9 Male student	4		
8.9 Wife of architect			1
9.3 Wife of psychologist			2
9.4 Female student		4	
10.6 Male furniture salesman	5		
11.6 Female furniture saleswoman		5	
12.8 Wife of advertising agency secretary			3
13.1 Male office messenger	6		
13.5 Wife of student			4
13.9 Female office messenger		6	
15.1 Wife of furniture salesman			5
16.3 Office messenger's wife			6

(*Data from Haavio-Mannila 1969, Table 6.*)

These are signs that the ranking of 'wife' or 'housewife' is low relative to other occupations – signs which indicate that there may be a measure of agreement in society generally about the status of wife (such agreement being a crucial determinant of social prestige hierarchies).[39] If this were so, then an incorporation of this rank into stratification theory would give rise to a more accurate picture of women's position in the class structure, and it would increase the validity of stratification measures. A second possibility is that social ranking of wife or housewife roles varies with different socio-economic contexts. As Acker puts it:

> . . . the position of upper-class housewife may be much more highly valued in the overall structure than the position of lower-class housewife. It may be that the valuation of this position rises as its functions become more symbolic and less utilitarian. Or, to put it another way, the value may rise as functions become centred more around consumption and less around productive activities.[40]

These criticisms of stratification theory derive from the known importance of gender as a criterion of social differentiation in modern society. Sociologists have paid very little attention to the significance of gender in this context – much less attention than has, for example, been paid to age or ethnicity. Gender differentiates; it may also stratify – that is, the attributes of femininity and masculinity may be systematically ranked differently.[41] Although there are scattered suggestions in the stratification literature that gender forms a criterion of stratification,[42] such a statement tends to be either treated frivolously, or rebutted by a neat process of tautological argument. Hence (to take the former method of dismissal first) Randall Collins' account of 'A Conflict Theory of Sexual Stratification' claims that stratification by gender is based on 'sexual property' – the notion of exclusive sexual rights.[43] Men are bigger and sexier than women; every encounter between them is a sexual encounter, the only important market is the sexual market, and therefore women's resources, life-styles and class position are ultimately determined by the 'biological facts' of female sexual attractiveness and male sexual aggression. The argument is frivolous firstly because conceptually it is full of elementary mistakes, the primary one being the equation of 'sexuality' with 'gender'. This is a common confusion and accounts for many weak arguments in sociology and elsewhere. Social classification as masculine or feminine (gender) is not the same as biological maleness or femaleness, nor is 'sexuality' a synonym for it.[44] In other words, relationships between the sexes are not necessarily sexual relationships. Sexuality may be a component in stratification by gender but it cannot be assumed *a priori* by a process of projection in which the male sociologist, himself accustomed to thinking of women in these terms, imposes his own proclivities and preoccupations on the data he is analysing. Secondly, Collins' argument is deficient on the level of empirical evidence. For example, the description of different sexual stratification systems, on which the theory rests, makes an appalling number of generalizations which can be falsified by a random search through the ethnographic literature.[45]

In *Class Inequality and Political Order*, Frank Parkin unwittingly provides an illustration of how stratification by gender can be tautologically argued away.[46] The steps in his argument are summarized below.

1   The family is the unit of the class system: hence people are wrong in saying that sex or gender stratification exists.

2   Women are certainly oppressed, but these sex-based in-equalities do not constitute a stratification system: for most women social and economic rewards are determined by the position of the male head of the family.

3   Only if the disabilities associated with female status were 'felt' to over-ride class differences would sex/gender represent an important dimension of stratification.

4   Women see themselves as members of a kin group rather than as women.

5   Because the major unit of reward is the family, most women do not feel that their interests conflict with those of men.

6   Therefore gender is not the basis of a stratification system.

This is a classic case of an argument which purports to take into account the female point of view, but which fails because the reference is merely token. Parkin asserts that only if women see themselves in non-family terms is stratification by gender meaningful, but he presents no *evidence* as to what women actually feel in relation to their family or class position. He simply asserts that their perceptions are congruent with his own view that the family is the important unit.

Women's role and position in the social stratification system exceed, and are possibly very different from, the secondary and vicarious role they are assigned in the sociology of stratification Even in 'family' stratification the role of women is hidden. The relevant questions which sociologists fail to ask include: to what extent do housewives influence family status-rankings through their consumption or general housekeeping behaviour? Does a married woman's adherence to stereotyped ideals of 'feminine' behaviour in dress, appearance and so forth, have any influence on social perceptions of her family's status?[47] How far do women determine the occupational positions and behaviour of their husbands? How is a family's social ranking affected by both husband and wife in a paid job or career?

This kind of amendment to traditional stratification analysis would still, of course, leave standing the major objections to it. In the end there has to be some way of restructuring the mode of

analysis to take account both of gender differences in role, status
and resources within the family, and also outside it. This is a
major task, but its importance is affirmed by the attention
feminists in general, and Marxist-feminists in particular, are
giving to the problem of women's place in the class system.[48]

(c) Power

The phenomenon of power is closely allied with that of stratification. Rather than examining the visibility of women in all the
various types of sociological analyses of power, I am going
instead simply to draw attention to an area in which the un-
doubted social power of women has not been considered at all.

While occupancy of the traditional wife/mother/housewife
constellation of roles – the manner in which much sociology
represents women – is correlated with certain types of powerless-
ness, it also has its own avenues of influence. For example, since
women are the main socializers of children, they have an
enormous capacity to affect patterns of personality and
behaviour. The incidence and patterning of illness among
members of a family is interlocked with the emotional interior
of the family: thus another logical corollary of women's pivotal
position in this unit is their capacity to affect not only health,
but ill-health.[49]

Women have power as housewives, wives and mothers, and
as members of the community. As the 'degree of control a person
or a collectivity of people exercises over the actions of others' [50]
the sociological examination of power is conventionally linked
with male-oriented stratification analysis, and with the analysis of
formal institutions such as government. This line of thinking
presupposes that there is only one kind of power. Attention is
thereby diverted from another variety: informal or unarticulated
power. This kind is more often exercised in private than in
public places, the concept of 'legitimate authority' tends to be
irrelevant to it, and it is less visible and less easily amenable to
sociological analysis. A distinction proposed by Peter Worsley
between two kinds of politics is relevant here. 'Politics I' is concerned with 'the exercise of constraint in any relationship . . .
Looked at this way, there is no such thing as a special kind of
behaviour called "political"; there is only a political dimension

to behaviour . . .' [51] The field of 'Politics II' is much narrower. It is concerned with the machinery of government, state and party political administration.

An example of the difficulties associated with the analysis of informal power – the political dimension to behaviour – in the case of women is given in a footnote to Katz and Lazarsfeld's study of *Personal Influence*:

> In the study of voting behaviour during a presidential campaign, it was found that while wives frequently referred to discussions with their husbands, the latter rarely returned the compliment. The husbands apparently did not feel that they were 'discussing' politics with their wives. Rather, they were telling their wives what politics was all about.[52]

Were the women influencing the voting choices of their husbands or not? Katz and Lazarsfeld's own study delineates the crucial role of women in the shaping of everyday decisions to do with consumption patterns, fashions, public affairs and cinema attendances in a mid-western American community. Female influence was greatest in consumer decisions, and least in public affairs (although, as in the above example of voting choices, the researchers say that the latter finding may be due to the men's unwillingness to admit to having serious political discussions with women).

Katz and Lazarsfeld found 'gregariousness' to be an important factor associated with the role of women in the formation of public opinion. Gossip, defined as 'idle, unconstrained talk especially about persons or social incidents' [53] is a function of many gregarious rituals. As a means of controlling other people's behaviour, it meets the essential criterion of power, but is largely unanalysed. (According to Worsley the associated notion of a 'pressure group' forms the bridge between formal and informal politics.) British and American community studies give the phenomenon of gossip some attention, but there is, so far as I know, no systematic study of gossip as a form of unarticulated female power.[54] While both sexes gossip, the literature suggests that they gossip differently.[55] Where opportunities for controlling situations and events in a more organized sense are constricted – as in the case of women at home – it is logical to assume that power to exert control through gossip becomes relatively more important.

Gossip has received some attention in anthropology. According to Max Gluckman, gossip and scandal are 'among the most important societal and cultural phenomena we are called upon to analyse'.[56] Although Gluckman does not consider the variable of gender, he describes some of the functions of gossip: the unification and affirmation of community values, the control of aspiring individuals and cliques within society, the selection of leaders, the maintenance of group exclusiveness. Gossip may not be a female prerogative, but it certainly is so in the social stereotype of women. For example

> Few would dispute that women excel at gossiping . . . In the seemingly endless, and to male ears repetitive, chatter that goes on among women . . . a massive and encyclopaedic confidence is built up in the gossipers . . . gossip serves exactly the same grooming functions for the women as poker for the men . . . As gossip is to ladies and gambling to gentlemen, flirting is to both together.[57]

There are intimate ideological connections between women's gossip on the one hand and sorcery and witchcraft on the other. Gluckman quotes one example of this from the ethnographic literature, an analysis of African village life in which gossiping between one lineage and another is believed to introduce a risk of sorcery. The fights of women (held to be the main culprits) who take their grumbles to outsiders provide an opportunity for these outsiders to bewitch the entire lineage. Another example, much closer to home, relates to the persecution of witches in pre-industrial Britain. A cursory glance at the literature in this field reveals the importance of suspicions concerning gossiping groups of women.[58] Witches were also often midwives and healers, and it is interesting that their persecution coincided with the beginning of a 'takeover' process in which the (predominantly) male medical profession acquired control over the care of women in childbirth – an area in which women were originally autonomous. In other words, one form of power was challenging another.[59]

(d) The Family

If women have no place of their own in much of sociology, they are firmly in possession of one haven: the family. In the family women 'come into their own'; they *are* the family. By far the largest segment of sociological literature concerning women is focused on their roles as wives, mothers and housewives – but not on the housewife's role as *houseworker*. Major topics in this literature are marital happiness, the division of labour and the general patterning of husband-wife roles; the combination of women's employment with marriage, and its consequences for husband-wife and mother-child relationships; the inter-relationships between the nuclear family and the wider kinship system; and the 'captive wife' syndrome – the socially isolated situation of women with young children. These topics are often looked at in an historical context: changes in the patterning of family life with industrialization and urbanization are examined. The general consensus of opinion among sociologists is that, compared with the state of affairs in the nineteenth century, the modern marriage relationship is happier, more egalitarian, more important, and therefore certainly more stressful.[60] Disputes wage over the issue of whether or not nuclear families today are isolated from their kin.[61] It seems to be generally agreed that young mothers run a far higher risk of isolation and loneliness than their Victorian counterparts.[62]

Where are women in all this? They appear to occupy the centre of the stage, but in what guise? A favourite word is 'role', and the dramaturgical metaphor is highly appropriate. In family and marriage literature women are entirely encapsulated within the feminine role. The psychoanalytic view has been very influential, leading to an implicit definition of women as wives and mothers to the virtual exclusion of any other life-area. In addition the literature has a definite 'social problem' orientation, which is shown most clearly in the vast number of studies of the 'working mother'.[63] The focus on the child-rearing implications of women's employment has led to such detailed considerations as the relation between the employment status of mothers and their children's health,[64] and the possibility of an association between employment and the nutritional adequacy of pre-school children's diets.[65] The problem of disturbances in the traditional pattern of domesticated-wife servicing employed-husband is also implied. As one of the earliest studies in this field expressed it:

many people see it [the employment of women] as a challenge

to society, because it breaks with long-established patterns of
family life, and with the values and beliefs supporting them . . .
It involves two of the most intimate personal relationships,
that of husband to wife, and of parent to child . . .[66]

Almost none of this literature is woman-focused. While considering the advantages and disadvantages to other family members
of new patterns of domestic life, the consequences for the
woman are often omitted. 'Role conflict' is talked about, but
this is not necessarily quite the same thing.

None of these criticisms of course implies that marriage and
family life are not important to women today: indeed, the
evidence suggests that these areas of experience are still critical.
But do we know *how* critical? Where is a sociological account
of the relative importance attached to these areas in the totality
of women's experience?[67] Possibly the family and marriage are
areas in which sociological visibility exceeds social presence;
certainly the presence of men as fathers is not matched by an
equal visibility in the discipline.[68] A sign of the over-exposure of
women in this area is the low status of family and marriage
sociology: as a radical young female sociologist asked the
feminist-sociologist Alice Rossi in a moment of unguarded
chauvinism: 'how did you manage to get stuck in a low status
field like marriage and the family?'[69] The status of this area is
low, because the status of its subjects – women – is also low, and
because attitudes prevailing among sociologists towards the
position of women as an academic subject serve persistently to
trivialize its importance.

Another consideration is whether conceptual distinctions and
classifications in family and marriage sociology are appropriate
to a female perspective. In Chapter 4 I argue that the concept of
women's 'domesticity' which is used loosely in sociological
writing needs to be broken down into a number of more precise
concepts before much sense can be made of women's similarities/
differences on this dimension. Other, broader confusions also
hide under the umbrella of 'the family and marriage'. These are
the areas in which sexuality, reproduction, child-socialization
and housework are carried out, yet rarely is an adequate
distinction made between the four kinds of experience. Popular
idiom has it that the four themes are very imperfectly combined
in the family: 'children ruin a marriage', 'sex and family life

simply don't go together', and so forth. There is a need to make this kind of distinction in sociology also.

(e) Industry and Work

By comparison with marriage and family sociology, women are conspicuous for their absence as data in the sociology of industry and work. This is in striking contrast to the important role they play in the occupational structure: currently some thirty-six per cent of the labour force is female.[70] Despite this fact, studies of employment are almost wholly male-oriented. There is a notable paucity of studies analysing (from the viewpoint of work-attitudes) the occupations in which women workers have traditionally been concentrated – food and clothing manufacture, retail sales work, clerical work, teaching, nursing and domestic work.[71] The employment of women tends to be studied as a deviation from the norm – i.e. when combined with marriage. (The fact that this pattern is yearly becoming less of a deviation is brushed aside: in 1971 forty-three per cent of all married women in Britain were employed.)[72] Married women are asked 'why do you work?', a question whose equivalent in the study of men's work–attitudes is 'why aren't you working?' The invisibility of women in the sociology of work is guaranteed by the choice of predominantly masculine jobs in research design. For example, the automobile industry, described as 'the most intensively studied industrial situation'[73] has a largely male work force. Whatever the specific features of the occupations chosen for study, samples tend uniformly to be male, or mostly male: this fact is hidden through the use of titles which purport to be describing work in general and the worker irrespective of gender. Arthur Kornhauser's *Mental Health of the Industrial Worker,* Herzberg, Mausner and Snyderman's *The Motivation to Work,* Walker and Guest's *Man on the Assembly Line* and Hughes' *Men and Their Work* are examples. (In the latter two cases 'man' and 'men' are generic terms.) Theoretical or descriptive surveys not based on empirical research commonly make no reference to women at all, or allot them a specific section on 'work and the family' or some such title.[74]

Since women's place in the sociology of work is very much a secondary one, it follows that we do not have enough empirical data to determine the relative importance to women of their experiences in the occupational sector. Fragmented evidence suggests that questions about married women's reasons for taking jobs tap the normative tip of the iceberg – that women say they work for the money because this is the socially acceptable reason.[75] Yet the prevailing treatment of women workers defines them as a particular and different sub-group of the general category 'workers' (this parallels the role they are assigned in the study of deviance). Such an astigmatic view of course excludes them from the main focus of research. Robert Blauner in *Alienation and Freedom,* an analysis of job conditions in four factory technologies, provides an excellent example of this traditional approach. He dismisses the women who make up almost half the workers in the textile industry he studied as 'a major safety valve against the consequences of alienating work conditions'. The high concentration of women in jobs which are, in Blauner's words 'the least skilled, the most repetitive, and the least free' makes it possible for men to have jobs with the opposite attributes. 'Women in the industry are not dissatisfied with such work' asserts Blauner, without giving his evidence for this statement: 'Work does not have the central importance and meaning in their lives that it does for men, since their most important roles are those of wives and mothers'.[76]

There may well be gender differences in attitudes to paid work, but these are not adequately demonstrated by the reiteration of the old adage that women's primary role is a family one. A study which adopts a critical attitude to this conventional axiom is Wild and Hill's analysis of job satisfaction and labour turnover among women in the electronics industry.[77] They show convincingly that the belief in women's capacity for boring and repetitive work is part of industrial folklore: if it were true, turnover rates should be no higher in industries which offer such work than in those where the work is more intrinsically interesting. However, this is not so. In the electronics industry that Wild and Hill studied particularly, female turnover rates showed a high relationship with job satisfaction/dissatisfaction: many women, like many men, express a need for personally satisfying work and the failure to find it is often a reason for changing one's job.

These brief and incomplete excursions through five subject-territories of sociology provide some examples of how male-orientation may be manifested. In exposing this it is possible to begin to see how and where the female perspective might usefully be introduced. Other areas which call out to be critically re-evaluated in this way are methodology and theory. For the former, Jessie Bernard has suggested an underlying distinction between two types of procedure that reflects traditional gender stereotypes.[78] 'Feminine' methods such as participant observation, small-sample depth-interviewing, and concentration on qualitative rather than quantitative variables, have less academic prestige and acceptability than their 'masculine' counterparts. This deserves further consideration. So far as the theorizing and model-building enterprises of sociology are concerned, these also require some assessment with the two criteria of sociological visibility and social presence in mind. Some problems in stratification theory and the theory of deviance are mentioned above. In the section below I make some observations on male-orientation in functionalist theory.

2 REASONS

I propose three main reasons for the present bias against women in sociology; the nature of its origins, the sex of its practitioners, and the ideology of gender roles, borrowed from the wider society, which is reproduced uncritically within it.

(a) Origins

The nineteenth century in Euro-American culture was one of the historical periods in which women have been most oppressed. Institutionally, they were deprived of most individual freedoms, rights and responsibilities, and ideologically they were little more than chattels, slaves or decorative ornaments (depending on their class position). This was also the period in which the foundations of sociology were laid. The so-called 'founding fathers' (an appropriate phrase) lived and wrote in an eminently sexist era. Of five such founding fathers – Marx, Comte, Spencer, Durkheim and Weber – Marx (1818–83) and Weber (1864–1920) alone held what could be described as 'emancipated' views about women. Marx provided the bones of an analysis of marriage as female domestic slavery, although he was personally something of a rearguard romantic;[79] Weber argued for sex-equality within marriage.[80] Herbert Spencer (1820–1903) protested that marriage was an unequal institution, and that women should have equal rights of competition with men, but in his later writing he reversed this opinion and declared that 'if women comprehended all that is contained in the domestic sphere, they would ask no other'.[81] August Comte (1798–1857) was a doctrinaire sexist and his philosophy about women is most clearly shown in his utopian 'positivist scheme of social reconstruction'.[82] Every social class except women was to be ranked on a hierarchical scale of importance and specialization of function. Women were to be in charge of domestic morality, and their moral influence was to be ensured by the rule of indissoluble monogamous marriage. Ultimately, his view reduced to a belief in the constitutional inferiority of women, whose maturation Comte considered to have been arrested in childhood.

The perspective Durkheim (1858–1917) held on women was also shaped by a biological doctrine: women belonged 'naturally' in the family. His analysis of the structure of the modern con-jugal family was phrased solely from the point of view of the man. He regarded it as essential that men become more deeply committed to their work through the formation of professional/occupational groups, since for them an involvement in the family did not provide a sufficiently sound moral basis for continued existence: 'Men must gradually become attached to their occu-pational or professional life . . . In the hearts of men, professional duty must take over the place formerly occupied by domestic duty'.[83] Meanwhile, the family (as the province of women) would continue to be a centre of moral education and security.

This axiom was one that Durkheim carried out in his private life. Indeed, the intellectual achievements of these men rested in a personal way on the basis of women's domestic oppression. (The Webers' marriage is, to some extent, an exception here: Marianne Weber was a feminist and a writer in her own right. Of the five, Herbert Spencer never married.) It was said of Comte that 'the woman he chose as his wife was nothing more than a means for the immediate gratification of his crude sexuality'.[84] The prototype of many a wife, before and after, was Marx's wife Jenny, who dedicated her whole being to his life and his work. It was an entirely happy marriage. She loved, admired and trusted him and was, emotionally and intellectually, entirely dominated by him. He leaned on her unhesitatingly in all times of crisis and disaster, remained all his life proud of her beauty, her birth and her intelligence . . . In later years when they were reduced to penury, she displayed great moral heroism in preserving intact the framework of a family and a household, which alone enabled her husband to continue his work.[85]

Similarly, Durkheim's marriage

could not have been happier, both personally and in creating an atmosphere conducive to his work . . . the domestic ideal that is evident in his writings (the family being his favourite subject of study and lecturing) was most clearly represented by his own home life . . . his wife created for him the respectable and quiet familial existence which he considered the best guarantee of morality and of life. She removed from him every material care and frivolity . . .[86]

These comments probably portray accurately the role-segregation of Marx and Durkheim's marital relationships, but it is perhaps reasonable to question the assumption of female happiness they both make. Jenny Marx's life was at times appallingly wretched and difficult. Durkheim was a very austere man who led a rigidly timetabled existence and refused to talk to his family except at mealtimes.

Such points could be made repetitively. Domestic sexism does not guarantee sexism in public affairs, although one is often a symptom of the other. Both can be presumed to matter most when and where they are most influential – as in the charting of the interests, concerns and methods of analysis that make up a new academic discipline. The early sociologists established a number of traditions that have subsequently moulded the place of women in sociology. These include a biological reductionism applied to gender roles, a presumption that women belong in the family but hardly anywhere else, and a 'functionalist' analysis of the family and its connections with the rest of society. The American school of sociology had no less sexist beginnings. In particular Lester Ward and W. I. Thomas took over themes from Comte and Spencer and developed their own form of biological dogma and social prescription applied to women's place.[87] Their view of women as solutions to the Hobbesian problem of order repeated values dominant in

America in the early years of this century, according to which oppression by sex, colour or class could be justified in a laissez-faire, utilitarian philosophy of human relationships.

(b) A Male Profession

As Wright Mills observed in his critique, 'The Professional Ideology of Social Pathologists': 'If the members of an academic profession are recruited from similar social contexts and if their backgrounds and careers are relatively similar, there is a tendency for them to be uniformly set for some common perspective'.[88] This applies both to the origins of sociology and to the characteristics of its practitioners since the beginning. Gender was not a variable that Wright Mills considered in his analysis of the social backgrounds of social pathologists (thus indicating his own low level of awareness about such matters).[89] Systematic data on the sex of sociological personnel now exists. An American report, *The Status of Women in Sociology*,[90] documents the existence of tokenism – in eighty-five per cent of sociology departments there is at least one woman. It shows the pattern of the gender hierarchy – five per cent of full professors, sixteen per cent of assistant professors, but thirty per cent of lecturers in 1972 being female. It demonstrates the under-representation of women in sociological publications and in editorial positions. Similar inequalities are to be found in British sociology.[91] Such facts are highly relevant to the continuing message of sexism transmitted by all aspects of the discipline.

(c) The Ideology of Gender

'Perhaps the most enlightening part of the Committee's investigation was the discovery that many able sociologists . . . abandon the empirical stance and rely upon folk myth and stereotype'.[92] This observation from the American *Status of Women in Sociology* report draws attention to the underlying ideology of gender roles which is responsible for all the various manifestations of sexism. Ideology in this context may be defined as 'a set of closely related beliefs or ideas, or even attitudes characteristic of a group or community'.[93] This ideology relating to gender roles underpins the structure of sociology much as it does the structure of social life. But while the dominance of folk myth discussed above, for example, the 'sexual' and 'conformist' stereotype of women has acted against their presence in the about women in popular thinking is well documented,[94] no such critical stance has been taken to the persistence of these stereotypes in sociology itself. Implicit assumptions about how women do, and should, behave colour all subject-areas. In those study of deviance; a belief that the family is the only important vehicle of reward and realization for women has led to a distortion of their role in the stratification system; and an unspoken devaluation of female types of power as trivial and insignificant has led political sociology towards a one-sided examination of formal constraint–and authority-systems.

A multitude of *particular* inter-related notions about women may be identified as shaping research and theory in all areas of sociology, but a *general* set of axioms is responsible for the place of women in the two areas of family and marriage, and industry and work. The neglect of housework as a topic is also anchored in these axioms. They can be stated thus:

1 women belong in the family, while men belong 'at work';

2 therefore men work, while women do not work;

3 therefore housework is not a form of work.

The first two of these assumptions have been illustrated above. The third appears to be a deduction from the first two, but the syllogism is false. Its falsity hinges on the fictional nature of the dichotomy between 'family' and 'work' and on the meaning of the term 'work'. Although the work/family distinction expresses the separation between these two spheres of life brought about by industrialization, it does not follow that one is the world of men while the other is the world of women. Many women go out to work; many women (and some men) work in the home, but one would never guess the facts from this kind of statement:

> The adjustment of female workers to their jobs is often made more difficult by the peculiar problems of the employed woman who must divide her interests and attention between the *working world* and her *traditional role as a woman*. (Italics added)[95]

Confusions are compounded by the assertion of biological determinism:

> The situation confronting the woman in our society is somewhat different [from that of the man]. Because she alone has

the capacity to give birth to and nurse children, her primary function is seen as one of mother and homemaker . . . it is clear that *working* occupies a more important place in the lives of men than women. (Italics added)[96]

Both these quotations are representative of many studies in this field.

What is 'work'? According to one definition,[97] a work role has five properties. It requires the expenditure of energy; it permits a contribution to the production of goods or services; it defines patterns of social interaction; it provides social status for the worker, and, lastly, it brings in money. The only difference in this definition between employment work and housework is housework's lack of pay. But because work is not a component of the feminine stereotype housework lacks any conceptualization in sociology *as* work.

The 'dual role' concept which is in common currency validates the denial of housework's status as work. Again, the two worlds are work and home. Alva Myrdal and Viola Klein's *Women's Two Roles* was one of the first studies to adopt this concept: its focus is the position of women in the labour force and the problems of combining home and work. In this analysis housework is a side-issue.[98] The American habit of referring to housework as 'homemaking' neatly cements the ideological division between home and work. In turn this paves the way for another procedure which acts against the conceptualization of housework as work activity, and that is the confusion between the four words/roles housewife, wife, mother and woman. For example, Helen Lopata in her study *Occupation Housewife* discusses the 'life-cycle of role involvements', and says

> Although women state that they are tied down by the responsibility of small children, they also experience satisfaction with several aspects of their role [which role?]. In the first place, becoming a housewife impresses them by the very openness of the role [?] and by the freedom they now have from constraining supervision . . .[99]

Housewife and mother roles are synonymous in this quotation, although Lopata herself presents considerable evidence as to the differences and disjunctions between them. Hannah Gavron in *The Captive Wife* is aware of the political implications of the 'dual role' concept:

Women today are considered to have two choices – to work or to stay at home. This implies that staying at home does not involve work. Yet at a time when the rest of the industrialized world is moving towards a forty hour week, women, many of whom may work at least eighty hours per week, are encouraged to regard this as not being work.[100]

Yet Gavron's own chapter 'Mothers and Work' uses the term 'work' to mean employment work, not housework. In her five-page chapter on the running of the home she considers only two topics: financial arrangements between husband and wife, and the extent to which men share housework and the care of children. The women's own attitudes to, and perceptions of, housework are left unanalysed.

These are examples of the way even studies of women's domestic roles tacitly subscribe to the myth of feminine passivity. Although housework *is* work they say, we would have to turn the ideology of our culture on its head to analyse it in such a manner. The most serious consequence of this mystification is a failure to represent the meaning of housework to the actors (actresses) themselves. This point is expanded in the next chapter. Other consequences follow. The attitudes of women to work in the home are very likely to be related to other attitudes they hold – such as those to paid employment, to marriage, to child-socialization, to leisure activities and so on. But the failure to see housework in this way is endemic to sociology, and so these possible relationships have not been explored.

A way of seeing is a way of not seeing. One example is functionalist theory, a school of sociology which, as a distinct 'way of seeing', has had a pervasive influence. Other feminist critics have pointed out how functionalist theory effectively presumes that the domestic oppression of women is necessary for the stability of the social order.[101] Elsewhere, I have criticized functionalism as a myth of the division of labour by sex to which ethology and anthropology make their own contributions.[102] But functionalism also operates specifically to deny housework's status as work; indeed, one of its main premises is that the feminine role in the family is opposed to the masculine role precisely on this dimension. According to functionalist theorists, the role of 'task leader' in the family involves 'instrumental' activities such as decision-making, earning money and 'manipulating the external environment'; the role of 'sociometric star' carries 'expressive' duties such as the expression of emotional warmth and the integration of internal family relationships. Men perform an instrumental role, women an expressive one. Put in plain language, the women stay at home and provide *emotional* support while the men go out to work and provide *financial* support. The gender division is reducible to biology. According to Zelditch, 'a crucial reference point for differentiation in the family . . . lies in the division of organisms into lactating and nonlactating classes'.[103]

The distinction between the two kinds of role in functionalist theory is simply the stereotyped separation between women/home and men/work. The qualities of the feminine expressive role, as defined by Zelditch, Parsons and others, are directly opposed to the qualities of the housewife/houseworker role. For, to express warmth, to be constantly person-oriented and conciliatory, it is clearly 'necessary' that the housewife-wife-mother not be occupied with such highly instrumental tasks as cleaning the house, budgeting the housekeeping money, laundering the clothes, and throwing out the rubbish.

In functionalist theory, as in most family and marriage literature, women are over-visible. This is because the areas of women's greatest visibility in sociology tend also to contain examples of the most rampant sexism. The ideology of feminine passivity not only runs right through sociology, but is the cornerstone of that zone within it where women are least hidden. A correction of this distorted male-oriented perspective involves going back to women themselves and looking through their eyes at the occupation of housewife.

2 Description of Housework Study

Despite a reduction of gender differences in the occupational world in recent years, one occupational role remains entirely feminine: the role of housewife. No law bans men from this occupation, but the weight of economic, social and psychological pressures is against their entry into it. The equation of femaleness with housewifery is basic to the structure of modern society, and to the ideology of gender roles which pervades it.

About eighty-five per cent of all British women between the ages of sixteen and sixty-four are housewives, according to the findings of a national survey described by Audrey Hunt. The definition of who is, and who is not, a housewife is phrased in terms of *responsibility*: thus a housewife is 'the person, other than a domestic servant, who is responsible for most of the household duties (or for supervising a domestic servant who carries out these duties)'.[1] A housewife may be married or not, and she may or may not have a job outside the home. In Hunt's survey, nine out of ten non-employed women were housewives, but so were seven out of ten employed women. Thus, not only is the housewife role specifically a feminine role, it is also women's major occupational role today: the responsibility for running a home is one which is shared by the majority of all adult women.

This, then, is the main justification for a study of housework. It is a daily experience in the lives of most women, who in turn make up statistically the greater part of the population. Another reason for looking at women's attitudes to housework comes from surveys of gender differences in the areas of education and employment over the last few decades. These fields, in which

29

there has been a growing attempt to eradicate sex inequality, still show the persistence of women's domestic commitments as a barrier to equality.[2] This division between the life-styles of men and women is well documented, but little is known about the precise form or effect of housework attitudes.

The sociological neglect of housework was demonstrated in the last chapter. Because so little material exists, the study presented in this book was conceived as an exploratory, pilot survey. As Margaret Stacey observes in *Methods of Social Research*:

> Hypotheses which are worth testing can only be developed in areas about which a good deal is known, i.e. where a great deal of empirical field data has already been collected. Before this stage most research is of an exploratory nature . . . It is only after much empirical data has been collected and a series of simple relationships, close to reality, have been established, that either precise hypotheses can be enunciated for testing or theory derived inductively from empirical data.[3]

A first aim is to *describe* the housewife's work situation and the housewife's attitudes to housework. A second is to examine *patterns of satisfaction and dissatisfaction* with housework in relation to a number of variables, including social class, education, the division of labour in marriage, technical equipment, patterns of social interaction and so on. A third aim is to suggest possible *hypotheses* directed towards explaining differences between housewives in attitudes to housework and the housework situation.

The sample consisted of forty London housewives. All were aged between twenty and thirty at the time of interview, and all were mothers. They were selected from the medical records of two general practices (details of sample selection are described in Appendix I). The area of London remains unspecified, and the names of the women have, of course, been changed in order to preserve anonymity. The women were interviewed in early 1971 using the interview schedule reproduced in Appendix II; the interviews were tape-recorded and lasted on average about two hours. A number of 'ratings' of satisfaction and other aspects of the work situation were based on the interview responses and used in the analysis of data. These include: ratings of satisfaction/dissatisfaction with housework, child-care, marriage, employment work and life generally; an assessment of the women's level of identification with the housewife role, and the level of definition applied to housework standards and routines; an assessment of the marriage relationship as 'segregated' or 'joint' on the two dimensions of leisure activities and decision-making, and, lastly, an assessment of the husband's part in the division of labour as reported by his wife. All these ratings are discussed in relevant parts of the following chapters. Further information about their use is given in Appendix I.

A sample of forty is undoubtedly on the small side; most sociological research studies using empirical data obtain it from larger samples than this. What kind of universe does this small sample of forty women represent? Are generalizations from the sample population warranted? These questions are common reactions to the notion of a research study based on 'only' forty interviews. I will provide brief answers to them here, since the general relevance and acceptability of the findings presented in the rest of the book clearly depend on the methodological status of the sampling, data-gathering and measurement procedures used.

There is a widespread tendency in social science and in more popular discussions of opinion/attitude surveys to assume that a large sample provides some automatic guarantee of reliable results, while a small one promises unreliability. This misconception is based on a naive idea of what constitutes 'validity' and 'representativeness' in research procedure. Statistical representativeness is not, of course, assured simply by means of large numbers; a large sample, running into several hundreds or thousands may be selected in a way which makes it unrepresentative of the general population, while a small sample may, conversely, meet more precisely the criterion of representativeness. The classic example of large sample research involving an inadequate sampling frame is the *Literary Digest*'s attempt to forecast the results of the US presidential election in 1936. The sample was picked from telephone directories which did not cover the poorer segments of the electorate. C. A. Moser in *Survey Methods in Social Investigation* identifies three sources of bias in sample selection: (1) the use of a sampling frame which does not cover the population adequately, completely or accurately; (2) the use of a 'non-random' method of sampling, so that the selection of subjects is consciously or unconsciously affected by human judgement; and (3) the refusal to co-operate among some segments of the chosen population.[4] Non-response is liable to be more of a problem in the larger-sample surveys, particularly those using postal questionnaire methods. Even where the data is collected by trained interviewers, non-response probably remains a greater problem than with small samples, since the requirement of having a team of interviewers (rather than one or two) may result in a lower commitment to the goal of obtaining a high response rate. A response rate of seventy to ninety per cent is common in professional surveys involving large samples; for instance, the 1,928 individuals interviewed in the main sample of Young and Willmott's recent study of work and leisure in the London region represented seventy-three per cent of those chosen as being eligible.[5]

Lack of representativeness through inadequate sampling and high non-response rates are not the only sources of invalidity and unreliability, however. An equally crucial (though much less often discussed) area in which errors can arise is that relating to the interview itself – to the content of the schedule and 'the measurement and/or classification of the resulting data. Bias may creep in through the wording of questions (which may be ambiguous, unintelligible or suggestive of a particular answer), through the careless recording of answers, through the interviewer's (perhaps unwitting) influence over response-patterns and through a general failure of the interviewer to establish the kind of rapport with the respondent that enables him or her to give truthful answers on personal matters. The manner in which the interview data is subsequently classified and processed may lead to other kinds of distortion.

These problems in the collection of data, like the question of sample representativeness, are not endemic to large sample research, nor are they magically solved by the use of a smaller sample. On the other hand they are more likely to arise with larger samples simply on common sense grounds: the investigator's distance from the data is increased through the involvement of others (interviewers, research assistants, coders, etc) in data-gathering and processing, and possible occasions for the introduction of bias are thereby multiplied. Very careful training of all the research workers is needed to avoid the various pitfalls. In addition, the investigator must not make the (conscious or unconscious) assumption that the size of the sample makes careful attention to the wording of the interview unnecessary. The interview is a research instrument and the research findings are only valid if the questions 'get at' the areas the researcher claims (or assumes) they do.

What all this amounts to is a proviso that research based on samples of five hundred, a thousand, or more individuals should not be uncritically accepted as 'good' research while surveys using small samples, say a hundred or less, are dismissed as invalid. Careful attention needs to be paid to the aspects of research procedure mentioned above. The evaluation of the findings of any piece of research must also, of course, take into account its nature and aims. Is the research mainly descriptive? Is it hypothesis–testing? What claims does it make as to the universal applicability of its results? Every research study needs to be assessed on the criterion of whether it measures up to its own stated objectives.

For the goals of mapping out an area, describing a field, and connecting events, processes or characteristics which appear to go together, a sample of forty individuals is certainly adequate. This type of taxonomic approach may, perfectly appropriately, give rise to explanatory hypotheses,[6] and particular, well-defined hypotheses may also be tested with samples of this size. In *Theory and Methods of Social Research* Johan Galtung makes a useful distinction between a 'substantive' hypothesis 'which is about social reality and to be tested by means of the data' and a 'generalization' hypothesis 'which is about the data'.[7] The question as to whether a specific hypothesis is confirmed or not confirmed by the data is in principle different from the issue of whether the research findings can be generalized to a wider population. For testing substantive hypotheses Galtung considers a sample of forty perfectly acceptable (the criterion being the minimum number of cases required for statistical tests to be applicable). On the other hand, to be on the safe side for the purposes of *generalization,* a sample size of around eight hundred individuals is needed.

Important contributions to sociological knowledge have been made using data from small samples. For instance, Elizabeth Bott's influential study *Family and Social Network*[8] is based on interviews with twenty couples. J. M. and R. E. Pahl's study of middle-class career and family relationships[9] derives its material from questionnaires completed by eighty-six managers and their wives, supplemented by home interviews with sixteen couples. Hannah Gavron's *The Captive Wife*[10] is based on interviews with forty-eight middle-class and forty-eight working-class women. Each of these works incidentally illustrates one or more of the problems discussed earlier. For example, twenty-seven per cent of Gavron's middle-class sample was drawn from the London Housebound Housewives Register, a self-selected group of 'dissatisfied' housewives: this reduced the representativeness of the sample. The Pahls in their study had quite a high rate of non-co-operation: twenty of the group of 113 managers whom they wanted to study did not complete the questionnaire (although the response rate was higher from the wives' postal questionnaire); of the twenty-nine couples who were asked to give home interviews, six refused and six did not answer the letter.[11] Elizabeth Bott and her colleagues had considerable difficulty finding families to take part in their project: they used forty-two 'contact agencies' ranging from general practitioners, clergymen, students (taught by one of the researchers), and a branch of the Labour Party to simply 'friends and colleagues'. Altogether forty-five couples were suggested, and twenty-five were willing to be interviewed, although five of these did not meet the research criteria. This is also a sizable rate of refusal, and the nature of many of the contacts used casts some doubt on the representativeness of the sample population. However, Bott's aim was not to test well-defined hypotheses, but to carry out an intensive exploratory study of a small number of families, with the idea of furthering psychological and sociological understanding of urban family life.

In the presentation and analysis of the interview data which follows, the conclusions I draw do, strictly speaking, apply only to the research sample. However, there is no reason to believe that the sample is *unrepresentative* in any way. Referring to Moser's three sources of sampling bias mentioned earlier, it is clear that the sampling frame used (two general practice records) does not cover the whole population of housewives; yet there is no evidence that these records represent a particularly unrepresentative sub–sample of the population. Neither general practice has a reputation for being outstanding or different from the normal run of practices. Two practices were employed rather than one because one did not provide enough names fitting the research criteria, and also because both working-class and middle-class respondents were required: one practice was in a working-class and one in a middle-class area. Names were selected from the practice records on an alphabetical basis (see Appendix I), which, although not strictly speaking a 'random' method, is not obviously biased in any particular direction. Although there were some failures to contact patients selected, there were no refusals to co-operate among the housewives who were contacted. These considerations generate confidence in the representativeness of the women studied.[12]

In analysing the relationships between particular variables in the housewife's work situation I use a number of statistical tests, chiefly the chi-square test of significance. This procedure might be criticized on the grounds that the sample is too small to justify it. There is, however, no statistical reason why these tests should not be employed on such data, although clearly the probability of any result being due to chance is more likely to be lower as sample size increases. It should not be forgotten that in general, statistical tests of this kind are aids to interpretation. There is a difference between 'statistical' and 'theoretical' significance.[13] A relationship may be statistically significant but theoretically non-significant (because it is tautologous or trivial). The more difficult case is when theory suggests that a relationship should exist that seems to the researcher to be present in the data, but on a statistical level the relationship is not confirmed. In the end, the interpretation of research data and the results of statistical tests applied to them rests squarely on the researcher's shoulders:

> There is after all more to research than can be seen from the tables, and the researcher in interpreting his [sic] results is inevitably – and rightly – influenced by all that has gone before, by his acquaintance with the raw material behind the figures and by his own judgement ... The researcher who cautiously confines his conclusions to those strictly justified by the data may be safe from criticism, but he is not making his own full potential contribution.[14]

It would be shirking one's responsibility not to speculate on how one's findings may or may not be generalizable beyond the research universe. Important connections to draw are those between one's own findings and the conclusions of other, related research. These are broadly the approaches I adopt. I also operate with the assumption that, although my results pertain strictly only to the sample of forty housewives I interviewed, there is no reason why they should not relate to the wider population of housewives, since it cannot be shown that the forty women are unrepresentative of the larger population. Nevertheless, the crucial test must be whether further research along similar lines duplicates these findings.

In an important sense a piece of research planned, executed and analysed by one person derives both its strength and its main weakness from this source. The strength comes from the coherence and consistency that a single perspective makes possible. The weakness hinges on the fact that the research is only as 'good' as the integrity and judgement of the person who carries it out. This applies particularly to the interpretation of interview responses and the use of rating scales. On the first point, I aimed to make the questions as 'factual' as possible. Thus for example the questions about domestic routines and husband's participation in the division of labour were geared to specific activities and time periods rather than to the more attitudinal or normative dimension of who 'usually' does what at what time. These procedures minimize the task of interpretation. As for the use of rating scales, Goode and Hatt have pointed out that pooled judgements increase the accuracy of any rating scale: the use of one judge only reduces accuracy.[15] Limitations of time and money acted as major constraints in the design of my research. The research was carried out for a doctoral dissertation on the princely sum of £410 per annum (this was the 'married woman's' rate of postgraduate grant at the time, £120 lower than the full grant).[16] These limitations affected the size of the sample and also made it difficult to employ such procedures as the multiple judging of rating scales. However, a number of techniques which it is hoped reduced the possibility of bias in this stage of the research are described in Appendix I.

To return to characteristics of the sample: the forty women interviewed were all aged between twenty and thirty, were married, and the mothers of at least one child under five. In addition, all the women were born either in Britain or Ireland. These criteria were used in selecting the sample. The idea was to get a fairly homogeneous sample, to look at housework attitudes in a group of women with similar backgrounds. In this way gross dissimilarities in housework attitudes due to different cultural backgrounds, different age groups, and so forth, would be avoided, and the task of analysing the relationships between certain kinds of attitude and other facets of the work situation would be simplified. Including Irish women – six of the forty fell into this category – might be seen as contradicting this objective. But studies of traditional working-class life in rural Ireland (from which the Irish-born women in this sample originally came) and in urban Britain show many similarities. The division of labour by sex, the segregation of male and female roles in marriage, and the socialization of females for domesticity are all aspects in which the two cultures closely resemble one another. In fact, analysis of the interview material did not mark out the Irish women as particularly different from their British-born counterparts on any dimension of attitudes or behaviour. In two respects – the nature of their self-concepts and their social networks – their position was quite highly domestic and kin-oriented, but they shared these characteristics with other women in the sample.[17]

Half the forty women were 'working class' and half 'middle class'; social class was assessed in the conventional way, on the basis of husband's occupation. This use of conventional methods runs counter to the criticisms offered in Chapter 1 of traditional stratification analysis. At the time I selected my sample (late 1970) my objections to male-orientation in stratification theory and practice existed only in embryonic form, and discussions among sociologists (feminist or otherwise) of the place of women in sociology were non-existent. There was, however, one over-riding reason for taking the conventional approach: much of the existing literature on women's domestic roles draws attention to social class differences in women's satisfaction with domesticity; middle-class women are supposedly more dissatisfied than working-class women. Therefore, for meaningful comparisons to be possible between my own findings and those of other researchers, social class had to be assessed in the same way. Although the analysis focuses on social class, other variables relating to the housewife's own education and previous (or present) employment are also examined: in some cases it is these factors rather than social class itself which turns out to be important.

The Registrar-General's classification of occupations was used in making the social class assessments: classes I and II (professional and managerial) were termed 'middle class' and classes IV and V (semi-skilled and unskilled) 'working class'. Class III was divided into (1) white collar and (2) skilled manual occupations. The former were counted as 'middle class' and the latter as 'working class'. In three cases of clear-cut discrepancy between the social class classification arrived at in this way and the wife's previous occupation, education or general life-style, social class was upgraded or downgraded to take account of the contradiction. This is the somewhat rough-and-ready solution to the problem of male-biased occupational classification followed by John and Elizabeth Newson[18] and others.

Two other characteristics of the sample population require some comment: the incidence of employment, and of domestic help. Six of the women were employed outside the home at the time of interview. One had a full-time secretarial job, one had a part-time factory job (for four hours each morning), three did part-time cleaning jobs (two in the evening, one in the morning) and one housewife had a Saturday job as a hairdresser's receptionist. Does the inclusion of these women affect the survey findings? In Hunt's national survey of women's employment between fifteen and twenty per cent of women responsible for children aged five years or under were employed nationally, over half of them part-time.[19] The percentage in the present sample is fifteen (six out of forty); on this score it is not unrepresentative. It might be suggested that the employed women make up a particular group with respect to housework attitudes: women who are dissatisfied with housework may turn to employment as a palliative. Research does not generally support this conclusion.[20] Of the six employed women among the present forty, two were assessed as satisfied with housework, two as dissatisfied and two as very dissatisfied. This spread is similar to that in the sample as a whole.

The addition of paid work to the housewife's activities does not mean she is no longer a housewife. The definition of housewifery is cast in terms of *responsibility* for the running of a home. For this reason, the fact that three of the forty women had paid domestic help does not disqualify them from the title 'housewife'. (None of the three had living-in domestic help.)

The area from which the working-class housewives come is an area of mixed housing in which rented flats and rooms are interspersed with some owner-occupied dwellings. The houses date mostly from the 1910–20 era, and are in poor condition. The general appearance of the area is a drab one: there are few green spaces and few trees break up the uniform lines of terraced and semi-detached housing. Shopping amenities of the area are good. On the main street, running directly into central London, a Woolworths, a Marks and Spencer and several other department stores preside over a range of smaller shops. Transport amenities are poor, with the nearest London underground station a twenty-minute bus ride away. Since a major redevelopment plan is currently being implemented, many areas of slum and semi-slum housing are being demolished and families are moving to new council estates. Such a move had already affected three of the twenty working-class housewives interviewed. The impression of a shifting population given by this redevelopment is intensified by the proximity of the area to a major immigrant settlement zone.

By contrast the middle-class area has a relatively stable and prosperous population. Most homes are owner-occupied and most are well maintained. Several new privately developed housing estates are prominent landmarks, developments of homes with the distinctly middle-class assets of laundry rooms, ground-floor children's playrooms, integral garages and so forth. The streets are well provided with trees, and green spaces abound. Like the working-class area to which it is geographically close, the nearest shopping centre contains department stores and supermarkets, along with the usual variety of smaller shops. However, unlike the working-class area, the shopping centre is also a transport centre: there is a main line station on the national rail network and two underground lines connect it with the rest of London.

These, then, are the contexts from which the forty women come. Although they represent a particular group in modern society – young mothers – they are also representative of that much larger heterogeneous population which occupies the suburban fringes of our cities. In this sense the picture of the housewife which emerges in the present study not only bears on an understanding of the situation of *women* in society today; it also illuminates one face of urban family life. With this background in mind, the next chapter begins a discussion of some of the conclusions arising out of the interview material.

3 Images of Housework

Two conflicting stereotypes of housework exist in popular thinking today. According to one, the housewife is an oppressed worker: she slaves away in work that is degrading, unpleasant and essentially self-negating. According to the other, housework provides the opportunity for endless creative and leisure pursuits. In this view housework is not work but homemaking, and the home is a treasure house

> of unsuspected joys...the delectable smell of her own bread as it emerges crisp and brown from the oven, and the satisfaction of stitching up a new print dress on her own sewing machine...the smell of fresh earth in her own backyard...[1]

The aesthetic appeal is strong. But how does this argument – and its converse – measure up to the reality of the housework situation as perceived by housewives themselves?

Throughout the forty interviews a clear perception of housework as work emerges. The women in the sample experience and define housework as labour, akin to that demanded by any job situation. Their observations tie in closely with many findings of the sociology of work; the aspects of housework that are cited as satisfying or dissatisfying have their parallels in the factory or office world. This equivalence is emphasized further by the women's own tendency to compare their reactions to housework with their experience of working outside the home.

A number of interview questions in particular provided answers on which these generalizations are based. The first two of these are questions about the 'best' and 'worst' aspects of being a housewife. Over half the answers to the 'best' aspects question refer to what could be called the work dimension of the role, as do almost all the answers to the 'worst' aspects question – even though these questions do not specify housework, but permit answers relating to marriage, motherhood and home life generally. (The answers are shown in Tables 3.1 and 3.2.) Of course it could be objected that the responses highlight this facet of the housewife role because much of the rest of the interview was taken up with questions about housework. Yet this generalization is consistent with the line taken by the women in many other comments made spontaneously – unprompted by questions from the interviewer. In addition, groups of questions were devoted to marriage and to child-care, so that there was no pressure on the women to feel that responses on these subjects would be out of order.

Autonomy is the most valued quality of the housewife role: housework is the worst. Joanna Giles, an ex-computer programmer married to a radio producer, described her feeling of autonomy thus:

> To an extent you're your own master . . . you can decide what you want to do and when you want to do it . . . it's not like being at work when somebody rings you up and you've got to go down and see them or you've got to do this and that within half an hour.

The impression is given that, rather than being *positively* valued for its autonomy, housework is *negatively* valued as a retreat from a disliked alternative – employment work. This is a common feature of many responses:

> (What would you say are the best things about being a housewife?) Well, you don't have to get up early in the morning and go out to work, do you?
>
> (Factory machinist's wife)

> The thing that's nice about being a housewife is you have your own time – there's nobody behind you with a punch card . . . You're your own boss, like.
>
> (Painter and decorator's wife)

Many of the answers – nineteen in all – used this phrase 'you're your own boss' to describe the housewife's feeling of being in control.[2] The phrase presents a direct analogy with the paid job situation. Autonomy, in the sense of freedom from supervision and ability to determine one's own work rhythms, is an important dimension of employment work. Martin Patchen, in a study of 834 US government employees found that the factor of control over work methods consistently emerged as most closely associated with high job motivation.[3]

Table 3.1 Answers to the question 'What would you say are the best things about being a housewife?'

'Best things'	Number of answers mentioning:
You're your own boss	19
Having the children	9
Having free time	5
Not having to work outside the home	4
Having a husband	4
Having home/family life	3
Housework	1
Other	2
Total*	47

*Total adds up to more than 40 because some housewives gave more than one answer.

Table 3.2 Answers to the question 'What would you say are the worst things about being a housewife?'

'Worst things'	Number of answers mentioning:
Housework	14
Monotony/repetitiousness/boredom	14
Constant domestic responsibility	6
Isolation/loneliness	4
Must get housework done	3
Being tied down	3
Children	2
Other	2
Total*	48

*Total adds up to more than 40 because some housewives gave more than one answer.

In the housewife's case autonomy is more theoretical than real. Being 'your own boss' imposes the obligation to see that housework gets done. The responsibility for housework is a unilateral one, and the failure to do it may have serious consequences. As itemized by these women, such consequences include the wrath of husbands and the ill-health of children (through lack of hygiene):[4]

Why do I clean the kitchen floor twice a day? Well, it's because she's all over it, isn't it? I mean it's not nice to let a child crawl on a dirty floor – she might catch something off it.

(Lorry driver's wife)

What this means is that the taking of leisure is self-defeating; the fact that one is one's own boss adds to, rather than subtracts from, the psychological pressures to do housework. Joanna Giles, the ex-computer programmer, went on to make this point:

The worst thing is I suppose that you've got to do the work because you *are* at home. Even though I've got the option of not doing it, I don't really feel I *could* not do it, because I feel I *ought* to do it.

In the words of a lorry driver's wife:

It's not that anyone's going to whip me if I don't do it – but I know there's going to be double the quantity tomorrow, so really I'm just beating my own brow.

Thus housework – the actual work involved – is the other side of the coin from the nominally high evaluation attached to autonomy. Twenty-eight replies to the 'worst things' question mentioned housework or its monotonous, boring quality as the most disliked dimension; a further six described negatively the women's feeling of being constantly responsible for home and children. To use Eleanor Driscoll's words:

(What would you say are the worst things about being a house-wife?) Having to get up *every* morning ... you think 'Oh heck I've go to do the place today, and I've got to do the dinner' – that's something I can't stand, thinking I've got to do the dinner.

(Shop manager's wife)

The housewife is 'free from' but not 'free to'. That is, she is exempt from supervision but not wholly free to choose her own activities.

If housework is work, what kind of work is it? Answers to two other questions give information on this point. The first invited the women to compare their own work (housework) with that of their husbands. This is a sensitive issue on which many wax indignant. Deborah Keyes, an ex-typist, says:

I think housewives work just as hard. I can't stand husbands who come home and say 'Oh look you've done nothing all day, only a bit of housework and looked after the child'. But I reckon that's tiring myself, well, not tiring, *it's just as hard as doing a job – I don't care what any man says* ... My husband says this – that's why I feel so strongly about it. (Italics added)

Deborah Keyes has one child, is married to a central heating fitter and lives in a 'high-rise' flat. She is dissatisfied and tends to comment apathetically on her dissatisfaction, but her observations at this point in the interview were very lively indeed:

I say to him [husband] I'm going to clear off for the day and you can do it all one day, and you'll see what it's like.

Of the forty women, twenty-six claimed that they worked harder than their husbands, seven said the men worked harder, and seven that it depended on personality or on the kind of job the husband had. There are explicit comparisons of one set of work routines with the other:

Housewives work harder. My husband's always coming home and saying 'Oh I sat down and talked to so-and-so today' or 'we had a laugh today with so-and-so ... ' I don't do that, I never sit down.

(Plasterer's wife)

Or:

I always say it's harder, but my husband doesn't say that at all. I think he's wrong, because I'm going all the time – when his job is finished, it's finished ... Sunday he can lie in bed till twelve, get up, get dressed and go for a drink, but my job never changes.

(Wife of a driver's mate)

A painter and decorator's wife produces conclusive evidence on this point:

The husbands never look very tired do they? It's always the woman that's tired isn't it? When they've finished, they've finished ... Things like road digging might be harder [than housework] but there again, when they've finished, they go and have a drink and a cigarette and that's it.

Housework is described as a never-ending job – in the stock phrase 'a woman's work is never done'. It is said by some to be more tiring physically than a paid job, by others to be less tiring: some women say it takes a greater emotional toll, others that the drain is less than other work. Reference is made to the *unconstructive* nature of housework tasks, to the emotionally frustrating sense of being on a treadmill that requires the same action to be repeated again and again;

> Housewives tend to be busy all the time but they're not really doing anything constructive, are they? Well, I suppose it is constructive in a way, but you never really see anything for it and it's all routine.
>
> > (Statistician's wife)

Miles are walked in exchange for a feeling of perpetual defeat. In the eyes of Jean Bevan, an ex-nurse married to an office manager, housework is 'real' work and employment work is not:

> (Do you think housewives work as hard, not so hard, or harder than their husbands?) Harder. He doesn't work you see – he just sits in an office and tells other people to work.

Before Jean Bevan's husband was promoted to an office job, he did, in his wife's opinion, do 'real' work, i.e. manual work, like housework. This is an interesting point. The denigration of office work as inferior, non-manual labour, has a key place in the sexual transformation of clerical work around the turn of the century.

> 'Don't we lose our manhood?' asks the blackcoated hero of an early twentieth century novel as he reflects on his job. 'What do we see of real life? What do we know of the world? . . . We aren't real men. We don't do men's work. Pen-drivers – miserable little pen-drivers – fellows in black coats, with inky fingers and shiny seats on their trousers – that's what we are.[5]

To class housework as manual work is thus to put it higher up the scale of job prestige.

This defence of housework is all the more necessary because housework passes unmentioned in the predominant stereotype of the housewife as a leisured homemaker. Yet another reason why the women's comments are phrased in this way derives from the low social ranking women see as attached to the occupation of housewife.

When asked how they felt about writing this occupation on a form, twenty-one housewives 'minded' and nineteen did not see anything disadvantageous in it. A journalist's wife makes reference to the social stereotype:

I only think of myself as a housewife when I have to fill up a form. Sometimes I'd like to put something a bit more interesting. I think it's a *menial* sort of job – *people look upon it like that.* (Italics added)

It is clear from this comment that the question of occupational classification is closely linked to the self-concept: it involves the issue of whether, and to what extent, women see themselves as housewives. This is explored in more detail in a later chapter. But whatever their level of personal identification with the housewife role, the denigration and trivialization of housework is such a pervasive cultural theme that the message is likely to have filtered through to the housewife in some form or other. The need to disassociate oneself from it then follows.

Mixed with low social ranking are the related notions of housework as 'dull' work and the housewife as a 'dull, boring' person. A warehouse foreman's wife says:

I mind writing housewife on a form. I'd like to put 'secretary' or something – it sounds better. The majority of people are housewives. It sounds dull – you've nothing else to do except clean and dust and cook.

The image of the housewife as a cabbage makes a number of appearances in answers to the question about writing housewife on a form (it is mentioned by twelve of the forty women).[6] A 'cabbage' housewife is someone entirely immersed in domestic affairs, a colourless personality, a drab, uninteresting automaton. Eleanor Driscoll, a working-class housewife who has recently moved from a two-room slum into a local authority house, puts it like this:

I did [think of myself as a cabbage] when I was living at the other place doing all that washing by hand . . . I had no facilities, no money, I was bored, fed up, had nothing to look forward to. At least now I know that perhaps one day we might get a car – even save up for a house – and that's something to look forward to . . . so I don't think of myself as a cabbage.

Another woman resolutely described herself as a 'shrink wrapper' rather than a housewife. This is the definition of her part-time factory job, which consists of wrapping tins in cellophane paper. She gets a certain amount of amusement from describing herself in this way, but the verbal presentation of self has a serious purpose:

> I think of myself as a housewife, but I don't think of myself as a cabbage. A lot of people think that they're housewives and they're cabbages; I don't like to think I'm only a house-wife . . . I usually say 'I'm a wife and a mother and I've got a part-time job'. People look down on housewives these days.

'Only' or 'just' a housewife is the ubiquitous phrase. Its implica-tion is that being a housewife is something so eminently inferior to every other occupation; it also belittles those other roles of wife and mother. Elaine Cawthorne, another working-class housewife, expresses it splendidly:

> I'm not married to a house! I hate the word 'housewife' . . . they say to you 'what are you?' and you say 'I've got a baby. I'm a mother, a wife' and they say, 'oh just a housewife'. Just a housewife! The hardest job in the world . . . you're never just a housewife . . . Into that category comes every-thing.

Resentment is compounded because 'housewife' contains 'wife' and 'mother'. The social denigration of housework overflows into the even more highly valued (to the women themselves) occupations of wife and mother. Women must consequently separate out these different roles, and a way to begin is to protest that the whole image is wrong.

Another message that comes over clearly is the need to separate out the different tasks that make up housework. House-work is not a single activity. It is a collection of heterogeneous tasks which demand a variety of skills and kinds of action. Washing a floor contrasts with shopping for groceries: peeling potatoes with washing dirty socks and planning a week's meals. To call all these jobs by the same name is to disguise their differences, to reduce them all to the same common denominator. In fact, some are more liked than others; some are more repeti-tive, some less tiring, some more potentially creative and so forth. Each of the tasks that the housewife does – cooking, laundering the clothes, cleaning the house and so on – can, after all, constitute a paid work role in its own right. The role of chef is very different from the role of commercial laundry operator or the job of 'domestic help'.

The six core housework tasks – cleaning, shopping, cooking, washing up, washing and ironing – can be arranged in a kind of league table of likes and dislikes. Table 3.3 is such a table. It shows the percentage of the sample who say they 'like', 'dislike' or 'don't mind' each task when asked a direct question about that task. Two percentages are shown in each case: one relates to first responses to the question 'Do you like . . .?' and the other to all responses. By asking the women what they liked or disliked about the task in question, and whether their attitude was reversed in any particular circumstances, I was able to get a more complete picture of their experience of each task, and also to learn something about the characteristics these different housework tasks are seen to possess.

Table 3.3 Answers to questions about housework tasks

| Housework task | Percentage of forty women giving answers: | | | | | |
| | Dislike | | Don't mind | | Like | |
	First answer*	All answers†	First answer	All answers	First answer	All answers
Ironing	75	75	20	33	5	15
Washing up	65	70	28	30	8	8
Cleaning	50	68	20	20	30	38
Washing	33	65	35	40	33	38
Shopping	30	60	20	20	50	55
Cooking	23	48	18	18	60	60

* To the question 'Do you like . . .?'
† With probing, e.g. 'What do you like about it?' 'Is there anything you dislike about it?'

Of the six tasks, ironing is most disliked: three-quarters of the sample report a negative attitude. It is disliked because it is physically an exhausting activity; more than any of the other tasks it consists of actions which have to be repeated time and time again with little variation.

> I loathe ironing. It's just standing there, and you take one [garment] from the pile and stick it on the ironing board and iron it, fold it, and put it down, take the next one – and it's as though it's never going to end.
>
> (Plasterer's wife)

> What I don't like about it is standing over the board, moving the iron back and forth.
>
> (Wife of a driver's mate)

It's a boring job – ironing. Moving the iron back and forwards
the whole time.

(Factory hand's wife)

Ironing consists of repetitive actions which tire specific muscles
without engaging the attention of the mind or the concentrated
energy of the whole body. The obvious comparison here is with
the assembly line worker in a factory, tied machine-like to a
mindless and endlessly repetitive task. No other aspect of housework presents quite this parallel. Only one woman out of the
forty actually claimed unequivocally to like ironing, and she said
she knew she was unusual, particularly in the satisfaction she
gets from ironing shirts, an activity which many of the other
housewives said was the most intolerable of all. Those housewives who 'don't mind' ironing make it clear that they dislike
the task itself, yet have found conditions under which it becomes
bearable. Having the radio or television on is one such ploy;
another is to plan the ironing to coincide with the husband's
presence in the evening. Similarly, a negative attitude may turn
to a 'don't mind' one under certain conditions, for example when
the items ironed are less intrinsically boring (baby's clothes are
said to come in this category).

Washing up is next in the 'dislike' section of the table: taking
first responses together with later ones, seventy per cent of the
women describe a negative attitude. Like ironing, it tends to have
assembly line aspects, though these are not so pronounced. One
'just stands there washing plate after plate', or 'it just tires one
out'. It is also a *dirty* job; in an ex-fashion model's words:

I hate it. I dread it. I just can't bear mucking around with
dirty greasy things.

The unpleasantness is stressed because it is usually preceded by
an enjoyable activity – eating a meal. Every meal is followed by
washing up: washing up is a recurrent event,

It's never ending. You've no sooner done one lot of washing
up than you've got another lot, and that's how it goes on all
day.

(Lorry driver's wife)

If you could have paper things . . . sometimes it seems to be
putting out fresh plates, eating off them, washing them, and

then putting them out again . . . some days you seem to be
at it all day long.

(Food wholesaler's wife)

This inevitability is not present in the same way with ironing.
Those who say they like washing up do not like the task itself –
one woman likes it because she has a dishwasher, one because
she has just acquired a new stainless steel sink, and the third
likes it merely 'to get it out of the way'.

Attitudes to cleaning – the third in the 'dislike' list – are a
little less negative: twenty of the forty women dislike or hate
cleaning, eight 'don't mind' it, twelve like or 'love' it. Typical
responses are:

> I dislike cleaning. I don't really know why. Probably I feel
> there's always something else I could do and it never seems
> to stop.
>
> (Statistician's wife)

> I don't really mind it. It's something to do. I'd be bored if I
> didn't have it to do.
>
> (Carpenter's wife)

> I like cleaning – polishing, everything. I like to see a nice
> shine.
>
> (Wife of a driver's mate)

These are the first answers given, but in reply to further questions
the number of women making at least one negative reference
increases to twenty-seven – sixty-eight per cent of the sample.
Many women say cleaning is boring: you do it one day and
there it is to be done again the next. Cleaning a house is

> just like working in a factory – you dust the same thing every
> day and it's never appreciated. I mean I could get this whole
> place so tidy and the kids come home from school and it's
> like a bomb's exploded and nothing's appreciated about it,
> whereas if you're decorating or teaching children there's
> something always gained out of it . . . as far as actual house-
> work goes, I don't see how anyone can like it. It's boring, just
> like a robot.
>
> (Shop manager's wife)

The comparison with repetitive industrial work is thus articulated.

This comparison is not confined to the middle-class half of
the sample, but is an observation that working-class housewives

also make. A working-class housewife married to a machine operator declares:

> Housework is boring. The same old thing – cleaning the same things all the time, that's what gets me. When a man goes to work, he might be only making things, but at least they're *different* things . . .

While a middle-class housewife, the wife of the director of a publishing firm, comments:

> Yes, I think I do find housework monotonous, if you think one has to get up, make the beds every day, wash up every day, one should dust every day – I mean it *is* monotonous, isn't it?

Unlike shopping, cleaning is a lonely duty. The felt need to get the cleaning done conflicts with the desire to be sociable; one can iron, or perhaps cook, while talking to a friend or neighbour, but one cannot wield a vacuum cleaner and carry on a conversation at the same time. The conflict is clearly illustrated in the interview with Marilyn Thornton, a plasterer's wife with five children. She does her own housework in the mornings and spends every afternoon cleaning the bedrooms in an overnight transport café belonging to a friend of hers. She takes her eighteen-month-old twins with her to work. While the point of the job is to make money, it is also to get out of the house and talk to other people. (When doing her own housework Marilyn Thornton has the radio on constantly 'for company'.) Because she has this afternoon job, she must get through her own work in the mornings; but she gets her work done in the mornings in order to create time for a job. Significantly, another housewife mentioned the fact that housework is not paid work as a reason for disliking it; she said she would be happier doing someone else's housework for pay than doing her own work.

The example of Marilyn Thornton emphasizes sharply the association of housework with social isolation. The importance of this in relation to work satisfaction patterns is discussed in Chapter 5. Two other common reasons for disliking cleaning concern technical aspects of the work environment and one's 'mood'. The housewife says she has an old and inefficient vacuum cleaner: this is a statement about the inappropriateness of the tool to the work. Or she may describe the interior of the home as difficult to clean:

I've been on at my husband to get a fitted carpet in this room
because this lino drives me mad. It gets so dirty and it *looks*
dirty if it's not polished every day.
(Policeman's wife)

This carpet's navy and it's terrible, it shows everything. You've
got to do it again and again. Invariably if I leave it, someone
walks in. So I feel happier in my mind if I do it every day.
(Retail chemist's wife)

A frequent claim is that cleaning is only a bore when one's
mood is out of tune with it: conversely, in the 'right' mood,
cleaning is cheerfully and quickly done. Perhaps this can be seen
as a statement of a general condition that obtains for all workers.
Or is it a typically 'feminine' response? Connections can be
traced with the imagery of advertisements which portray harassed
housewives overcome by sudden headaches while coping with the
demands of husband, home and children; on these occasions the
mood is corrected by the appropriate painkiller or vitamin pill
and then the housewife proceeds to go happily about her work.
On a more basic level the attribution of dislike to a personal
deficiency (the wrong mood) also probably reflects on the deeply
personal nature of the housewife's relationship to her role. The
housewife, in an important sense, *is* her job: separation between
subjective and objective elements in the situation is therefore
intrinsically more difficult. This is an important point which is
crucial to the whole question of attitudes to, and satisfaction
with, housework:

I like housework. I'm quite domesticated really. I've always
been brought up to be domesticated – to do the housework and
dust and wash up and cook – so it's a natural instinct really.
(Supermarket manager's wife)

The indistinguishability of the housewife and her work provides,
if anything, a motivation to be satisfied – whether with cleaning
specifically or with the whole complex of housework activities
generally.[7]

So far as washing – the fourth most disliked task – is concerned, attitudes are more evenly divided between positive,
negative and 'don't mind' categories. Thirteen housewives say
they 'like' washing, fourteen 'don't mind' it and thirteen 'dislike'
or 'hate' it. Although both washing and washing up are activities
in which dirt is removed from objects, the pleasure inherent in

washing seems to be greater. Possibly this is because of the
personal associations that clothes have. The clothes that are
washed belong to and are used by someone, normally the housewife, her husband and children. It depends, of course, on the
particular item. For example, Elaine Cawthorne says

> I like washing his [the baby's] clothes, but I hate washing his
> nappies. I find them tiresome . . . It's not that they're his
> nappies and he wets them – it's nothing to do with that – it's
> just that they're endless. Whereas if you're washing his clothes,
> you're washing one jumper and it's not the same as the next
> jumper; nappies are one square after another, like a night-
> mare . . .

If washing can be repetitive in this way, a counterbalancing
image is suggested by the next quotation from the interview
with a supermarket manager's wife:

> Once the washing's on the line, I think that's *nice* – *nice* and
> clean. I suppose it's a satisfying thing – to know you've done
> it at last and it's all there, *nice* and clean. It's always a *nice*
> sight to see a line of washing blowing. (Italics added)

Why is a line of washing a 'nice' sight? Mass media advertising
reiterates the message of white clothes gently blowing in the
wind, transmitting a feeling that 'whiteness' or 'cleanliness' is
the housewife's moral obligation to her family.[8] Perfect cleanliness is the commercial ideal, but the clothes must also be *seen*
to be clean. Public visibility is achieved when the clothes hang
in the garden, and the advertising image adds the alluring finishing touches to this picture with cloudless skies, matched only by
the cloudless smile on the housewife's face and the unbelievably
perfect condition of the white garments on which her attention
is perfectly focused. (According to these advertisements a large
proportion of the population wears white from head to toe,
especially for the more messy activities. Is your son a champion
dirt collector? If so dress him in white and use sunshine soap-
flakes to get the dirt out.) Seven out of the forty women
specifically mention the pleasure they obtain from seeing a line
full of clean clothes; some explain it is because they anticipate
the silent admiration of neighbours at this visible (though short-
lived) achievement. Others do not mention the possible approval
of others, and apparently have no idea why the image attracts

them, nor why they should feel an inner compulsion to conform
to it.

Automation makes a difference here. Eleven of the working-
class and fourteen of the middle-class housewives had washing
machines: [9] use of a machine in one's own home lightens the
task. As Eleanor Driscoll recollects

> At one time I had this scrubbing brush and I used to spend
> the whole day scrubbing and I used to have a big pan and I
> used to boil my clothes up in it – it drove me round the
> bend . . . I've got this washing machine now, thank goodness.
> A washing machine cuts housework really down.

'I don't know what I did without it' is the sentiment. There is
a difference between fully automatic washing machines – which
change the nature of the task altogether – and 'twin tub'
machines where the hot wet washing has to be lifted manually
into a separate drying compartment. The women who had this
type of machine complained about the considerable amount of
work still required of the housewife, and the mess on the kitchen
floor to be cleared up afterwards. In a similar way the launderette
does not remove the physical drudgery of washing. The housewife has to get the washing there in the first place, she has to
unload it, sort it, sit and watch it wash and dry (or dash out to
shop in the interim) and then pack it all up again. This, when
there is a baby in the pram and a two- or three-year-old to attend
to, is no mean feat.

Against launderettes it also has to be said that they do not
fit the media image of the perfect housewife. 'I don't *believe* in
the launderette', said one working-class housewife. 'They don't
seem to get the clothes clean – you have to boil them when you
get back.' In part this is a complaint about the inferior service
these establishments offer. But it is also an ideological statement: the housewife's place is in the home washing and hanging
out her own clothes; not in the launderette where they are
processed for her. The ethic of the 'little woman in the little
house' is surreptitiously eroded, for launderettes are meeting
places where housewives collectively discuss their work – and
who knows what else besides?

By contrast with these other tasks, the housewife's role as a
consumer is a more public one; it requires an absence from her
work-place – the home. Largely for this reason, answers to the

question 'Do you like shopping?' are predominantly favourable; many women mention 'getting out of the house' or 'meeting people' as advantages of shopping. A carpenter's wife and a policeman's wife describe their feelings:

I like shopping. You see people when you go out – it's a change from the house.

I like it because I'm out, I think, and I like looking in the shops and sometimes I bump into people I know, and it just makes a little break . . .

Not surprisingly, shopping tends to be a daily event. As Table 3.4 shows, most of the women shop six times a week, only four shop two or three times a week, and no housewife does all her shopping once a week. The social class difference in frequency of shopping is negligible.

Table 3.4   Frequency of shopping and social class

| Social class | Frequency of shopping | | | | |
| | Six times a week | Four or five times a week | Two or three times a week | Once a week | Total |
	No.(%)	No.(%)	No.(%)	No.(%)	No.(%)
Working class	14(70)	5(25)	1(5)	0(0)	20(100)
Middle class	12(60)	5(25)	3(15)	0(0)	20(100)
Total	26(65)	10(25)	4(10)	0(0)	40(100)

The proliferation of shopping excursions as a relief from domestic captivity is recognized:

I do my big shopping on Tuesday – but I go for odds and ends every day. I make these journeys just to get out of the house. Otherwise I'd be in the house all the time.
(Policeman's wife)

I go shopping nearly every day – although that's not really necessary. But I do because I combine it with taking her [the child] for a walk. And it does me good to get out of the house.
(Journalist's wife)

As an earlier comment mentioned, another merit of shopping is that it can be expanded to include (or even defined to consist of) window shopping. This is self-consciously an escapist activity, its main value being that it avoids the careful budgeting and penny-counting which shopping itself entails.

Thus, not enough money or impossibly high prices are reasons why shopping is disliked. A clear distinction is made between the two sorts of shopping:

> I don't mind shopping on Saturday when I've got the money, but I don't like it during the week – I'm usually broke by Monday – so I keep it down to a minimum. I don't really like walking around thinking I'd like to buy that – I'd rather not go.
>
> (Machine operator's wife)

Of course a limited budget could be seen as a challenge. Only two housewives actually see it this way without reservations; Dorothy Underwood, a cinema manager's wife and the mother of three children under four, and Sandra Bishop, the wife of a painter and decorator and the mother of one child:

> I quite enjoy shopping. It makes a change from housework – getting out of the house – and it's a bit of a challenge too, budgeting and trying to get the cheapest of everything.
>
> (Dorothy Underwood)

> I like it. But I don't just go in one shop, and I never buy anything without looking at the price. I'm terrible with prices. Some people say 'you're mad – just go in one shop' but I can't. I usually go in at least three. Like tea – we have the same brand each week – but if I know it's cheaper in one shop I go into that shop, just to get that one thing – like I got it for 1/6 this week and it's usually 1/11 – I like to get the best, but cheaper.
>
> (Sandra Bishop)

Other complaints about shopping cite physical difficulties. Having to take children along imposes both a physical and mental burden; there is the problem of managing children and shopping simultaneously, and the housewife's attention is distracted by the need to pacify a crying child or by the knowledge that a baby in a pushchair is parked out of sight. Consequently she becomes a less efficient shopper and a more frustrated one. Queueing or having to wait in shops is disliked; so are certain kinds of shops – in some the large supermarket, and in some the small corner shop. The more shopping resembles work, the less it is liked. Small semi-serious shopping expeditions are valued as a relief from the social isolation and the work of housework. But major expeditions for food are disliked. All except two of these forty women do their 'big' shopping once a week – that is, stocking up on goods like sugar, flour, etc. – and it is customary to combine this with shopping for the weekend. Virtually all dislike this kind of shopping. The mental strain of trying to concentrate on it with small children is considerable, and so is the physical strain of getting it all home. Only five of the forty had the regular or occasional use of a car for shopping and other activities.

Of the six basic housework tasks cooking is, according to these women, potentially the most enjoyable activity. It presents a challenge; it can be an art:

> Cooking doesn't bore me like cleaning does. I enjoy it – I enjoy trying new recipes.
>
> (Cinema manager's wife)

> I get fed up with cooking the same old thing – I like it if I can experiment. We [herself and the housewife in the next flat] try new recipes off the Jimmy Young show, and see how they turn out.
>
> (Lorry driver's wife)

No doubt this perception – of cooking's creative potential – is also influenced by advertising and by the attention devoted to cooking in women's magazines and similar literature. The object of the exercise as presented in such channels of communication is not how to get the most nutritious meals prepared in the shortest possible time but rather how to go beyond the usual range of meals with time-consuming inventiveness and culinary skill. The aim is not simple efficiency. Instead it is an *elaboration* of the task, designed to subtract it from the category of 'work' and add it to the creative pleasure dimension. This treatment of cooking, reflected in the comments of these housewives, is a particularly clear demonstration of how the social denial of housework as work operates.

They say it can be creative, but is it, in practice? A lorry driver's wife:

> I do like cooking if I've got time to do it properly. But the way I'm doing it now I don't like it. I used to love concocting meals . . . really love it. But now the quickest and most nourishing meal is the winner.

Limitations of time (and money) act as brakes on the enjoyment of cooking. The housewife is not only a chef but also a washer up, a cleaner, a nanny, a childminder:

> I mean I can't get my hands covered with flour and egg and stuff if he's going to cry and I've got to pick him up, can I?
> (Lorry driver's wife)

> I think if I was left in peace to cook, then I'd get pleasure from it. But as it is . . . if I make pastry, there's usually pastry from one end of the house to the other, because the kids have got to have their little bits, and in the end you think, 'Oh was it worth it?'
> (Food technologist's wife)

In reality husbands demand meals at specific times, small children cry when their stomachs are empty, the hour that might be spent cooking competes with the hour that ought to be spent washing the floor or changing the beds. 'Thinking what to eat' is an endless duty, however creative the actual task may be. Thus one latent function of the creative cookery ideal is the production of dissatisfaction. Standards of achievement exist of which the housewife is permanently aware, but which she cannot often hope to reach due to the other demands on her time.

In sum, one could list certain properties of housework tasks, their context, or the housewife's approach to them, which make recurrent appearances in answers given to the section of the interview dealing with what is liked and disliked about the six core housework tasks. Attributes referred to as promoting a positive attitude include (in order of importance):

1 Being able to talk to other people while working;
2 Being in the 'right' mood;
3 Having enough time;
4 Having the right work environment or tools of work;
5 Having enough housekeeping money;
6 Having one's work appreciated.

The following factors are mentioned as associated with a negative attitude:

1 Monotony and repetitiousness;
2 Having the wrong environment or tools of work;
3 Being in the 'wrong' mood;
4 Children getting in the way;
5 Not having enough time;

6   Social isolation;
7   Having to think about work.

These points reinforce the generalizations made at the beginning of this chapter, that housewives approach housework as work, analogous with any other kind of job. Their comments about the 'best' and 'worst' aspects of housewifery refer predominantly to the work dimension of the role; freedom from supervision heads the list of positive qualities, while the work itself is the major negative aspect named. Housework is defended as 'real' and 'hard' work, a defence made all the more necessary because of the low status and value conventionally accorded to it. While the stereotyped image of housework treats it as a single activity, women see it as consisting of many disparate ones. Feelings about these different tasks do not seem to be dependent primarily on temperament or on personal background; rather they emerge as related to the kind of conditions under which the tasks are performed.

The picture thus sketched is in strong contrast to the popular view of housewives as a leisured class. Housewives cannot be accused of 'doing nothing all day'; nor can it legitimately be said that their only 'work' is 'creative' and thus intrinsically pleasurable. As to that other view of housewives as oppressed workers, we need to look more closely at the extent of women's overall satisfaction or dissatisfaction with housework. The impression already given that, by and large, the women interviewed did not enjoy their work, is dissected and examined more thoroughly in the next chapter.

4 Social Class and Domesticity

Out of the conceptualization of housework as work which is a major theme of this study arises the need to spell out the different components in what is broadly termed women's 'domesticity'. One of the most important of these is the concept of overall satisfaction with housework. Other components relate to attitudes to housework and the perceived status of housewifery. The discussion in this chapter has a two-fold purpose. On the one hand the aim is to describe patterns of domesticity in the present sample of housewives. But these findings are also tied in with assertions about social class differences in domesticity which abound in much of the literature dealing with women's place in the family.

Various authors have suggested or claimed that working-class women are satisfied with housework while middle-class women are not. For example, the psychological dilemmas of women's two roles discussed in the late 1950s by Myrdal and Klein are said by them to affect only the minority of educated middle-class women.[1] Discontent with the traditional role of housewife is seen as a middle-class prerogative. In *The Family and Social Change*, an account of kinship in a South Wales town, Rosser and Harris make a similar assertion, that 'for a variety of reasons' the 'domesticity' of working-class wives is higher than that of their middle-class counterparts.[2] Strangely, they do not examine these reasons, although the level of feminine domesticity is a crucial link in their argument about the existence of close-knit kinship networks in working-class communities. Mirra Komarovsky, in her study of American *Blue Collar Marriage*, finds that higher education is correlated with a 'less favourable' attitude to housewifery,[3] and a number of other studies back up this contention as applied to the American scene.

None of these writers looks at housework satisfaction; the notion of feminine domesticity is undefined and usually rather vague. The categorization of social class used in these studies is the conventional one based on husband's occupation. For the present sample the relationship between housework satisfaction and social class assessed in this way is shown in Table 4.1.

Table 4.1   Work satisfaction and social class

| Social class | Work satisfaction | | | | |
	Very satisfied No.(%)	Satisfied No.(%)	Dissatisfied No.(%)	Very dissatisfied No.(%)	Total No.(%)
Working class	1(5)	5(25)	9(45)	5(25)	20(100)
Middle class	2(10)	4(20)	9(45)	5(25)	20(100)
Total	3(8)	9(23)	18(45)	10(25)	40(100)

The concept of 'satisfaction with housework' follows the concept of 'work' or 'job' satisfaction as used in the sociology of industry and paid work; it represents an overall assessment of the degree to which housewives are positively or negatively oriented to their work. The four categories shown in Table 4.1 are collapsed into a simple dichotomy – satisfied, dissatisfied – in subsequent discussions of the relationships between satisfaction patterns and other factors. The placing of each housewife in a satisfaction category was done by the interviewer-researcher, on the basis of the overall interview response; further details for the methodologically curious are given in Appendix I.

As Table 4.1 indicates, there is no social class difference in the frequency with which housewives are satisfied or dissatisfied with their work. The predominant feeling is one of dissatisfaction – twenty-eight of the forty women come out as dissatisfied. If education is taken instead of social class, there is still no difference between groups of women: equal proportions of those educated to sixteen and beyond are satisfied and dissatisfied with housework. In this context it is interesting to note a finding from Arthur Kornhauser's study of industrial workers. Kornhauser found that occupational differences in mental health (broadly equivalent to 'satisfaction') persisted apart from the influence of education.[4] Proportions of workers having good mental health persistently decreased from higher to lower level occupations for each of three educational categories separately. In other words, mental health is likely to be reduced in low skill occupations (like housework) irrespective of the worker's previous educational background.

The best way to make these somewhat abstract concepts of satisfaction and dissatisfaction more concrete is to give some illustrations from the interviews. One 'very satisfied' housewife is Sandra Bishop, the twenty-three-year-old wife of a painter and decorator, an ex-factory machinist and the mother of one daughter aged eighteen months. Here are some of her comments.

> Yes, I do like housework. I like to make it [the house] nice, you know, and I like to spend quite a bit of time cooking and that. I like to put it on the table and hear the comments afterwards, and I'm pleased to bits if it's been all right . . . I don't mind cleaning at all . . . I like shopping . . . I like to get the best as cheaply as I can . . . I like washing up. When I first came here [a new council maisonette] I went mad on it, because of this sink, and I washed all my wedding presents. At my Mum-in-law's the sink was in the corner, not under the window where it is now . . . I do more washing up than anything now!
>
> I do think of myself as a housewife. Some days I think I'm only young – I fell straight away for her [the baby] – I used to think before I was married I'd better get all the clothes I want now because I'll never get them when I'm married – but I was wrong, because I can really have all I want now . . . I like being a housewife. I never did have any ambitions really – I never did want to do anything.
>
> (Is there anything else you would rather be doing at the moment, apart from being a housewife and a mother?) No, not really.
>
> (When you feel really happy these days, what sort of thing is it that makes you feel like that?) The weather, and I like entertaining, I couldn't do any when I lived with my Mum-in-law . . .

Overall, the tone is highly positive; certainly it is so in relation to the impressions created by some other women in the sample. Norma Larkin, a police sergeant's wife, an ex-hairdresser, and the mother of one son, is 'very dissatisfied' with housework:

> I don't like housework particularly – it's just a bore, it's so

monotonous, and with a child you've done it once and five minutes later it just doesn't look as though you've done it at all. (Cooking?) No, not particularly, but you've got to eat. (Washing?) No, I can't say I like any of these jobs – I do them because they've got to be done: I'm here and I've got to do them (all said in a dragging monotone).

(How far do you really think of yourself as a housewife?) I've gradually got accustomed to it. Being stuck at home and always told 'that's your job'. It gets my goat sometimes. Because I used to earn a bit of money and be independent, and now I've got to rely on every penny from my husband.

(Do you ever feel there is anything else you would rather be doing now . . . ?) No, if I could see myself as anything else it would be in a career that I was doing, but then I wouldn't be married. (Marriage and a career aren't compatible?) They are, but not as I saw things at the time – I didn't think I would marry. I thought I would go on in that job – hairdressing. Things changed and I got married and I should accept things as they are.

(When you feel really happy these days . . .) Life's not monotonous – but it's very much the same. I feel very happy when there's a holiday coming up – just because it's a change of routine. I think to myself 'what a rut to be in!' I mean I wouldn't change things for the world with him [the child] but how else can you do it? You've got to stay at home and have children – men can't have them. But being at home and doing housework all day – I really don't like that. You don't get any permanent satisfaction from it.

To count such comments as these as indicative of satisfaction and dissatisfaction with housework may perhaps be criticized on the grounds that what these women are talking about is not the housework situation, but marriage. However, neither of them makes any reference to her husband, or to the dynamics of her marriage relationship in these comments, though Norma Larkin makes some (implicit) observations about marriage in general. The economic dependence to which she refers is not a facet of marriage as such, but a facet of marriage in which the wife is not employed. It is an aspect of full-time housewifery as a work role, not of the marriage relationship itself. For all but the most privileged housewives, economic dependence is a fact of life, and dependence on the husband for money with which to feed and clothe the family and run the home constrains the freedom which women might otherwise have to control their work situations.

The issue of satisfaction with housework is more complex than has been suggested so far. Twelve of the forty interviews contained interesting contradictions between the overall assessments of satisfaction and answers to the direct question 'Do you like housework?' asked in the early stages of the interview. These contradictions throw some light on the social class question. They fall into three groups: (1) eight working-class women who say initially that they 'like' or 'don't mind' housework, but turn out to be dissatisfied with it; (2) two middle-class women who follow the same pattern; and (3) two middle-class women who say they dislike housework but are satisfied with it. These contradictions cannot simply be explained in terms of the satisfaction assessments being incorrect; the disjunction between the two factors – initial answers and overall feeling – is too complete. The following example comes from the interview with Sally Jordan, a factory worker and a dustman's wife; she belongs in the first group of working-class women whose early positive or non-committal response turns into predominantly negative feeling:

(Do you like housework?) I don't mind it . . . I suppose I don't mind housework because I'm not at it all day. I go to work and I'm only on housework half a day. If I did it all day I wouldn't like it – woman's work is never done, she's on the go all the time – even before you go to bed, you've still got something to do – emptying ashtrays, wash a few cups up. You're still working. It's the same thing every day; you can't sort of say you're not going to do it, because you've got to do it – like preparing a meal: it's got to be done because if you don't do it, the children wouldn't eat . . . I suppose you get so used to it, you just do it automatically . . . I'm happier at work than I am at home . . .
(What would you say are the worst things about being a housewife?) I suppose you get days when you feel you get up and you've got to do the same old things – you get bored, you're stuck in the same routine. I think if you ask any housewife, if they're honest, they'll turn round and say they feel like a drudge half the time – everybody thinks when they get up in the morning 'Oh no, I've got the same old things to do today, till I go to bed tonight.' It's doing the same things – boredom.

These comments reveal obvious discontent.

An interesting methodological and theoretical problem is posed by these contradictions. How can they be explained? One major reason why it is important to provide an explanation hinges on the discrepancy between the present finding of no social class difference in housework satisfaction and the widespread notion that middle-class women are more likely to be dissatisfied. The tendency of working-class women to respond positively or non-committally to a question about 'liking' housework (whether or not they actually experience a basic dissatisfaction) may be one reason why other researchers have concluded that fundamental social class differences exist on this dimension.

Answers to the question 'Do you like housework?' are not evenly distributed between the two class groups, as Table 4.2 shows.

Table 4.2   Answers to the question 'Do you like housework?' and social class

Social class	Answers to question			
	Like No.(%)	Don't mind No.(%)	Dislike No.(%)	Total No.(%)
Working class	6(60)	8(10)	6(30)	20(100)
Middle class	4(20)	2(10)	14(70)	20(100)
Total	10(25)	10(25)	20(50)	40(100)

$x^2 = 7.2$; d.f. $= 2$; $p < .05$

The working-class housewife is more likely to say that she 'likes' or 'doesn't mind' housework, and the typical middle-class response is one of dislike. In his work on social class and linguistic styles, Basil Bernstein has identified two different modes of language use.[5] These he began by terming a 'public' and a 'formal' language, but later called 'restricted' and 'elaborated' codes. It would not be in order to list fully here Bernstein's distinctions between the two codes; however, one of these distinctions is of direct relevance to the question of social class differences in answers to the question 'Do you like housework?' Describing what could roughly be termed the 'working-class' code, Bernstein says

A public language is one which contains a large number of idiomatic, traditional phrases from which the individual chooses. Instead of an individual learning to create a language-use within which he can select to mediate his individual feeling, a public language user tends to attach his feelings to social counters or tags which maximize the solidarity of the social relationship at the cost of the logical structure of the communication and the specificity of the feeling.[6]

In contrast to this, the speech mode more characteristic of the middle class

facilitates the verbal elaboration of subjective intent, sensitivity to the implications of separateness and difference, and points to the possibilities inherent in a complex conceptual hierarchy for the organization of experience.[7]

Whereas the (predominantly) working-class mode of language use inhibits the verbal elaboration of individual differences, the (predominantly) middle-class code is precisely oriented to this dimension of experience.

Bernstein's work has come in for some strong criticism recently.[8] Although much of this criticism centres on the misuse of his work by others, some more substantive arguments are that middle-class values inform his conceptual distinctions and that these are insufficiently grounded in the raw data of speech patterns. Without engaging in the details of this debate, and having presented what is an admittedly brief over-simplification of Bernstein's work, I would nevertheless venture to say that the different response patterns of working-class and middle-class women in the present sample do seem to fit into the broad outlines of Bernstein's scheme. My suggestion is that the eight working-class women who say they 'like' or 'don't mind' housework but show evidence of being dissatisfied with it, are in fact committing this contradiction because the speech mode they are used to makes the presentation of individual feelings difficult. The linguistic style of the middle-class housewife more easily permits her to describe her own individual feelings about housework than does that of her working-class counterpart. This does not mean, of course, that the working-class respondent is unable to produce complex verbal structures. The point seems to be one of the relative facility with which working-class and middle-class housewives can, in response to a direct question, immediately describe their individual feelings about housework. In the working-class group the use of similar phrases ('I like', 'I don't mind' housework) may overlay differences in experience which are not readily articulated.

Several riders must be added to the bald statement that class-differentiated linguistic codes help to explain the contradiction between initial statements of attitudes and overall feelings. Why should the working-class housewife say she 'likes' or 'doesn't mind' housework – why should this be the typical response? It has been observed by others that housewifery as a role for women is more positively evaluated in traditional working-class communities than in middle-class social networks.[9] In other words the dominant norm is one of feminine satisfaction with housework. A tendency to repeat this norm follows. This tendency is illustrated succinctly in the responses of two working-class housewives to a question about general satisfaction asked at the end of the interview:

(Would you describe yourself as generally satisfied or unsatisfied with life – or neither, particularly?) Generally satisfied. Well, I mean to say *you have to make the best of things.*
(Painter and decorator's wife)

I don't really know. Satisfied, I suppose. I suppose I have to be. What's the point of being the other way when *you know you've got to be satisfied.*
(Factory hand's wife)

For those who are dissatisfied with housework, a statement of this feeling is problematic because the break between socially acceptable behaviour and individual experience has first to be made.

The converse point may help to explain the phenomenon of the two middle-class women who said they 'disliked' housework yet showed evidence of satisfaction with it. Their reference is to the middle-class norm of the discontented housewife. This explanation is borne out by the remark of one middle-class housewife: 'I don't go about feeling discontented', the implication being that she thinks she might be expected to do so. The fact that many of the twenty middle-class women did not say they disliked housework does not rule this explanation out of court. In neither class group is either norm – satisfaction *or* dissatisfaction – adhered to absolutely. While most middle-class women say they dislike housework and most working-class women say they like or don't mind it, there are some in each class group who deviate from this pattern. It is simply that one is a more *likely* response for the middle-class housewife and one is more *likely* for her working-class sister. Since the social class assessment is based on husband's occupation, it may also be that the 'deviants' are more 'working class' or 'middle class' on several important dimensions than their class-categorization itself indicates. This is certainly true of the two middle-class women who said they liked or didn't mind housework but were dissatisfied with it. One, Clare Pullen, was married to a supermarket manager, but had herself been a machine operator before giving up work to have a baby. The family lived in a two-room rented flat in a predominantly working-class area. Jean Bevan, the second of these two, had a middle-class previous occupation – nursing – but also lived in a working-class area. Her methods of child-rearing stand out as being more 'working-class' than 'middle-class'; for example she smacked a lot and expected the three year old to be clean and tidy all the time: both these are areas in which the Newsons found social class differences in their study.[10] As they point out, child-rearing patterns may provide a better indicator of social class than the more conventional criteria. However, to date no systematic method has been devised of assessing social class in this way. Most researchers are at some stage forced up against the inadequacy of the social class classification. To define away every social class difference on the grounds that the social class division itself is erroneous would clearly be a pointless procedure, but the researcher does have an obligation to note those cases where it seems to her/him that faults in this classification 'explain' the pattern in the data most closely.

To summarize this part of the argument, it can be said that the contradictions found in these forty interviews between housework satisfaction patterns and answers to the question 'Do you like housework?' may be interpreted as evidence of class-differentiated linguistic styles and norms of feminine domesticity. These weight the balance of responses in each class group in a particular direction, while the actual experience of doing housework is a dimension on which the classes are not divided. Rather than proving an insoluble methodological problem, these contradictions are, in fact, a key finding in the research. As later chapters show, answers to the 'Do you like housework?' question are also related to the kind of standards and routines adopted in housework, and to women's self-concepts as expressed in a written statement. These connections suggest that what a woman says about housework at the beginning of her interview does not only reflect on the mode of feeling-expression general in her class-specific linguistic code. A 'like' or 'don't mind' attitude seems symbolic of a search for satisfaction in housework; the declaration of 'dislike' appears to indicate the recognition of dissatisfaction. This crucial distinction is expanded in Chapter 10.

Before leaving this issue, I will note a methodological moral. The lesson learnt is that simple questions produce simple answers. Not a great deal in the way of interpretation or conclusion should be hung on answers to a single question about 'liking' housework. Only a depth interview of several hours can be expected to provide a complete picture of overall positive and negative feelings experienced by the housewife in relation to housework.

Thus far the major burden of the evidence seems to be *against* the view that social class differences in women's domesticity exist. Working-class and middle-class women are satisfied and dissatisfied with housework in equal numbers: different patterns of response to a particular interview question are interesting, but do not affect this basic conclusion. The conclusion is confirmed by the social class distribution of positive, negative and neutral responses to questions about housework tasks, some of which were described in the last chapter. These are shown in the table below.

Table 4.3   Average rate per person of different answers to work task questions, by social class

| | First answers | | All answers | |
Kind of answer	Working class	Middle class	Working class	Middle class
'Dislike'	2.60	2.90	3.85	3.75
'Don't mind'	1.40	1.40	1.65	1.50
'Like'	2.00	1.70	2.25	2.15
Total	6.00	6.00	7.75	7.40

Average rate per person

In this table there is very little difference between one social class group and the other.

On another issue, that of the way in which the status of housewifery is perceived, both class differences and similarities in women's domesticity are found. While thirteen out of twenty middle-class women (sixty-five per cent) 'mind' describing themselves as housewives on a form, only eight out of twenty working-class women (forty per cent) state this objection. (The difference is not statistically significant.) Mirra Komarovsky comes up with the same finding in her survey of American working-class marriage. She says:

> The discontent of the housewife is often attributed to contemporary values. She chafes, it is said, because of the low prestige society attaches to her role ... Such an explanation of discontent may perhaps apply to educated middle-class housewives, but we find little evidence of status frustrations among working-class wives.[11]

This perception of the low social esteem in which the housewife role is held, charted in the previous chapter, is associated with work dissatisfaction. Of twenty-one housewives who mind being labelled a housewife, nineteen (eighty-six per cent) are dissatisfied with work; of the nineteen who 'don't mind' this label, ten (thirteen per cent) are dissatisfied. (This difference is significant at the five per cent level.) Thus, in so far as middle-class women are more likely to perceive the low status of the housewife role, they are more likely than their working-class sisters to be dissatisfied with it.

What is the logic of this process? The sociological theory of 'status crystallization' or 'status congruency' is relevant here.[12] Broadly speaking, this theory states that stress or dissatisfaction is more likely to be experienced by an individual if her/his ranks are discrepant – for instance the ranks associated with income, education and ethnic group. If all are at the same level, there is a high degree of status crystallization, and stress for a status-related reason is improbable. In the case of the housewife there are two possible discrepancies which might be connected with dissatisfaction: that between the status of housewife and the status of the husband's work, and the discrepancy between the status of the housewife's own present or previous employment work and her status as a housewife. While the former is not

associated with work satisfaction patterns in this sample,[13] the
latter is – or at least the relationship is in the expected direction.
In Table 4.4 'status' was assessed using three criteria of skill,
training and social prestige.[14] In evaluating the social prestige of
each occupation I have placed special emphasis on 'feminine'

Table 4.4. Social class, employment and dissatisfaction

Employment:	Social class	
	Working class	Middle class
1 Low status	12	1
Unskilled factory work	8	1
Retail sales work	3	0
Domestic work	1	0
Percentage of all with low status occupations dissatisfied with housework — 62%		
2 Intermediate status	8	13
Typist	3	2
Office worker	3	5
Receptionist	1	0
Secretary	0	3
Library assistant	0	1
Hairdresser	1	2
Percentage of all with intermediate status occupations dissatisfied with housework — 67%		
3 High status	0	6
Manicurist	0	1
Fashion model	0	1
TV/radio production assistant	0	2
Nurse	0	1
Computer programmer	0	1
Percentage of all with high status occupations dissatisfied with housework — 100%		

Association between occupational status and work satisfaction not significant at 5% level.

rewards – that is, those dimensions of a job that have relatively
high prestige within the feminine job world. These include
'glamour', the opportunity to mix with high status men and
women, and the intrinsic reward of doing a 'worthwhile' job.[15]
Of course qualities like money, responsibility and promotion

opportunities still remain important, but a degree of gender-differentiation in the dimension of prestige follows from the broad structure of gender-differentiation in the occupational world.

In Table 4.4 sixty-two per cent of the housewives with low status occupations are dissatisfied with housework, sixty-seven per cent of those with intermediate occupations are dissatisfied, and, of those with high status occupations, all are assessed as dissatisfied with their present work – housework. This suggests that, in part, the housewife's dissatisfaction with her work is a function of downward social mobility. The connection is articulated by some women in the sample. Mary Byron, a middle-class housewife married to a sales representative, talks about her previous job experience:

> I did hairdressing for five years and then I had a job as a manicurist at Claridges. Manicuring is boring actually, but it was meeting all those people, there was always something interesting to talk about because the people were so knowledgeable and travelled . . . you get all the kings and dukes and lords. It's like a different world there, and they treat you so nicely . . . They treat you like a lady, it was fabulous.

By comparison housework is boring, lonely, unrewarding work, and it has none of the prestige associated with meeting famous people and working in a glamorous establishment like Claridges. Being a fashion model is also a 'nice' job:

> Sometimes actually I think 'Oh I'd like to go back to work' – to be in that hubbub – because I always worked in the West End and there was something about the atmosphere – being dressed all day . . . I adored it – the glamour, the feeling of being in the hub of things which I love – I love clothes – I used to make up every day and make myself look nice and meet people . . . to me it wasn't work, every minute of it was enjoyment . . . I didn't have to think 'Well, if I put that dress on I'll only get it dirty because the baby will be sick over me' – to be dressed up all day and feel you can be clean and only have nice jobs to do and always be with people . . .

Or there may be regret for the loss of the rewards of professionalism, as in this woman's comments about nursing:

> I very often miss nursing. I thoroughly enjoyed it. I found it extremely satisfying, which was something I never found when I worked in an office . . . I didn't ever seem to get the same sort

of satisfaction out of getting something to balance properly as I did out of seeing a patient recover, which was something you'd helped them to do. There's just something special about it. Nothing else is like nursing – it's a job on its own.

But the status frustrations of moving from an interesting and professionalized work-world into the world of the housewife stand out most clearly in the interview with Juliet Warren, an ex-television production assistant. She says:

> I would hate to think of myself as just being a housewife . . . I think that's why I'm so frustrated. I really cannot come to terms with the fact that I am . . . there's lots of interesting work to do – there was in the job I did – and I want so much to identify with that rather than just sit back here and say 'I'm a housewife and I'm happy' . . . because I couldn't be. I think 'housewife' is like 'spinster' and 'spinster' is a terrible label to put on anyone. 'Housewife' is a terrible label too.

For Juliet Warren the comparison between her previous and present work is not merely provoked by the interview. It is brought home to her every day in the person of her husband, a television documentary director. She reports one recent incident and her reactions to it:

> The thing that made me a little envious was this girl – she's his assistant on this particular film – ringing up, and there was a slight chance they would be going to Switzerland that day, and suddenly I was in there again and I thought how exciting it all was and how nice it would be to go off filming again. I said so to Tom and he said of course this girl isn't all that popular with the men – that's an important part of a production assistant's job – and he said 'she'd give anything to be in your place – to be married and have a baby'. Then I could remain sane about it, by thinking I'm being stupid: I've really got the best world. It's just that having known it, I do get fed up sometimes.

This connection between high status employment work and present dissatisfaction with housework holds only for the middle-class women, but there is evidence that the tendency to be dissatisfied with housework in relation to the status of one's previous job may involve the question of a 'reference group'. There are no women with high status previous jobs in the working-class group, so that those with an intermediate status job hold the highest status jobs in the working-class group as a whole. Among the working-class women, eighty-eight per cent of those with jobs whose status is 'high for class' are dissatisfied with housework; in the middle-class group, the figure is a hundred per cent. Conversely, of those women with jobs whose status is 'low for class', a lower proportion is dissatisfied with housework; fifty-eight per cent in the working-class, and fifty-seven per cent in the middle-class group. Thus, while middle-class women are more likely to object to the label 'housewife' on grounds of its low status, there is a general tendency for downward mobility on the status dimension – from paid work to the job of house-wife – to be associated with present dissatisfaction.

Beyond this particular question of status, middle-class and working-class women in this sample have in common a deep-seated appreciation of the rewards experienced in outside work. The resultant comparison with housework persistently brands it as a less enjoyed and less enjoyable occupation. This is all the more remarkable since many of the jobs held by these women are not, at first sight, particularly rewarding ones. Nearly a quarter of the forty were in unskilled factory jobs and over a third have done typing or general office work. Thirty of the forty fall into the four occupations of factory work, retail sales work, domestic work, and office or secretarial work. All, with the exception of Joanna Giles, an ex-computer programmer, were engaged in occupations stereotyped as feminine and thus traditionally low paid.

Housework contrasts with employment work in its lack of economic reward, its isolation and the lack of social recognition accorded to the responsibilities carried by the housewife. Helen Crane, an ex-secretary, valued her job because it not only gave her the experience of autonomy, but it publicly valued her exercise of this responsibility:

> I was my own boss for a start – the man I worked for left after about seven months, and the man who took over didn't know anything about it: I knew more about the job than he did, so I had to tell him what to do for the first six months . . . in fact he tried to get the job upgraded anyway. He did get it upgraded from a secretary to more of an assistant . . .

The extreme depth and detail in which these women describe their job experiences – often of five or more years ago – is an index of their continuing significance. Carol West, an ex-sales ledger clerk, reiterates the importance of job responsibility:

> I worked at City Motors and I stayed there for seven years –
> I had quite a few jobs before that, but I liked that one. I
> enjoyed the work there – dealing with customers on the phone
> – there were two of us girls . . . the other girl was in charge and
> we had a man over us, but it was between us two . . . we had
> to get all the statements out at the end of the month . . .

Janet Gallagher worked in a factory:

> I didn't like the beer factory all that much – it was wet all the
> time, but in the yeast factory I quite liked that, because I was
> working with machines . . . I tell you one thing I used to enjoy,
> on this particular belt there were so many girls, what I used
> to enjoy was sending plenty of work down to them – I was
> responsible for how much work they got out . . .

June Doyle's pre-marriage job was equally 'menial'; she was a
chambermaid:

> I worked at the London Palace Hotel as a chambermaid for
> three years. I enjoyed it very much. It wasn't the work, it was
> the company – the environment. The variety of ages up there
> – old, middling and my generation. I was very, very happy.
> And I had a lot of time to myself. I finished every day mostly
> at one o'clock and I was to start at half past five the next
> morning. I missed it when I gave it up to get married. I'd like
> to be back in that time again . . . You can't really explain it . . .

Although she gave up this job eight years ago, she has a lasting
identification with it. When asked if she ever felt lonely in the
daytime as a housewife, she replied:

> Yes, sometimes, but then you get adjusted to it. I was lonely at
> first. Before I got married I was living in the London Palace and
> there was something like three hundred and sixty girls there.
> I have a card someplace and all their signatures are on it, when
> they gave me my dinner service [a wedding present]. There
> was always somebody there and we had a television set and rest
> room there, and there was always about twenty or thirty girls
> in it.

On the basis of their comments about their jobs, the women
were assessed as satisfied or dissatisfied with employment work.
Of twenty-seven who are satisfied, twenty (seventy-four per cent)
are *dissatisfied* with housework, and eighteen (sixty-seven per
cent) with life generally. Among the thirteen who are dissatisfied with their jobs, eight (sixty-two per cent) are dissatisfied

with housework and two (fifteen per cent) with life in general. Although only one of these relationships is statistically significant – that between employment work satisfaction and dissatisfaction with life generally – both are in the direction suggested by the women's own observations. Enjoyment of one's past job does not augur well for contentment in the role of housewife. Again, this conclusion runs counter to the general idea of class differences in women's domesticity. Even though most of the working-class women had low skill, repetitive jobs, they picked out certain qualities of these jobs as satisfying by comparison with housework, and they shared this tendency with the middle-class women.

The findings presented in this chapter, taken together, force a re-evaluation of the claim that the unhappy housewife is a purely middle-class phenomenon. Such a claim is too simplistic; it does not take into account the various faces of women's domesticity. Working-class women are no less likely than middle-class women to express dissatisfaction with housework. Their attitudes to the separate tasks which make up housework are on average very similar to the attitudes of the middle-class group. A drop in status from paid work to housework is likely to be associated with dissatisfaction in both social classes, and a simple enjoyment of the rewards of an outside job is also, for both middle- and working-class women, a bad omen from the viewpoint of housework satisfaction. The findings discussed in Chapter 7 should be added to these similarities: irrespective of their husband's social class, women share a similar childhood socialization for domesticity and a consequent personal identification with the housewife role.

Two differences between working-class and middle-class housewives coexist with these similarities. Complaints about the label of 'just a housewife' are more common in the middle-class group, and attitudes to housework as revealed by the question 'Do you like housework?' show a class-differentiated patterning. Both these differences suggest the importance of a distinction which I shall come back to later: attitudes to the role of housewife are in principle not the same thing as feelings about housework. A woman's attitudes to the housewife role may be positive – she may feel herself to be a housewife, and agree with the idea that housewifery is an appropriate role for women, but she may at the same time dislike doing housework. The reverse pattern is also possible. Feelings about housework are a question of the experience of doing housework and one's reactions to it; orientation to the housewife role involves the issues of self-concept, gender identity and sub-cultural norms of feminine role-behaviour. The data on domesticity presented in the preceding pages suggest that working-class women on the whole have different attitudes to the housewife role from their middle-class counterparts, but in the area of work activity, middle-class and working-class experiences are very similar.

5 Work Conditions

One preoccupation of the sociology of industrial work has been the *causes* of job dissatisfaction. What accounts for the fact that some workers are satisfied, while others are not? The difference cannot simply be dismissed as a question of personality, since certain patterns of job satisfaction or dissatisfaction seem to be associated with particular kinds of jobs. Thus jobs which involve social interaction with other workers are generally more satisfying than socially isolated work; monotonous, repetitive work is more likely to be linked with job dissatisfaction than more varied work; jobs which involve responsibility and the ability to organize work time and work methods are generally preferred over those which lack these qualities, and so forth.[1] It would seem that one source of industrial discontent in the modern world is the structure and content of work itself.

This is a general conclusion. But does it apply to the case of the housewife? Answers given by the forty women in the sample to questions about work tasks suggest that certain characteristics of housework may be more or less uniformly experienced as dissatisfying while others are potentially rewarding. A look at the social class dimension also indicates that there is a considerable area of shared response to housework which may reflect on the nature of the work itself, and the conditions under which it is done. Hence it would seem both helpful and important to examine a number of aspects of work that industrial sociology has highlighted as critical in the explanation of job satisfaction. These are the experiences of monotony, fragmentation and excessive pace in work and social interaction patterns. Two other dimensions of work which have been found less important in the case of the industrial worker are also looked at in this chapter: working hours and the technical environment.

1 MONOTONY, FRAGMENTATION AND EXCESSIVE PACE

A common charge levelled against housework is that it is inherently monotonous and repetitive. Although the tasks that make up housework are dissimilar, there is said to be a 'sameness' about them which derives from their frequent need to be repeated, their lack of intrinsic meaning, and the impermanence of the goals they achieve. There is nothing more 'automatic' than the perfect housewife, mechanically pursuing the same routine day in and day out. The Peckham Rye Women's Liberation Group speak from personal experience when they say that housework is:

> An endless routine; it creates it own high moments of achievement and satisfaction so as to evade...futility. The bolt you tighten on the factory floor vanishes to be replaced by another: but the clean kitchen floor is tomorrow's dirty floor and the clean floor of the day after that. The appropriate symbol for housework (and for housework alone) is not the interminable conveyor belt but a compulsive circle like a pet mouse in its cage spinning round on its exercise wheel, unable to get off . . .
> But the routine is never quite routine, so the vacuum in one's mind is never vacuous enough to be filled. 'Housework is a worm eating away at one's ideas'. Like a fever dream it goes on and on, until you desperately hope that it can all be achieved at one blow. You lay the breakfast the night before, you have even been known to light the gas under the kettle for tomorrow's tea, wishing that by breakfast time everything could be over...[2]

The monotony of housework turns it into a mindless task. Without calling for one's whole attention, it so persistently demands a small part of it that concentration on anything else is ruled out. Thus monotony and fragmentation are intimately connected, and through the need to accomplish a long series of jobs each day, a feeling of always having too much to do may be added.

Is this a very one-sided picture, as it is sometimes claimed to be? Perhaps monotony, fragmentation and excessive pace are noted by few housewives and are not bound up with a dominant feeling of dissatisfaction. One way to test this possibility is to ask direct questions about the incidence of these experiences in housework, and compare them with that reported by other groups of workers. In their study of affluent workers' attitudes to work John Goldthorpe and his colleagues asked three questions designed specifically to measure the extent to which industrial work is experienced as intrinsically unsatisfying. These questions were: 'Do you find your present job monotonous?' 'Do you find you can think about other things while doing your job?' and 'Do you ever find the pace of the job too fast?'[3] On the basis of the answers they received to these questions Goldthorpe and his colleagues concluded that monotony is a definite source of job dissatisfaction. Fragmentation and excessive pace were also found to be important variables bearing on job satisfaction, with many workers, who did not find their work monotonous, stating that it did not absorb their full attention or that they found the pace of it too fast. These three questions were used in an adapted form for housewives in the present sample.

When asked, 'Do you find housework monotonous on the whole?' thirty out of the forty women said 'yes':

It's the feeling that although you've done the job for today you've still got to do it tomorrow. It's one of the things that gets me down about it.

(Journalist's wife)

Dissatisfaction is higher among those who report monotony. Eighty per cent of the women who said 'yes' to the monotony question are dissatisfied with housework, compared with forty per cent of those who said 'no'. (This difference is significant at the five per cent level.) The conclusion to be drawn is that monotony is clearly associated with work dissatisfaction, and this is supported by the large number of housewives who mentioned monotony *spontaneously* at various points in the interview. A cinema manager's wife and a toolmaker's wife provide examples:

I like cooking and I like playing with the children, doing things for them – I don't like the basic cleaning. *It's boring, it's monotonous.*

It's the monotony I don't like – *it's repetitive and you have to do the same things each day.* I suppose it's really just like factory work – just as boring.

Fragmentation – the experience of work subdivided into a series of unconnected tasks not requiring the worker's full attention – is also a common experience. Thirty-six of the forty women said 'yes' to the question 'Do you find you can think about other things while you're working?', and most of the women then went on to offer examples of topics they thought about. From these answers it is clear that fragmentation is an expected and accepted quality of housework. The women were on the whole surprised at the question, apparently assuming that a dispersal of concentration is intrinsic to housework. As Dawn Abbat, a middle-class housewife, answered the question:

> (Do you find you can think about other things while you're working?) *Oh, of course.* Today I've been thinking to myself, I've only got the sleeves to put in that dress – when am I going to have the time to do it?

Perhaps for this reason, fragmentation is not associated with work dissatisfaction: there is little difference in the percentages dissatisfied in the two groups – those who report fragmentation and those who do not.[4] This is an instance of the general finding that aspects of work activity have the capacity to satisfy or dissatisfy people only in relation to the personal value put upon them.[5] Job satisfaction or dissatisfaction is a function of the perceived relationship between what one wants from one's job and what one sees it as offering or entailing. Since women do not see housework as a coherent, meaningful structure of tasks demanding their full attention, they are not made dissatisfied by its fragmented nature.

What are the kind of thoughts that occupy the housewife while she works? The list of topics given in answer to the fragmentation question is as follows: fantasy, eighteen replies; leisure/social activities, seventeen replies; housework, fourteen replies; child-care, twelve replies. (These add up to more than forty because some women mentioned more than one topic.)

'Fantasy' comes first on the list. The housewife's name for this is 'daydreaming':[6] Sally Jordan, a dustman's wife, says:

> I daydream when I'm doing anything. I'm always going off into a trance. I don't hear people when they talk to me. I stare into space. I'm working at the same time.

Favourite topics for daydreaming are housing and holidays. The significance of fantasizing about a new house or a new flat is that one is visualizing a change in one's work environment. Pauline Cutts, a secretary who lives in a rented furnished flat with her husband and one child, says:

> Usually I dream about having my own house. I think about that most of the time. I think there's more reward in housework if you've got your own house – even with an unfurnished flat there is.

The dream of 'my own house' holds out the prospect of perfect satisfaction with housework. This seems to be because owning the floors one cleans promises such a harmonious alliance between the worker and her work that dissatisfaction is (in theory) ruled out.

Although the desire to become a home-owner may represent a genuine social aspiration for these women and their families, there is no evidence that it guarantees satisfaction with housework: the housewives in the sample who did own their homes were no more satisfied than those whose homes were rented. The ideal of 'each woman in her own house' is certainly one fostered by advertising, and thus it may be, in part, a stereotyped response to the boredom of housework. The same holds true of holidays as themes of mental activity while working:

> (Do you find you can think about other things . . . ?) Yes – a summer holiday in Ibiza! – No – seriously – I'm usually thinking about what Susan is up to, planning what to do.
> (Machine operator's wife)

Holidays are avenues of escape:

> I think about how I could get dressed up and go out somewhere, for a couple of hours, and just leave it all, because I get so sick of it sometimes . . . I do get very irritable with myself very often. I often feel like I could pack up and go home for a holiday in Ireland.
> (Painter and decorator's wife)

The status of daydreaming about holidays, housing and related themes as conventional ways of expressing discontent is suggested by a passage from the interview with Elizabeth Gould, an ex-fashion model. She lives in a new four-storey house on a recently completed private estate, and typifies the perfect housewife of television advertising: her house has fitted carpets throughout, gleaming unmarked white paint, and every modern gadget, and it is impeccably maintained by Elizabeth, who describes herself as a housewife with very high standards. She explains:

> I don't daydream about things in my future very much because I must admit I haven't got much to daydream for – because I'm very lucky, I've got a lovely house, a lovely husband; we go on lovely holidays, we lead a nice social life, I've got lovely clothes –I can't really daydream and say I wish I was this, I wish I was that.

As answers to the 'fragmentation' question the category of leisure activities tends to merge into that of fantasy. 'Getting out for the day/away from the house' are ubiquitous topics; there is also a focus on social life:

> (Do you find you can think about other things while you're working?) Yes – what I've done the night before, the day before – thinking about parties and that. What people said, the things that happened, what we might do next Saturday night – that kind of thing.
>
> (Van driver's wife)

Although fourteen answers to the fragmentation question concern housework, the housewife rarely thinks about the work she is actually doing. Instead there are references to past and future performances:

> I think about the carpet that's got to be laid, and I must clean those windows tomorrow . . .
>
> (Lorry driver's wife)

> I think about what I'm going to do next . . . what I'm going to cook, the children, where I'll take them out . . . this sort of thing.
>
> (Sales director's wife)

This is a crucial finding. Housework is such fragmented work that almost never does the housewife report thinking about the task in hand. Whatever skills are needed, complete mental concentration is not one, and the effect of having many different tasks to do is a dispersal of the housewife's attention in many different directions. Children amplify this fragmentation effect. They make perfect concentration impossible and are often the cause of breaks in work activity. The extent to which children are thought about while housework is done is not only a reflection on housework's fragmented quality; it also signifies the basic difficulties which inhere in the combination of housewife and mother roles.[7]

All these strands of thought fulfil a latent function for the housewife. They enable her to get housework done; thinking about something else is a weapon deliberately employed in the attempt to combat boredom. The case of bakery workers provides a parallel: 'For those trying to survive, empty stretches of time must be structured, and an alternative content – some psychological colour – must be injected into the present in order to make it tolerable'.[8] In this sense, daydreaming is purposeful – not merely a random response to a superfluity of mentally unoccupied time:

> Daydreaming? That's what keeps me doing it [housework].
> (Factory hand's wife)

The alternative strategies of having the radio or television on 'to take my mind off it' or 'so I don't realize I'm doing it' are also mentioned.

Like fragmentation, the experience of time pressures in housework is not associated with work dissatisfaction. The women were asked 'Do you find you have too much to get through during the day?' Roughly half of those satisfied and half of those dissatisfied with housework say they have too much to do.[9] Neither do feelings of 'having too much to get through' relate to the number of children the housewife has, or to the kind of aids and amenities she possesses.

This finding is inconsistent with the conclusions of various surveys of job satisfaction in industry, according to which a feeling of excessive pace is a potent cause of dissatisfaction.[10] For the housewife the situation is complicated. Apart from the deadlines created by husbands' and children's needs, she imposes her own time pressures; these follow from the way she organizes her work and the kind of standards she sets herself.[11] The interviews suggest that satisfaction or dissatisfaction are the prior conditions here, and that the feeling of having too much to do or not flows from them. A woman who is generally satisfied[12] will organize her days so that she is not overcome by the many demands on her time. One such housewife is Barbara

Lipscombe, the wife of a car patrolman and the mother of three children aged four, two and one. She says of ironing, for example,

> I don't let the ironing build up too much. I wait until my husband's doing the late shift, and I wait until the children have gone to bed, and I sit down in front of the television. I find I can do it much easier if I've got one eye on the television. I seem to get through it easier and it doesn't worry me at all then.

Lack of organization creates work and may be a consequence of feeling dissatisfied, as in Juliet Warren's case:

> My standards have definitely dropped since I've been at home with the baby. I suppose it's because I can't do anything uninterrupted and I still can't get used to that. It takes a lot of effort. I'm very aware there's lots of jobs I ought to do – I used to be pretty thorough – and there are things I haven't got the time to do. I might start off the day with lots of intentions and by the end of it I'm so fagged out I just collapse. It worries me, because it's there again tomorrow . . . in my mind I've got a fixed routine, but I know I haven't got one really . . . I'm just badly organized.
> (Wife of a television documentary director)

Another facet of work is that of limits or deadlines. As Chapter 4 showed, the need to complete a task within a set period may produce a negative attitude towards it. Cooking is especially subject to this limitation, although it is in theory one of the most liked activities. This finding *is* echoed in one study of job motivation among industrial employees. The author sums up:

> Members of groups which have frequent time limits express significantly *less* pride in their work . . . The finding that those who more frequently work under time limits are *not* more interested in their work and take *less* pride in their job . . . is arresting. It may be that time limits, even when employees help set them, are not viewed as a standard of excellence by most employees in these job settings. Another possible explanation is that, while time limits may provide one standard of excellence, the attention which they focus on the speed of work diverts attention from the possibility of doing work which is creative or innovative, thereby reducing achievement incentive.[13]

So far as the housewife is concerned, time limits imposed by factors outside her control mean that the pace of her work is too fast for each task to get the attention she would like to give it. Unlike many jobs, housework can often be done in a very short space of time without actually failing to be done at all. Cleaning may consist of a quick dust or 'whip round' for the harassed housewife, and to some eyes at least it will still look as though the house has been cleaned – hence the expression 'eye service' ('I've just given the house eye service today'). However, it is the housewife's ultimate responsibility to see that all tasks get done properly. Neglect or minimization of a task is at best only a short-term expedient, and the housewife's awareness of this fact causes time pressures to be felt possibly more acutely than they are in other kinds of work.

To summarize therefore, monotony, fragmentation and time pressures are aspects of housework commonly experienced by housewives. In reply to three direct questions ninety per cent report fragmentation, and seventy-five per cent monotony, but the percentage drops to fifty per cent in the case of time pressures: these are more often referred to spontaneously in the course of discussing housework tasks. In Table 5.1 housewives' experiences of monotony, fragmentation and speed are compared with those of a sample of factory workers.

Table 5.1 The experience of monotony, fragmentation and speed in work: housewives and factory workers compared

| | Percentage experiencing: | | |
Workers	Monotony	Fragmentation	Speed
Housewives	75	90	50
Factory workers*	41	70	31
Assembly line workers*	67	86	36

* These figures are taken from Goldthorpe et al. The Affluent Worker: Industrial Attitudes and Behaviour, p. 18. The assembly line workers are a sub-sample of the factory workers.

Housewives experience more monotony, fragmentation and speed in their work than do workers in the factory. But when a particular sub-group of workers is taken – assembly line workers – the gap is narrowed. The inherent frustrations of assembly line work are also to be found in housework. This gives substance to the contemporary feminist polemic which brands housework as 'alienating' work.

2 SOCIAL INTERACTION

From the direct comparison of housework with factory work we move to an aspect of work which many studies agree has possibly the strongest influence on a worker's satisfaction. This is social interaction. Research has shown that loneliness is an occupational hazard for the modern housewife, who is often cut off not only from community life but from family life – in the wider sense – also. According to Gavron's survey of ninety-six urban housewives, the feeling of being tied to the house and isolated from meaningful social contacts is a common one for both working-class and middle-class women.[14] Herbert Gans in his study of American suburbia *The Levittowners* reports that boredom and loneliness affect women more than men, because of the women's housebound role.[15]

The forty women interviewed were asked early in the interview to give an account of their daily routines. This enabled the topic of social relationships to be covered, although a direct question was also asked: 'Do you ever feel as though you're on your own too much in the daytime?' Of the twenty-two women who said 'yes', seventeen (seventy-seven per cent) were dissatisfied with housework, while eleven (sixty-one per cent) of the eighteen who said 'no' were also dissatisfied. The difference is in the direction of more dissatisfaction in the lonely group (but it is not significant at the five per cent level). These bare figures do not give the whole picture, however. The women vary a great deal in their patterns of social relationships. In some cases only two or three people are seen in the course of a week; in others, there are two or three social contacts in the course of each day. Compare the description of her social life given by Linda Farrell, a delivery man's wife, with that given by Margaret Nicholson, the wife of the director of a publishing firm.

Although I'm quite happy to be indoors and getting on with my work – I don't say I'd be outside gallivanting everywhere –

it'd be nice to know people. I'd like just to pop round to my sister's – that sort of thing . . . The only person I really see is my neighbour next door. I suppose I see her once or twice a week – she comes in for a cup of tea, or I go to her. She's got one child at school. My other neighbour's working. I don't like this area at all – you just don't know people. My mother comes once a week, for the day. She phones me every other day. I look forward to my husband coming home in the middle of the day – it makes a break, breaks the day up. Normally I don't see anyone till my husband comes in – it *is* lonely really. When I first got married I got terribly depressed, because coming from a big family there was always something going on at home. I somehow regretted getting married at first. I couldn't get used to it at all. I used to hate coming home here. I'd wait till he came home, and then go to my mother's . . . it sounds childish, doesn't it? (Linda Farrell)

I suppose I have a friend in to tea nearly every afternoon – that is, a friend with children. We come back from fetching the children together, and then she'll stay till about 6.30. I get tea for all the children. Then there's a friend next door I see an awful lot – every day, certainly. My children play in her garden. About twice a week I go to lunch with a friend, and again about twice a week I have someone to lunch here. Monday afternoons I have to keep free because I like to take Mrs James – the domestic help – home and Friday afternoon Lucy has a dancing lesson. On Friday morning I take my neighbour shopping. I do it because she relies on me, she can't get down there on her own. Oh, and I belong to a Young Wives' group, we meet once a fortnight, and I see people from that quite often. (Margaret Nicholson)

Linda Farrell's social circle is much more restricted than Margaret Nicholson's. It is also more narrowly focused on the kinship group – relationships with her parents, brothers, sisters, in-laws and so on are the ones she most values. Not surprisingly, her main aim is to move back to the area where her family live – preferably to buy a house there. With two small children and no transport, like most of these women, the daytime journey across town is problematic, and the idea of going on one's own in the evening (leaving one's husband to baby sit) is seen as imposing too much of a strain on the marriage relationship. The pattern of kinship relationships extends to other women in the working-class half of the sample, particularly to those who come from a large family. For several women an attachment to one sister, also married with young children, is the chief social focus of the week. In these cases there are also younger sisters, un-married, who come visiting in the evenings or at weekends, and during the day if they are ever 'off' work. Mothers are important: so are mothers-in-law. In two cases the housewife's father is a regular visitor in the day time, and in one case the father regularly combines a social visit with a trip to the launderette to dry clothes on his daughter's behalf.

The social relationships engaged in by Margaret Nicholson include a wide variety of friends and the stress on family ties is missing. This is much more the stereotyped picture of middle-class coffee mornings, flower arranging, and other 'feminine' cultural activities. There is more stress on the companionship of the husband-wife relationship: an ethic of 'being on our own together'.

Taking the criterion of the number of 'social contacts' the housewife has during work time, an association with work satisfaction patterns does emerge. A 'social contact' here is any individual, not a residential member of the housewife's family, with whom she experiences social interaction. This may vary from a few words exchanged over the garden fence, to visits which last all day. The total amount of time taken up in such social exchanges or interactions in this sample is in fact relatively small: a division of housewives into three groups according to the proportion of work time thus occupied – less than twenty-five per cent, between twenty-five and fifty per cent, more than fifty per cent – revealed the majority of women to be in the first group; there was no significant relationship with work satisfaction patterns. What seems to be important is the number

Table 5.2　Work satisfaction and social contacts

Social contacts per week	Work satisfaction		Total No.(%)
	Satisfied No.(%)	Dissatisfied No.(%)	
19 or less	5(19)	21(81)	26(100)
20 or more	7(54)	6(46)	13(100)
Total	12(31)	27(69)	39(100)

$p < .05$
(The figures in this table add up to 39, not 40, since the one housewife who was employed full time was excluded from this analysis; her housework routines were not comparable with those of the others in this respect.)

of people the housewife sees. Twenty-six of the forty women have nineteen or fewer social contacts a week; thirteen have more. (I excluded the one woman who had a full-time job from this tabulation since this was the one respect in which her housework situation was not directly comparable with that of the other women.) The relationship with work satisfaction patterns is shown in Table 5.2.

Some women expressly blame loneliness for their dissatisfaction. As a supermarket manager's wife put it:

> (Do you ever feel you're on your own too much in the daytime?) Yes. The last couple of months it's been dragging: you feel 'I wish I could talk to somebody' . . . not knowing anybody else you tend to get this feeling that unless you go out and talk to someone you'll go stark raving mad . . .

A feeling of loneliness is connected with a feeling that nothing is happening:

> (Do you ever feel you're on your own too much in the daytime?) Yes. Very often. I could be murdered here and no one would know. When the milkman comes, it's an event.
>
> (Lorry driver's wife)

The general impression conveyed is that these women would not necessarily be *more satisfied* with work if they saw more people, but that they would certainly be *less dissatisfied*. It is interesting to note here that similar findings have been reported for employed workers. The quantity and quality of social interaction during work time can apparently act as a 'dissatisfier' but not as a 'satisfier'.[16]

Some degree of isolation is entailed by the housewife role, simply because housework is 'home' work, privatized and solitary. The housewife's only faithful companions are her children. Satisfactory social relationships with adults thus have a heightened importance. But for some women, seeing and exchanging a few words with a number of other people during the day may actually be a source of negative feelings. The superficiality of these 'social contacts' acts to remind the housewife how critically important to her are the deep and meaningful relationships she lacks. In the words of a working-class housewife living on a new council estate:

> *It depends what you call friends.* You see everybody here

practically every day. There's about six or seven mothers with children in this corridor I see every day. I've got one neighbour who's a friend – we go in each other's homes.

3 WORKING HOURS

The housewife's working hours are among the longest in contemporary society. Hours worked by housewives in this sample ranged from forty-eight (the one housewife who had a full-time job) to 105. The range of variation is shown below in Table 5.3 in relation to number of children. Most of the women – twenty-five out of the forty – work between seventy and eighty-nine hours a week. Only ten work less than seventy hours, and five do ninety or more hours of housework a week.

These calculations of working time are taken from the accounts of daily routine obtained in the interviews. They include all time spent in housework, including shopping, and in childcare or supervision. Not counted as 'work time' are periods described by the housewife as spent in leisure occupations – watching television, reading and so on. Time away from home, visiting relatives, neighbours or friends, is not included in the total. The care or supervision of children, though not strictly speaking housework, is included because in practice it was impossible to make an adequate distinction between the two activities of housework and childcare. From these women's descriptions of their days, it is clear that rarely, if ever, is it possible for them to make this distinction either. (A distinction between *attitudes* to housework and child-care is a different matter from a temporal merging of the two activities.)[17] While doing housework they are responsible for children and must know what the children are doing: while looking after children they are almost always involved in housework activities. Changing a baby's nappies involves washing those nappies: feeding children entails (eventually) tidying up, cleaning, and washing up.

There are two exceptions to the inclusion of child-care in housework time. One is the counting of visiting as leisure which from the viewpoint of child-care it really is not. Wherever the housewife-mother is, she retains the responsibility for the care

Table 5.3   Weekly* housework hours and number of children

Number of children	Weekly hours spent in housework							Total
	40–49	50–59	60–69	70–79	80–89	90–99	100+	
One	1	2	5	5	1	1	1	16
Two	0	1	1	5	4	0	1	12
Three or more	0	0	0	2	8	2	0	12
Total	1	3	6	12	13	3	2	40

* 'Weekly' means a seven-day week.

of her children. The other exception is time when children are asleep. Here again, the responsibility for children is maintained and the housewife must be prepared to interrupt whatever she is doing at a moment's notice if her children wake up and require her attention. Neither of these categories of time is included in the assessment of working hours unless of course, in the latter case, the housewife is actually doing housework during the hours 'freed' by children's sleep.

The average working week of housewives in this sample is seventy-seven hours – almost twice as long as an industrial working week of forty hours. This figure is in agreement with other information about housework hours gathered by other researchers: Table 5.4 contains a comparison of results from a range of different studies. These studies cover three countries and a period from 1929 to 1971. The division into 'rural' and 'urban' studies suggests that housework hours are longer under urban conditions. But the figures in both groups indicate that there has been no decrease in housework time over this period. In the United States in 1929 rural housewives put in a sixty-four-hour week; in France, thirty years later, a sixty-seven-hour week. Comparing urban Britain in 1950 and in 1971, housewives have added seven hours a week to their working time during this period. This lack of change contrasts with the situation of employed workers. For example, between 1920 and 1953 in the United States in the manufacturing industry the average hours of work decreased by ten: from fifty to forty hours.[18]

These various surveys use different methods and different kinds of sample for the computation of housework time, so precise comparisons are difficult. However, if one looks at the size of family, the findings are fairly consistent: in the 1948 French

Table 5.4   A comparison of data on housework hours

Study,[19] and country carried out in:	Date	Average weekly hours of housework
I Rural studies		
Wilson: United States	1929	64
US Bureau of Home Economics:		
United States	1929	62
Cowles and Dietz: United States	1956	61
Girard and Bastide: France	1959	67
II Urban studies		
US Bureau of Home Economics:		
United States	1929	51
Bryn Mawr: United States		
(i) small city	1945	78
(ii) large city	1945	81
Stoetzel: France	1948	82
Moser: Britain	1950	70
Mass observation: Britain	1951	72
Girard: France	1958	67
Oakley: Britain	1971	77

study, for instance, housewives with one child put in on average a seventy-eight-hour week; in the 1950 British study a sixty-seven-hour week, and in the present study a seventy-one-hour week was the average figure for housewives in this group. The French studies which contain the most sophisticated breakdown of housework hours, according to a number of variables, suggest that, on average, one child adds twenty-three hours to housework time, two children add thirty-five hours, and three or more add forty-one hours. Of the twelve housewives with three or more children in the present sample none works less than seventy hours a week, eight work eighty or more hours, and two ninety or more.

Somewhat surprising is the fact that the longest hours are *not* put in by the women with the largest number of children. In the group with one child, Elizabeth Gould works eighty-four hours, Clare Pullen ninety-one hours, and Elaine Cawthorne 104 hours. In the group with two children Jill Duffy puts in a 105-hour week: of the forty she is the most industrious. (I discuss this paradox in Chapter 6.)

Is a long working week connected with work dissatisfaction? In this sample there is no statistical relationship.[20] This of course might be due to the fact that the sample as a whole has a long working week; it certainly contradicts the impression given by the women themselves that 'women's work is never done':

> The worst thing is, you've never finished. I always go to bed knowing that there's something I should have done – often the housewife slaves all day and the husband just comes home and puts his feet up.
>
> (Cinema manager's wife)

What then, accounts for the absence of a relationship between work hours and satisfaction patterns? The interviews suggest two answers to this question. First of all, it seems that the housewife's resentment of her long working hours is located by her in the context of a comparison between her own and her husband's situation. As earlier quotations have indicated,[21] the assertion that women work harder than men is part of a constant dialogue between husband and wife. A second answer is that long working hours are not a cause of housework dissatisfaction because they are an expected part of the housewife role. Like its fragmented nature, housework's 'never-endingness' is so much bound up with the idea of housework that the two are not conceived apart. Housewives simply do not expect to work the same hours in the home as they would in an office or factory.

The relative unimportance of extended work time as a determinant of dissatisfaction is confirmed by studies of industrial work. In one review of job attitudes research, working hours come out as less important than any other aspect of working conditions, and working conditions as a category come ninth in a ranked list of ten job factors. Not surprisingly, working hours are more important to employed married women than to employed men, since they have the double burden of employment work *and* housework.[22]

4 THE TECHNICAL ENVIRONMENT

Is the modern housewife's malaise due to deficiencies in her work environment? Lack of proper equipment, inadequate housing – are such considerations in fact a cause of dissatisfaction?

Or is dissatisfaction actually unrelated to these features of the home as the workplace?

The women interviewed were assessed on the number of amenities – running hot water, nearness to shops and so on – and aids – vacuum cleaners, washing machines and so forth – they possessed. (For a full list see the interview schedule in Appendix II.) A score was then obtained by assigning a value to each item. The average score for amenities was 7.5 and for aids 3.1. As was expected, scores were higher for both aids and amenities in the middle-class group (8.0 and 3.8 as opposed to 7.0 and 2.4 in the working-class group).

A housewife with an average 'score' was Joan Hubbard, an ex-shop assistant married to a toolmaker. She has two children aged four and two years, and lives in a privately rented un-furnished flat. It has two bedrooms, a kitchen, a bath and inside lavatory, and one living room, and is within five minutes' walk of the shops. The Hubbards have access to a small garden, but they have no running hot water: all water has to be heated on the gas stove. In the way of household appliances Joan Hubbard has a single tub washing machine (one that cannot rinse or dry the clothes), a vacuum cleaner and a fridge.

The highest score on amenities and aids was obtained by Sarah Maddison, an ex-office worker married to a food technologist, and the mother of three children. She lives in a house owned on a mortgage with four bedrooms and a large garden. In addition to such items as a fridge and a vacuum cleaner, she has a dish-washer, central heating, hired domestic help and the use of the family car in the day time. In these last two respects, Sarah Maddison is unusual. Only three housewives had paid domestic help at the time of the interview: two for six hours a week and one for five and a half hours a fortnight. None had living in domestic help. (A further two normally had help in the house, but were temporarily without it when interviewed.) All these housewives were middle-class. Similarly, out of the forty women, only five had the regular or occasional use of a car for domestic or leisure purposes, and this too, is an exclusively middle-class phenomenon.

Differential ownership of mechanical aids, and differences in the possession of amenities, may affect the *way* housework is done, and they may have some influence on attitudes to work tasks, but they do not appear to affect satisfaction with work. Neither scores for amenities nor those for aids are related to work satisfaction patterns in this sample.[23] In the interviews housewives sometimes expressed dissatisfaction with the aids and amenities they had, and a desire to replace them with 'better' ones: to substitute a fitted carpet for loose rugs, a stainless steel sink for a vitreous enamel one, an inside lavatory for an outside one. Complaints may range from criticism of the architecture of the house to criticism of the methods available for doing housework:

> I hate cooking more than housework. I'm bored with food. I think it's partly because of my kitchen actually – it's down those two little stairs, it's with the bathroom and it's away from the living room. It's not the sort of room that anyone wants to come and chat to you in. I couldn't have the baby in there, for example.
>
> (Radio producer's wife)

> Washing is a drag because I've got nowhere to dry it . . . these heating cabinets don't work . . . I have to put it in the bathroom. At my mother's I could dry it in the garden.
>
> (Lorry driver's wife)

The acquisition of a new machine may temporarily raise enthusiasm for a particular task, but it does not seem to affect the basic feeling of satisfaction or dissatisfaction:

> I don't really mind the cleaning. I just get on and do it. I've just had this new hoover bought me for Christmas, and he comes home from work and I say it only took me five minutes to do the stairs, and all this sort of thing, because it used to take so long before.
>
> (Office manager's wife)

But such stated satisfactions and dissatisfactions appear to be segregated from the housewife's general attitude to housework and the housewife role.

Some of the most satisfied women were actually those with the smallest number of aids and amenities. Sandra Bishop, who lives in a new two-bedroomed council flat on a new estate with her husband (a painter and decorator) and one child aged eighteen months, lacks several aids which many women would consider essential, including a hoover and either a washing machine or access to a launderette. She says:

I love housework. And yet some people come and say – 'Oh you have a hard time, with no washing machine and no hoover', but they're the ones who moan! I say I just get on with it . . . my Mum's managed – she still manages without a washing machine, and she washes every day, and I think *it's really how you are* . . . (Italics added)

In saying 'it's really how you are' Sandra Bishop is identifying other factors as more crucial determinants of housework satisfaction than technical aspects of the work environment. This insight is a valid one and is explored in Chapter 7.

The absence of a relationship between differences on the technical dimension and work satisfaction patterns in the case of the housewife cannot be directly compared with the factory worker's situation. The function of technology in the factory is quite different from its function in the home. Factory work is defined in a total sense by its technology; housework is not. (This, of course, is partly because the level of technology applied to housework is a long way behind that in industry. Domestic technology affects particular tasks but not the job of housework as a whole.) The industrial worker's control over the work process is shaped and generally reduced by technology; in the home, machines do not *themselves* determine the pace and rhythm of work. The housewife retains her control. However, the lack of relationship between the technical dimension of work and housework satisfaction patterns may point to the relative unimportance of working conditions as factors shaping work satisfaction generally. Here, research into the attitudes of employed workers to their work does support a parallel. Herzberg, Mausner and Snyderman observe in their study of *The Motivation to Work* that the provision of better working conditions has the effect of reducing dissatisfaction but not the effect of producing satisfaction.[21] Arthur Kornhauser reports for his sample of Detroit car workers that the physical conditions of work appear 'to have little or no explanatory value in accounting for poorer mental health at lower versus upper job levels'.[25]

In short, then, neither the technical environment of work nor the hours of work the housewife puts in at her job are linked with patterns of work satisfaction and dissatisfaction in the present sample. But a limited amount of social interaction is related to dissatisfaction with work, as also are feelings of monotony. The fragmented nature of housework is an accepted characteristic of it, and for this reason is not a source of dissatisfaction. Feelings of excessive pace are symptomatic of the housewife who is generally dissatisfied, and do not proceed directly from qualities of housework as work (although frequent time limits are intrinsic to housework and affect attitudes to work tasks).

6 Standards and Routines

'Work' has no single definition or shared meaning for the individuals who do it; the meanings of work are as various as the kinds of job that exist. Nevertheless for most people the idea of work contains some notion of externally imposed constraint. Even if one's occupation is freely chosen, it usually carries with it a set of rules about what should be done, when, how and to what standards. A train driver follows printed schedules and rules controlling speed and safety; a typist processes other people's material in accordance with pre-ordained standards of tidiness and literacy; accountants are accountable to their clients and are governed by rules of 'professional' conduct, and so forth. Not so for the housewife. Housewives, as Chapter 3 showed, are impressed by the freedom from the constraints of externally set rules and supervisions. However, a consequence of this autonomy is their responsibility for seeing that housework gets done. The housewife is her own supervisor, the judge of her own performance, and ultimately the source of her own job definition.

The two dimensions of this job definition are *standards* and *routines*. In describing her daily life every woman interviewed outlined the kind of standards she thought it important to stick to in housework, and the type of routine she used to achieve this end. There was, of course, a great deal of variation between one housewife and another. Some set what could be called 'perfectionist' standards, while others adopted a more casual attitude to order and cleanliness in the home. For some there were rigid routines repeated in the same way from one day to the next; for others, routines were more flexible. Different criteria are used in defining standards. Cleanliness may be the basic aim, with untidiness tolerated; or there may be an attitude of 'a place for everything and everything in its place' while the dust under the

beds and the dirt hidden in crevices pass relatively unnoticed.
Two portraits taken from the interviews will illustrate some of
these differences.

Barbara Lipscombe, a cheerful, warm, slightly dumpy woman,
lives in a rented three-bedroomed house and has three children
under five. She used to be a typist and is married to a car patrolman on shift work. The house is clean and tidy and most of the
Lipscombes' family life takes place in the room off the kitchen,
at the back of the house, furnished with a table and chairs, a
sofa and a television. Her day begins like this:

I get up when the children wake up about a quarter to eight.
I get a cooked breakfast, then I always get myself and my
little girl washed and dressed first, because I take her to school.
I take her to school, I come back, and my husband shoots off –
he minds the other two for me while I go to the school. I get
the other two washed and dressed. Then I like to get the
washing in the machine, because I can leave it doing while
I'm down the shops. I go shopping every day, and by the time
I come back it's usually time for the baby to have her food –
at about twelve – and then she usually sleeps till about two,
and then I cook lunch for him [the two-year-old] so that in
the evening it's a tea, although it's usually a cooked tea.

Usually we've finished with lunch by about a quarter past
one. Then I tidy round. I make the beds first thing in the
morning, but on Thursday I do enough shopping for Friday,
so that on Friday I don't go out, I do all my housework. I go
right through the house. Usually I start in my bedroom and
I like to get to the top of the stairs by the baby's lunchtime,
and then I stop and give them lunch and then I carry on and
get on quite well. I go through the front room and then I get
to this room [the 'breakfast' room] and I do the lunch washing
up then, and I wait till they go to bed to put the hoover over
this room and polish round. The rest of the week I just sort
of tidy round, dust, put the carpet sweeper over – that takes
me till a quarter past three, when I go to meet my little girl
from school, and I don't very often get much done once she's
home . . .

She goes to play with a little girl up the road, and then it's
usually time for the baby's tea. I feed her and get her washed
and undressed and ready for bed and then these two sit down
to tea. If my husband's going to be in about that time we all
have it together, but if he's going to be late they have theirs
first. Then quite soon after tea I wash and undress them, so
I've finished for the day. They play around for a bit, and he
goes to bed about half past six, and the little girl between

seven and half past – and then I can sit down! I do the washing up when the children are eating their tea.

Like the other women, Barbara Lipscombe was asked if she had 'particular ways of doing things' that she regularly kept to in housework:

> I think I like particular standards, but I don't think I always keep them. I like everything to be clean – not particularly tidy – I like the washing and ironing to be nice – nice and clean and nicely ironed. If I've got a lot to do I can't actually take as much time as I'd like over it. I like the beds changed often, which I find is hard to keep up with, because of drying the washing.
>   (Is it important to you to keep to these standards?) I find I've got to make excuses for myself if I don't, but I sort of think I've got this to do for the children, and that to do – and I'll have a grand old clean up next week, sort of thing. It's probably the wrong attitude, but I feel if I can't keep up, I can't keep up, so it doesn't really worry me.

This seems to be a fairly relaxed approach to housework, though the standards set are high ones and housework routines are defined and followed precisely and conscientiously. The daily schedule is recited almost automatically; Barbara Lipscombe gives the impression that it is well established and almost never disturbed.

A journalist's wife with one child paints a different picture altogether. Catherine Prince is tall, athletic-looking, easy going and sociable. Her home – owned on a mortgage – is still in the process of being 'done up': some rooms gleam with newly stripped floorboards and pristine white walls, while others have barely been touched. There is a feeling of disarray about the house; newspapers and books are mixed with the baby's toys and used cups and saucers draw the visitor's attention to the washing up left undone.

> I get up about 8.30 – when the baby wakes up. My husband gets up earlier and makes his own breakfast. I feed the baby and have something to eat myself and clear up a bit. About 9.30 I sit down with a cup of coffee to read the paper. After that I might do some washing – I'd rather do a little each day than a large amount at once. I tidy the beds. The baby sleeps for about an hour from 11 till 12 – I'm afraid I read a book then – I don't do very much housework!

When she wakes up we sometimes go shopping – though not every day, by any means; sometimes we don't go at all and sometimes we leave it till the afternoon. We have lunch between one and two and usually I cook, though if I don't feel like it, I don't bother. Then I play with the baby and we might go out for a walk or go and see friends – that sort of thing. From about 3.30 she plays quite happily by herself and I return to my book again! I give her supper about half past five and then she goes to bed. I tidy and vacuum the sitting room after she's gone to bed – I don't see any point in doing it in the morning because it'll only get messed up again. I can't spend much more than ten minutes a day cleaning altogether!

In the evening I get supper and we've eaten and washed up by eight. After that I knit or do some dressmaking and watch television.

(Would you say you have particular ways of doing things . . . ?) Yes, I've got very low standards! You see, I think housework is a waste of time, I don't do it, or I do a minimum. I do things like making the beds.

(How do you decide which things to do?) Well, as long as it doesn't make me feel uneasy, I'm a fairly tidy sort of person, so I do make the bed, and sort of tidy up in the bedroom, and I tidy up in here, when she's gone to bed. But if I don't think 'Oh God, that's dirty!' well, then, it's alright. But if I suddenly think 'that's a bit dirty,' then I do it.

These are 'low' standards compared to those of many other housewives in the sample, and the routine is there, but it is not anchored nearly so securely to set times of the day as Barbara Lipscombe's. All this fits in with Catherine Prince's professed anti-housework ideology, in contrast to Barbara Lipscombe's evident dedication to the housewife role.

The forty women were all assessed on this dimension of their approach to housework.[1] There are three categories: a 'high', a 'medium' and a 'low' specification of standards and routines. 'Specification' here describes a process of rule-definition to which

Table 6.1 Specification of standards and routines and social class

Social class	Standards and routines			
	High No.(%)	Medium No.(%)	Low No.(%)	Total No.(%)
Working class	11(55)	6(30)	3(15)	20(100)
Middle class	10(50)	8(40)	2(10)	20(100)
Total	21(53)	14(35)	5(13)	40(100)

housewives either implicitly or explicitly refer when describing
their standards and routines; the dictionary definition of 'specification' is 'detailed description'.² Barbara Lipscombe is assessed
as having a 'high' specification, while Catherine Prince has a
'low' specification of standards and routines. Table 6.1 shows the
spread of these assessments in the whole sample. Over half the
sample have a 'high' specification; about a third fall in the
'medium' category, and the rest are 'low'. There are no social
class differences.

The specification of standards and routines has four identi-
fiable functions. First, it provides a means of unifying the collection of heterogeneous tasks that make up housework; dissimilar
tasks are knitted together, and some kind of coherent job
structure emerges. Secondly, it serves as proof that housework
is *work*: the spelling out of these rules to be followed places
housework in the same category as other work – there are things
that simply *have* to be done. In this sense, the definition of
standards and routines can be seen as a defensive process: the
housewife is defending herself against the allegation that she
does nothing at all. Thirdly, rule-specification is a means of '*job
enlargement*', a process of elaborating housework tasks so they
take up endlessly increasing amounts of time. For the full-time
housewife, in particular, standards and routines thus serve to
keep the 'worker' employed. And, lastly, the definition of rules
for housework establishes a mechanism whereby the housewife
can *reward herself* for doing it.

The housewife receives no wage for her work. Rewards of a
more subtle kind thus have to be substituted. The husband is
one potentially appreciative figure in the housewife's landscape –
but does he play this role effectively? Among these forty women,
none referred spontaneously to her husband's comments as a
source of personal reward for doing housework. Eight women
said their husbands never passed opinions about how the housework had been done:

> I think I ought to keep the house clean, but I don't do it for
> my husband – because quite honestly he doesn't notice whether
> it's clean or not. He just takes it for granted that it always
> looks like this.
>
> (Retail chemist's wife)

Most of the housewives – twenty-four out of the forty – said

that their husbands *only* commented negatively, never apprecia-
tively. Linda Farrell's exposition of this tendency generalizes from
her husband to all men:

> I think if you *haven't* done something, it's noticed. If you *have*
> done something, it's not noticed. That's always true isn't it?
> I mind. I once said to him 'if you can't pay compliments, don't
> insult' I think they should do both.

And Jill Duffy's succinct comment summarizes the general
situation:

> I think if you don't do it, you get more thanks in the end –
> when you *do* do it.

For housewives who do receive appreciative comments from
husbands, this positive reward is often conditional, and therefore hardly an improvement on a situation in which only failure
is referred to:

> Sometimes when he brings someone home he says 'the place
> is looking nice today'. But he never says that any other time.
>   (Wife of a driver's mate)

Some reward may be obtained from neighbours' or friends'
comments, and some from a comparison of one's own work
achievements with those shown in the media. But in the end
the housewife has to encourage and reward herself. The existence
of this self-reward mechanism is demonstrated by the women's
answers to a question about how they felt when they had got
their work done as they liked it. These are three typical replies:

> I'm more satisfied in my mind when I know it's clean. Then I
> can sit down and psychologically I feel relaxed.

> Well, proud, I expect.

> Happy. Once it's all finished I can sit back and I think 'Oh
> that's lovely'.

Psychological reward is derived from simple adherence to standards and routines which, although originally emanating from
the housewife as worker, take on an *objective* quality. Of course
women do not define these housework rules entirely in isolation
from other influences. Media advertising almost certainly has
an effect, and so does the prior socialization of women for
domesticity. But these sources do not themselves set standards

and routines which are automatically taken up and followed. The paradox is that although standards and routines are, in the first instance, subjectively defined, they become curiously externalized. The housewife refers to them as external obligations to which she feels a deep need to conform.

A second paradox follows. This process of objectification effectively robs the housewife of her much-prized autonomy. She becomes bound by the constraints of pre-set work rhythms.

> The top of the cooker *mustn't* look dirty, whatever happens. So I clean it after every meal.
>
> (Policeman's wife)

> One thing that must be done is that my place *must* look respectable by 11 a.m. so that if anybody does come in, it looks tidy.
>
> (Accountant's wife)

A further implication is that, although standards and routines provide a basis for self-reward in housework, they also make possible less happy outcomes. 'Guilty', 'worried', 'miserable' and 'depressed' are the words which women use to express their responses to a situation in which they do *not* get their work done 'as it should be done':

> If I've got a routine I like to try and keep to it, otherwise I get very disorganized and upset. I feel very inadequate if I can't live up to the standards that I have and I start to feel guilty as well.
>
> (Cinema manager's wife)

> If the floor needs washing, okay, I won't wash it, but I know it needs washing and it'll go on nagging me until I've washed it – so you can't win really.
>
> (Lorry driver's wife)

This phrase, 'you can't win really' sums up the problem well.

Table 6.2　Specification of standards and routines and work satisfaction

Work satisfaction	Standards and routines		Total No.(%)
	High No.(%)	Medium/low No.(%)	
Satisfied	9(75)	3(25)	12(100)
Dissatisfied	12(43)	16(57)	28(100)
Total	21(53)	19(48)	40(100)

$x^2 = 3.22$; d.f. $= 1$; $p < .10$

What, then, is the relationship between the specification of standards and routines and work satisfaction? In Table 6.2 the two sets of figures are given.

The percentage of work-satisfied housewives is higher in the group with a high specification and lower in the group with a medium or low specification. It is possible to say on the basis of these figures that the higher the specification, the more likely it is that the housewife will be satisfied.

Yet less than half the women with a high specification *are* satisfied with work. One explanation here is that, rather than a high specification of standards and routines being a direct route to the achievement of satisfaction, it is instead *symptomatic of the search for satisfaction*. In Chapter 4 the discrepancy between responses to the question 'Do you like housework?' and the assessment of work satisfaction led to an explanation of these responses as (in part) expressive of norms to do with feminine domesticity and as indicative of two alternative approaches to housework: the search for satisfaction and the recognition of dissatisfaction. Those who said they 'liked' or 'didn't mind' housework seemed to be asserting their attachment to the norms of feminine satisfaction with housewifery. If the explanation of a high standards and routines specification as symptomatic of the desire to be satisfied is correct, one would expect some relationship between this measure and answers to the 'Do you like housework?' question. Table 6.3 shows the relationship.

Table 6.3 Specification of standards and routines and answers to the question 'Do you like housework?'

Answers to question 'Do you like housework?'	Standards and routines High No.(%)	Medium/low No.(%)	Total No.(%)
Like	8(80)	2(20)	10(100)
Don't mind	7(70)	3(30)	10(100)
Dislike	6(30)	14(70)	20(100)
Total	21(53)	19(48)	40(100)

$x^2 = 8.31$; d.f. $= 2$; $p < .02$

On the basis of this table, it can be said that the two variables are connected: a woman who declares a positive attitude to housework is likely also to have a high specification of standards and routines.

This whole question of housework behaviour raises an interesting issue: in what sense can a housewife who has very high standards and extremely repetitive routines be considered 'pathologically' obsessed with housework? In common parlance the 'houseproud' housewife is perfectionist in her approach to housework, but the term itself carries neither strong negative nor strong positive connotations. The psychiatrist John Cooper has carried out some work on the personality characteristics of 'houseproud' women.[3] He compared three groups of people: houseproud housewives, people suffering from chronic obsessional illness, and 'normal' women.[4] Cooper's method was to give the three groups an inventory of questions dealing with obsessional traits and symptoms; his results showed that the mean symptom score of the houseproud women fell between those of the normal women and the group of obsessional patients. Two scales of 'resistance' and 'interference', designed to measure the intensity of obsessional distress and the intrusion of symptoms on other activities, produced a similar result. Cooper's conclusion is that houseproud housewives *are* 'abnormal' in the sense that their behaviour has something in common with that of obsessionally ill people.

Some of the women with a high specification of standards and routines in the present sample did, indeed, demonstrate a strong emotional involvement in housework and their 'guilt', 'worry' or 'anxiety' about failures to meet housework standards does suggest some of the obsessional symptoms manifested by the patients in Cooper's survey. Jill Duffy, an ex-shop assistant married to a painter and decorator, is one of these women. She has two children aged three years and eight months, and her home is a two-room basement flat. It has a small kitchen and an outside lavatory, and the bathroom is shared with other people in the house. Heating is by means of one oil fire and a coal fire in the evenings. She has no refrigerator or washing machine, but she does have a vacuum cleaner. The flat is dark and somewhat damp but is meticulously clean and tidy. About housework she says:

I love it.
(Cleaning?) I just like it. I'm just happy when I'm doing it.
(Washing?) I love doing my own washing. I don't believe in
washing machines. (Why do you like it?) I don't know. I just
like it. I like to see what I've done. I do it every day – I hate
leaving it. If I did leave it, I'd stay up in the evening to do it,
it'd be on my conscience . . . I wish I didn't have to do it . . . I
wish I had the nerve just to leave it, but I can't.

Here is part of her description of daily routine, together with
some observations about the kind of standards she has (I have
used italics to draw attention to particular 'perfectionist'
remarks):

I go shopping after I've fed the baby every morning, and then
I come back and start my work. *I can always find something
to do.* I very seldom sit down – my God, I don't know where
to start!

I do my bedroom out every day – sweep it and dust the
furniture and I do something else every day, like I dust the
tops of the cupboards or I give the wardrobe a polish. Every
second day I wash out this room – because it's only lino. And
every fortnight I wash the curtains – the net ones and the
heavy ones too.

(So you don't do both rooms every day?) Oh I do. *I could
hoover this one twenty times a day.* I always feed Sharon [the
three year old] because if she feeds herself she gets it everywhere and the place is all messed up, and *I have to clean it
again.* It's the same when people come. If they drop cigarette
ash or crumbs on the carpet I'm out with the hoover again.

I wash every day and Sunday as well. *I never miss a day of
my life with washing on the line.* I know my standards have
dropped because with Sharon I used to change her clothes twice
a day. I really used to keep her lovely. I only change Roberta's
clothes once a day . . . When my husband takes his shirts off
I have to wash them straight away – like he wears two shirts
on Sunday and I wash them as soon as he takes them off.

(What do you do in the evenings?) I only sit down when he
comes in and he's not in much. *Friday night and Saturday
night are my busy nights. Friday night I wash the carpets – I
start about 10 p.m. and finish about midnight.* Saturday night
I always do the gas oven out. The other nights when he isn't
in I go into the kitchen and I find something to do – I clear
the cupboards out or something.

(Would you say you have particular ways of doing
things . . . ?) I suppose I have high standards but some others
are as good as me. My landlady doesn't spend nearly as much
time doing housework, but her place is always clean and nice

when you go into it. Some people don't do anything – some
people's places really aren't clean ... well, this one isn't very,
but I keep it the best I can.

Jill Duffy is certainly highly involved with the state of her
home and she does a great deal of housework that many other
people would consider unnecessary. Her response to 'free' time
is to fill it with more housework, and her housework ideals shape
the way she brings up her children (the insistence on not
letting a messy three year old feed herself, for example). However, rather than seeing Jill Duffy and others like her as 'pathologically obsessed' with housework (and thus as unrepresentative
of the wider housewife population) it makes more sense to view
their behaviour as a rational response to a problematic situation.
In the pursuit of housework satisfaction an impression of per-
fectionism is easily created. Because self-reward is gained
through meeting standards and sticking to set routines, in the
long run the tendency is to raise standards and elaborate routines
so that self-reward may continue to be achieved. The definition
of high standards and repetitive routines to be followed in housework is a means of 'job enlargement'. In industry the purpose
of this process is to make work more interesting, through the
restructuring of the components of a work role – either by
increasing the number of operations that each worker has to
perform or by making changes from one activity to another
more frequent.[5] The same idea of raising the satisfaction potential of work lies behind the housewife's elaboration of *her* work.
In her case, the function is not the straightforward reduction of
repetitiveness, but rather the creation of constantly rising
expectations which she can then try to meet.

Neither Jill Duffy nor any other of the high specification
women in the present sample were receiving medical treatment
for obsessional symptoms at the time of interview. Moreover,
slight degrees of guilt/worry/anxiety about failures to observe
housework standards and routines were also expressed by some
women in the low specification group. In Cooper's own survey,
the test scores of the houseproud housewives were closer to those
of the normal women than to those of the obsessional patients.[6]
A further important point is that on two scores – the overall
symptom score and the resistance score – there was a difference
between the normal women and a group of normal men who

were also given the inventory. The normal women showed more obsessional symptoms and more obsessional distress than the normal men.[7] This suggests that the personal identification of women with the housewife role weights the balance in favour of a psychological involvement in housework. A high specification of housework rules can be seen as a common response to a common problem – the problem being how to make sense of work that is intrinsically unsatisfying under conditions where less and less of it *need* be done (through automation, 'convenience' foods, better housing conditions, etc), but where the structural pressures which assign women to the home remain as strong as ever.

One consequence of 'job enlargement' in the housewife's case is an increase in working hours. This facet of housework, discussed in the previous chapter, is unrelated to such factors as number of children, technical aids and amenities, and so on. But there is an association between the kind of standards and routines followed in housework and the amount of time spent doing it. Jill Duffy's psychological involvement in housework, for example, manifests itself in a 105-hour week. The relationship between standards and routines and working hours in the sample as a whole is shown in Table 6.4.

Table 6.4 Housework hours and specification of standards and routines

| Standards and routines | Weekly housework hours | | Total |
	40–69 No.(%)	70 or more No.(%)	No.(%)
High	2(10)	19(91)	21(100)
Medium	4(29)	10(71)	14(100)
Low	4(80)	1(20)	5(100)
Total	10(25)	30(75)	40(100)

$x^2 = 10.84$; d.f.=2; p<.01

'Housewifery expands to fill the time available' – this principle was discovered by Betty Friedan in her 1950s tour of American suburbia.[8] The trend towards rising standards certainly provides an explanation of why housework hours have shown no notable decrease in recent years; pre-prepared foodstuffs, household

machines and equipment, and cleaner more comfortable homes
do not necessarily reduce the housewife's work-load. Betty
Friedan cites an apt illustration of this:

> The automatic clothes dryer does not save a woman the four or
> five hours a week she used to spend at the clothes line, if, for
> instance, she runs her washing machine and dryer every day
> ... As a young mother said, 'Clean sheets twice a week are
> now possible. Last week, when my dryer broke down, the sheets
> didn't get changed for eight days. Everyone complained. We
> all felt dirty. I felt guilty. Isn't that silly?'[9]

Silly it may be, but it is only by considering the way women
define their job as housewives that the housewife's long working
hours can be understood. This is one reason why standards and
routines represent an important dimension of housework behaviour.
But, more fundamentally, the unique quality of housework as a
job is precisely this dimension of self-definition. It explains why
housework is apparently so different from, and yet is experienced
by women as so similar to, other jobs. A lack of structure is
intrinsic to housework; thus a psychological structure is imported
to it. Women enter into a form of covert contract with themselves to be their own bosses, judges and reward-givers. Gaining
coherence and self-reward in their work, autonomy is relin-
quished and creativity constrained. To understand the processes
behind the definition of housework rules it is necessary to look
more closely at the way in which women identify with the role
of housewife; this is the subject of the next chapter.

7 Socialization and Self-Concept

The complex definitions of housework standards and routines described in the last chapter are not simply created as a response to the job situation; they antedate the time of 'becoming a housewife'. Their roots lie in the lessons of childhood, when girls learn to equate their femaleness with domesticity and female identities are moulded round the housewife image.

The performance of the housewife role in adulthood is prefaced by a long period of apprenticeship. Housework is not unique in this respect: other occupations also have apprenticeship schemes. But a female's induction into the domestic role – unlike these other schemes – lacks a formal structure, and consequently is rarely seen as an occupational apprenticeship. A main reason for this is that preparation for housewifery is intermingled with socialization for the feminine gender role in the wider sense. Neither in theory nor in practice is one process distinguishable from the other.

While the female's childhood preparation for domesticity is 'informal', there are, nevertheless, regular procedures involved which span many of the differences between groups in our society and act as a common denominator in the socialization of women. The American sociologist Ruth Hartley, in her study of feminine role development, has identified four of these processes.[1] They are 'socialization by manipulation', 'verbal appellation', 'canalization' and 'activity exposure'. An example of the first process is a mother's tendency to 'fuss' over a female child's appearance and to stress her prettiness – 'You *are* a pretty little girl'. The child takes over the mother's view of itself; verbal appellations reinforce the manipulative process. Canalization involves the direction of attention on to particular objects – in this case toys of the domestic kind: miniature washing machines, cookers, dustpan and brush sets, and so forth. (The world-famous toy department store in London, Hamleys of Regent Street, has a whole floor called 'The Little Housewife'.) Children are often socially rewarded for playing with toys of the appropriate gender, and this process lays down the basis of future adult pleasure in relation to similar objects – full-size washing machines, cookers and dustpan and brush sets. Lastly, there is actual exposure to adult activities in childhood. The future housewife is encouraged to participate in her mother's domestic activities – to help with the washing up, make the beds or lay the table.

These processes are all confirmed outside the family context. Recently various writers have drawn attention to the domesticated image of women put over in the mass media, in textbooks and reading books for children, and in school curricula.[2] Schools also encourage girls to play 'domestic' games and to behave in appropriately feminine ways. The latter goal may be achieved either indirectly, through teachers' attitudes, or, more directly, through the sex-segregation of play areas and particular activities. On a more general level, differences between adult feminine and masculine roles which persist as a (more or less) uniform feature of our society have a pervasive effect on the gender role perceptions and preferences children develop.

For girls caught up in this nexus of processes, the effect is that the feminine role, the 'little housewife' role and self-definition are blended together in an 'unselfconscious complex of unobstructed behaviour'.[3] Through the integration of feminine role learning with self-definition, housekeeping behaviours tend to be developed as personality functions. There may be very little awareness of their connection with sex status. As Ruth Hartley sums it up:

> with imitative activity filling the gap until the child is able to participate meaningfully as a partner in home-centred behaviours, the definition of this aspect of the female sex role [the domestic one] seems to proceed without interruption and with continuous reinforcement from the cradle on.[4]

These abstract generalizations take on substance in the words of many of the women interviewed in the present study. Faith

Abraham, who used to work in a factory making artificial jewellery, is married to a labourer; she was born and brought up in Ireland:

> We lived on a farm. My mother looked after the chickens. She was always busy – I've got seven sisters and three brothers. She used to do the cooking but we washed up, tidied up, made the beds and swept the floors. She wouldn't let us do the washing – she said we didn't wash properly. She loved doing the washing herself. My mother likes housework – she's a great housewife, very clean.
>
> When we were seven or eight we could clear the place up as good as my Mum ... but I've seen some girls – like my aunt's little girl and she's fifteen, she's just hopeless. She can't do a thing around the house.
>
> (What do you think about that?) I think it's terrible – she's just lazy. My sisters are all like me – they like cleaning, we're all alike in that way. (Your brothers?) My brothers didn't have to do housework!

Of her own housework behaviour she said earlier in the interview:

> I like cleaning . . . ironing is the only thing I don't like really. I like shopping. I like cooking. (Why?) I just like it. I like washing up ... I like washing – I wouldn't like to wash sheets and blankets and things, but I don't mind doing the children's things...
>
> (Would you say you have particular ways of doing things . . . ?) Yes, I think so. I like to keep the place tidy and clean. I think when we were young we always had to do housework really. There were such a lot of us ... I think that's why I like children – because there was always somebody smaller than me and I had to do everything for them really when I was younger – feed them, change their nappies...
>
> (When you were young, do you remember whether you wanted to be like your mother?) I did always want to get married. I used to say I'd love to get married and have children.

In this brief account three main aspects of Faith Abraham's socialization are mentioned: the direct rehearsal of housework tasks in childhood: a more general imitation of the mother as role model; and the repetition of the mother's housework behaviour in the daughter's own.

The section of the interview dealing with housework standards and routines was one in which references to the mother were very frequent. For example:

> I have the same standards as my mother. If anything needs doing, she does it. You don't have to look around and say 'that needs doing' because it's done. *I always try to model myself on her.*
>
> (Food wholesaler's wife)

Such references also tended to crop up in the earlier discussion of attitudes to particular tasks: this comment of Jean Bevan's is representative:

> I like washing. I like to see washing out on the line – especially sheets and the boy's shirts. *I think this is a bit of my mother –* she's extremely particular, my mother.
>
> (Office manager's wife)

One woman traced her like of cooking not only back to her mother but to her grandmother. The word 'inherited' is used here and the biological analogy is perhaps not inappropriate: a series of close mother-daughter relationships presents an invaluable opportunity for the perpetuation of feminine domesticity.

The mother may exert an influence even if she is not a 'perfect' housewife. This is brought out in the answers Joanna Giles gave to the question about standards:

> Housework-wise, I think I've got pretty low standards. But my mother's never been a great one for housework and I think my standards are probably like hers . . . as long as things don't get filthy, I'm happy, but a lot of people wouldn't be satisfied with that.

Also important is the fact that the attitude formed may be either one of continuing imitation or of direct rebellion against the mother's standards. Both are aspects of the same process:

> My mother's a terrible housewife. She's very muddly and disorganized and I can see so clearly where she falls wrong . . . when I lived at home it was always a bit of a nightmare because I was always trying to get things straight.
>
> (Juliet Warren, wife of a television documentary director)

The attempt to reverse one's mother's disorder is one form of rebellion, though its obverse – a general relaxation of maternal housework standards – is also possible:

> (Would you say you have particular ways of doing things . . . ?)
> Yes – keeping the kitchen clean . . . and also the meals I cook, but not very high standards where tidiness and dust are con-

cerned . . . I'm improving – in fact I used to be much worse. My mother doesn't work outside the home. She's very house-proud – obsessional. She's not a happy person.

(Dorothy Underwood, a cinema manager's wife)

The point is that in each case the woman is defining her own housework behaviour with reference to that of her mother. Maternal influence is paramount. To put it another way, mothers are by far the most important 'significant others' so far as house-work behaviour is concerned. For this reason an assessment was made for all the forty women of their levels of *identification* with the housewife role. This is defined as a condition in which the responsibility for housework is felt as a feminine, and there-fore a personal attribute, normally as a result of a childhood identification with the mother as role model.[5] The spread of identification levels across three categories – 'high', 'medium' and 'low' – is shown in Table 7.1 in relation to social class grouping.

Table 7.1 Identification with the housewife role and social class

| Social class | Identification with the housewife role | | | |
	High No.(%)	Medium No.(%)	Low No.(%)	Total No.(%)
Working class	11(55)	8(40)	1(5)	20(100)
Middle class	10(50)	9(45)	1(5)	20(100)
Total	21(53)	17(43)	2(5)	40(100)

There are no social class differences in this crucial area. Very similar childhood experiences are recalled by the forty women as influential in the formation of housework attitudes; this similarity is illustrated in the following two quotations, one from a 'working-class', and one from a 'middle-class' interview:

Anything my mother did was fine by me. Kids get idols – well, my mother was mine, and I'm not ashamed to say she still is, and she can't do anything wrong in my book. She's all for the finishing touches on everything. She's a fantastic cook, which I've followed in her footsteps. She does everything right; when I was young I helped with my small sister – she was born when I was fourteen – and I helped with the housework of course. From about the age of ten I remember that. I was scruffy until then – after that I was houseproud! I get on well with my mother. I'd love to be like my mother.

(Lorry driver's wife)

My mother was very particular. She still is. You could eat off
the floor in her house. When I was fourteen I can remember
being constantly nagged by her – our bedrooms were always
untidy. It's terrible but I find I do exactly the same with my
children now: they come in from school and everything is
dropped and I say 'pick them up' and I try to stop nagging
them because I remember how much *I* hated it. But I think
it does influence you . . . I remember coming home from school
and before you could do homework or go out to play there
were always chores to do – you know, our own set of chores.
We knew it had to be done and we used to accept it. She was
a hard worker, and I call myself a hard worker and I know
that some days I push myself too hard and my mother's done
that all her life.

(Food technologist's wife)

The conclusion that middle- and working-class women share
similar levels of domestic role-identification provokes an important question. How is it compatible with other findings of social
class *differences* in domesticity – both those discussed in Chapter
4 and those suggested by other writers?[6] One explanation is that
there *are* social class differences of a more superficial kind which
overlay the similarity in role-identification patterns. In discussing
(below) answers given by the women in my sample to a test of
self-attitudes, I shall present some evidence in favour of this
interpretation.

There are also indications from other sources that women's
basic allegiance to the housewife role is not class-dependent.
One American study of primary school girls found a class similarity in the range of behaviours, including domestic behaviours,
perceived as feminine.[7] Although some social class differences
in *preferences* for certain domestic activities were found –
middle-class women were more likely to dislike domestic service
activities such as washing floors and dishes – the more fundamental sense of these as a feminine responsibility persisted.
Another kind of 'test case' is the dual career family. Where
both husband and wife have substantial commitments to the
job world, one might expect domestic responsibilities to be
shared. This would be evidence *against* the present finding that
identification with the housewife role is not differentiated by
class. However, according to the Rapoports' analysis of the dual
career family, women remain the domesticated individuals.[8] The
diaries charted by the Rapoports portray a frenetic picture of

the career-woman-housewife-mother desperately chasing all her duties simultaneously. The women's daily routines contain a far higher proportion of domestic interruptions than do those of the men. For example, Mrs Benson, an architect married to an architect (they both work at home), begins her description of a weekday thus:

7.55 Remind son of time
8.45 Mend daughter's nightdress
9.15 Organize a party and the day's laundry
9.45 Go to shops, laundry, chemist – thread, plant, fish, buns, polish
11.05 Get office coffee, hang out day's laundry
11.40 Work finally started.

During the same period Mr Benson got up at nine, read his mail, started his office work at ten, and worked through till lunch at one.

A dilution of women's traditional commitment to the housewife role is, then, rare even in those families where there is symmetry between husband and wife on the paid job dimension. The Rapoports comment that the dual career pattern is actually liable to induce a reaction of overconscientious adherence to conventional gender role stereotypes in domestic areas. The woman responds to the negative image of the cold, 'masculine', competitive female, and her enduring dedication to the 'responsible housewife' pattern is a denial of gender role deviation and an affirmation of women's domesticated conditioning.

Beyond these specific studies there is little support for the view that the domestic theme in women's general situation has been substantially muted over recent decades. Employment figures show the continuing 'domesticity' of women's work roles: the bulk of women workers in all industrialized countries are in teaching, nursing, shop work, clerical work and factories making domestic products like clothes and food. In Britain the concentration of women workers in traditional female occupations has increased, not diminished, over the last ten years or so.[9] The expansion of educational and professional training opportunities for women has done very little to alter the concentration of female professionals in 'domestic' professions: most professional women are still teachers or nurses – both jobs closely allied with the traditionally 'nurturant' role of women.

One particular connection between the socialization of women and their later performance of the housewife role is elucidated by the present research data. Comments already cited from the forty interviews have demonstrated that women are often aware of a link between their own ways of doing housework and those of their mothers. This link can be more precisely stated. Table 7.2 shows that there is an association between the level of a housewife's identification with the housewife role and the degree to which she specifies standards and routines for housework performance.

Table 7.2 Identification with the housewife role and specification of standards and routines

Specification	High No.(%)	Identification Medium/low No.(%)	Total No.(%)
High	14(67)	7(33)	21(100)
Medium/low	7(37)	12(63)	19(100)
Total	21(53)	19(48)	40(100)

$x^2 = 3.55$; d.f. $= 1$; $p < .10$

Most of the women who are high on one measure are high on the other, and those who are low tend to show the same symmetry. This connection between the two factors suggests that the nature of a woman's early relationship to the housewife role helps to shape her own housework behaviour in later life.

What are the precise mechanisms involved in this process? An experimental study of children's behaviour outlines a possible answer.[10] In this study forty children with a mean age of four years and five months were divided into two groups: one group received 'nurturant' behaviour from a role model, while the other group was exposed to a non-nurturant relationship. The children were next asked to perform a two-choice discrimination problem – deciding which of two boxes contained a picture sticker – with a model who exhibited 'functionless' behaviour during the discrimination trials, that is behaviour not related to the stated task-goal (finding the sticker). The conclusion was that 'children display a good deal of social learning of an *incidental imitative sort*, and that *nurturance* is one condition facilitating such imitative learning'.[11] In particular, during the discrimination trials, the children 'dutifully' followed the example set by the model, even when she took an indirect route to the boxes, which more than doubled the distance to be travelled and 'was clearly incompatible with the subjects' eagerness to get to the containers'.[12]

A parallel with this behaviour can be found in the present study. Many of the women made it clear in the interviews that their concern is *not* simply to get housework done in the most efficient way and the shortest possible time. Instead, they are bound up in the replication of previously set standards and routines which may actually frustrate the straightforward goal of simply getting housework done. To the extent that these ways of behaving are inherited from the mother, it can be hypothesized that they are not directly taught from mother to daughter: rather they are indirectly and unconsciously assimilated. The 'nurturant' child-caring relationship that exists between housewives and housewives-to-be serves to make this assimilation more likely than not.

The learning lesson of domesticity sets up what is essentially a relationship between self (feminine) and role (housewife). *Is* a conception of self as housewife in fact articulated as part of the self-image? About half way through the interview, the forty women were given a test of 'self-attitudes' developed by the American sociologists Manford H. Kuhn and Thomas S. McPartland,[13] which provides data on this point. In its original form the test consists simply of asking respondents to complete the sentence beginning with 'I am. . .' twenty times over. In the present study the number of statements required was cut to ten, because the test was just one item in rather a long interview. The women were handed a sheet of paper on which the words 'I am . . .' appeared in a sequence numbered from one to ten. They were asked to write their statements down as quickly as possible and to answer as though describing themselves *to* themselves rather than to anybody else. According to Kuhn and McPartland, this procedure overcomes one weakness of direct questions aimed at uncovering people's self-images, which is that

> they provide no way of measuring the salience of an attitude; we never know whether the attitude would have been expressed at all, or in the same way, apart from the direct question . . .

When a respondent, in reply to the 'who am I?' question of the Twenty Statements Test writes 'I am a man', 'I am a student' . . . it is reasonable to believe that we have far more solid knowledge of the attitudes which organize and direct his behaviour than if, on a checklist and among other questions, we had asked 'do you think of yourself as a man?' 'Do you think of yourself as a student?' [14]

The particular dimension of the self-concept to which the test is oriented is thus that of *salience*. Kuhn and McPartland believe that 'the ordering of responses is a reflection of the makeup of the self-concept'. In their use of the test it was found that the order of salience of certain roles varied between different cultural groups. Ethnic group status was mentioned earlier in the case of negroes than it was in the case of white people, and gender role was mentioned earlier in the test and more often by women than by men.[15]

Each one of the forty women made some attempt to complete the test, though the number of statements made varied from three to eleven, with an average of 8.03 out of the desired ten per respondent. There were some clear social class differences in their answers. One difference was that working-class women were more likely to describe themselves as housewives and to give 'domestic' responses generally. Altogether twenty-five of the forty wrote 'I am a housewife' at some point in the test and seventeen of these were working class. Table 7.3 gives the relevant figures. These answers from a salesman's wife and a plasterer's wife are typical of this group; Linda Farrell writes:

I am a housewife
I am a mother
I am ordinary
I am a wife
I am happy
I am reasonably attractive
I am a sister
I am a neighbour
I am a friend
I am sociable

and Marilyn Thornton describes herself thus:

I am a housewife
I am a mother
I am a slave

I am energetic
I am a good worker
I am broadminded
I am nearly thirty

In fact, most of the women who describe themselves as housewives do so very early in the test; twenty of the twenty-five 'I am a housewife' statements occur in the first two places.

Table 7.3. Mention of the housewife role in the Ten Statements Test and social class

| Social class | Mention of the housewife role | | | Total |
	In the first two places No.(%)	Later in the test No.(%)	Not mentioned No.(%)	No.(%)
Working class	15(75)	2(10)	3(15)	20(100)
Middle class	5(25)	3(15)	12(60)	20(100)
Total	20(50)	5(13)	15(38)	40(100)

$x^2 = 10.6$; d.f. $= 2$; $p < .01$

One problem with the evaluation of these results is the possibility that the women who described themselves as housewives did so because this was an interview about housework. Even if some process of this kind was at work, one still has to explain the differences between women's responses – why did some women describe themselves as housewives and others not? Can this 'contamination' explain the social class patterning of the responses, for instance? Since the majority of the women were full-time housewives, some self-categorization as housewives can, in any case, be predicted.

The apparently greater salience to working-class women of self-conceptualization as a housewife is confirmed by a look at overall 'domestic' responses. Other statements such as 'I am a slave' 'I am a good worker' (referring to housework) are also statements of affiliation to the domestic role. Table 7.4 shows these statements and also 'personality' descriptions ('I am a happy person') and statements of mood ('I am depressed').

The majority of statements in every category of 'domestic' responses are in fact made by working-class women. Shirley Archer's list of statements illustrates the working-class stress on

Table 7.4 'Domestic' and other responses to the Ten Statements Test, by social class

Social class	Mentions of housewife role	Mentions of housework and house-work roles*	Responses to Ten Statements Test			
			Mentions of other domestic or family roles†	Total domestic responses	Personality descriptions	Mood descriptions
	No.(rate)	No.(rate)	No.(rate)	No.(rate)	No.(rate)	No.(rate)
Working class	19 (.95)	22 (1.10)	32 (1.60)	73 (3.65)	39 (1.95)	22 (1.10)
Middle class	10 (.50)	8 (.40)	23 (1.15)	41 (2.05)	81 (4.05)	23 (1.15)

* Excluding 'I am a housewife'. Examples are 'I am a cleaner', 'I am a hard worker', meaning housework.
† Examples are 'I am a mother', 'I am a sister'.

domesticity: here it is contrasted with Elizabeth Gould's more typically middle-class capacity to see herself in other terms:

I am a good housewife
I am good to my children
I am good at housework
I am good to my husband
I am good at washing
I am fed up at times
I am bad tempered at times
I am very happy with my work
I am happy with my children
I am seldom unhappy

(Shirley Archer)

I am moody
I am hard working
I am someone who talks too much
I am happy most of the time
I am a satisfied person
I am someone who needs other people all the time
I am a person who loves going out
I am often over bossy
I am a dreamer
I am a worrier

(Elizabeth Gould)

The first of these lists contains virtually no description of individual personality. Statements six and seven describe mood – being 'fed up' and 'bad tempered'. The last three statements are assertions of contentment, but only three statements – numbers six, seven and ten – do not refer in some way to domestic work or the work environment. But Elizabeth Gould's self-concept hardly refers to her domestic situation at all – except perhaps for the statement 'I am hard working'. What she is describing are characteristics of herself as a person, qualities of her own individual personality. This tendency she shares with other women in the middle-class group; the middle-class rate of personality descriptions is twice that of the working-class group.

The Ten Statements Test thus appears to reveal social class differences in self-concept of an unambiguous kind. To retain any coherence in the research findings it is necessary to reconcile this conclusion with the fundamental similarity between working-class and middle-class women on the dimension of identification with the housewife role.

There are three parts to the explanation. Firstly, the measure of 'identification' and the answers to the Ten Statements Test are probably tapping two different dimensions. Identification is a profound conformity-base, a fundamental and enduring facet of personality. According to the classical definition, identification is the major process leading to internalization, and internalization is 'a condition of incorporation of norms and/or roles into one's own personality, with a corresponding obligation to act accordingly or suffer guilt'.[16] When a norm is internalized, it is part of a person, automatically expressed in behaviour, rather than regarded in a more detached way as a rule external to the self. Actual statements about the self (such as those obtained in the Ten Statements Test) may not refer to this dimension at all, but instead relate to the psycho-linguistic question of the extent to which self and (housewife) role are differentiated in the self-concept.

We thus return, for the second part of the explanation, to the issue of class differentiation in linguistic styles discussed in Chapter 4 (pages 66–70). Following the lines laid down there, and using Bernstein's work on class and language codes, we could say that a language of *explicit* meaning (broadly speaking, the middle-class code) is a language in which what is expressed

is 'a function of the psychological qualities of the person'.[17] But
a language of implicit meaning (the working-class code) raises
the 'we' above the 'I' and encourages an assertion of role con-
formity. While all women are socialized for domesticity in much
the same way – by identifying with their mothers (and/or other
adult women) as housewives, internalizing the conviction that
they must be housewives in their turn – for the working-class
woman the linguistic process of role learning is such that 'I'
becomes part of the role. To put it somewhat differently, conceptual differentiation of self from role is inhibited by the mode
of language use which mediates the process of role learning.
Where this language stresses shared structure and identification –
'all women are housewives' – individuation becomes both less
important and less possible.

A third consideration draws attention to the association
between answers to the Ten Statements Test, and another set of
factors. In Chapter 4 social class differences in responses to the
question 'Do you like housework?' were noted. The social class
difference in statements of self-concept parallels the social class
difference in statements of attitudes to housework; there is a
close association between the two variables, as shown in
Table 7.5.

**Table 7.5 Answers to the 'Do you like housework' question, and
mention of the housewife role in the Ten Statements
Test**

| | Answers to 'Do you like housework?' question | | | |
Mention of the housewife role	Like No.(%)	Don't mind No.(%)	Dislike No.(%)	Total No.(%)
In the first two places	7(35)	8(40)	5(25)	20(100)
Later or not at all	3(15)	2(10)	15(75)	20(100)
Total	10(25)	10(25)	20(50)	40(100)

$x^2 = 9.8$; d.f. $= 2$; $p < .01$

This relationship does suggest that the syndrome of class-differentiated response styles (and the related question of class-differentiated norms of feminine domesticity) may be responsible for

the difference in mentions of the housewife role by class. Since answers to the Ten Statements Test represent, in part, expressed affiliations to the housewife role, language and subcultural norms relating to women's satisfaction with housework are likely to be important. (While, on the other hand, an assessment of identification with the housewife role by the interviewer is relatively free of these complications.)

This interpretation of class differences in answers to the Ten Statements Test – as entirely compatible with class similarities in domestic role-identification – does not, of course, mean that answers to the test have no meaning or importance in their own right. Conception of oneself as a housewife or not is liable to influence a woman's behaviour in a variety of ways. For example, it is probably important in relation to educational or occupational choices; it may affect the nature of the marriage relationship, and also, very possibly, the way in which a mother brings up her daughters. For these kinds of reasons, the finding that a significant minority of the forty women have a self-concept which is highly domesticated is an important one. Shirley Archer's list of statements, already quoted (page 124), is one example. Her amplification of the statement 'I am a housewife' to the later 'I am a good housewife' sets a pattern followed by others:

I am a woman
I am a housewife
I am a mother
I am happy
I am a good housewife
                    (Olive Brennan, a factory hand's wife)

I am a housewife
I am going to the shop
I am a mother
I am a good housewife
I am a mother of four children
I am a hard worker
I am a wife
I am a good cleaner
I am a good washer
I am always working
                    (Janet Gallagher, wife of a driver's mate)

I am a very busy housewife
I am always on the go

I am not lazy
I am a good housewife, I think
I am a soft person
I am very fond of style [fashion]
I am all for my children
I am fond of shopping
I am fond of washing
I am fond of cleaning
                    (Jill Duffy, a painter and decorator's wife)

In these cases a perception of competence and achievement is not in any way separated from the affirmation of domesticity. Sally Jordan's statements illustrate another aspect of this tendency:

I am a working housewife
I am a weak-willed person
I am a very lonely person
I am domineered by my husband
I am a conscientious person
I am a part-time worker
I am a tidy person in the home
I am neat in the way my children are dressed
I am a worrier over money
I am a very friendly person

Here the first statement 'I am a working housewife' refers to the fact of Sally Jordan's employment outside the home (part-time in a factory) but makes no linguistic separation between domesticity and employment work. (It also, of course, embodies the usual assumption that housework is not work.) Later on, statement six amplifies this to 'I am a part-time worker', an assertion which is immediately followed by a reference to housework behaviour.

The reiteration of domesticity in these responses represents an inability to break out of the circle: the circle of definitions which enclose women within a domestic identity. Another sign of this is a straight inability to think of self-descriptions. Given fifteen minutes to complete the sentence 'I am . . .' ten times, two women write the following:

I am a housewife
I am friendly
I am a mother
                    (Beatrice O'Leary, a machine operator's wife)

I am a housewife
I am a mother
I am a wife
I am a woman

(Faith Abraham, a labourer's wife)

The version of the test given by Olive Brennan (page 127) is abbreviated in the same way. None of the women was able to write anything else: one wrote her responses in about a minute, and then said 'I can't think of anything else, really'. She went on staring at the paper for some minutes, but was unable to get any further. The behaviour of the other two women was similar: two of the three were very talkative during the rest of interview and only Beatrice O'Leary's Ten Statements Test occurred in the context of a generally unforthcoming interview.

A degree of insight into the pronounced domesticity of some women's self-concepts can be gained by looking at a particular group of six women within the working-class sample of twenty: the six women who were all born and spent their early years in Ireland. These six include the three who were unable to write more than a few statements, and also Jill Duffy and Janet Gallagher who repeated the domestic theme. The sixth in the group, June Doyle, gave essentially the same picture of total domesticity, but included two 'personality' statements: like some of the other women she found the Ten Statements Test difficult to complete. Having written the first two statements, she said 'I can't – after that "wife and mother and housewife" I've never given it much thought'.

Comments made by these Irish women in the interviews support the interpretation that the traditional upbringing of Irish women places a greater and more restrictive emphasis on the value of feminine domesticity than does that of English-born women. The crucial factors as described by the women are (1) the mother's own role as housewife – with a large number of children and a low degree of household mechanization and amenities generally producing a large amount of domestic work to be done, and encouraging a high level of domesticity in the mother herself; (2) the housewife's own childhood role as domestic helper; and (3) the very limited opportunities for Irish women outside the home.

Of the six Irish women three left school at fourteen. The

background of a large family and a highly domesticated mother is common to all of them. Faith Abraham's recollections on this theme were quoted earlier (page 115). Jill Duffy was one of fourteen children and of her mother she says:

> Some nights she didn't go to bed . . . she used to work all night, doing washing and ironing when we were little. We girls helped her, the lads didn't. I used to love doing the ironing and cleaning, I used to love doing the bedrooms out . . . *It was my job.*

The same attitude is evident today: 'I just like cleaning' she said early in the interview: 'I'm just happy when I'm doing it. No matter how dirty it is, I don't mind'. Or take June Doyle's memories of childhood domesticity:

> (Do you like housework?) Well, I do you know. I was brought up to it – we had a big family, and we more or less helped since we were so big – all housework except washing.
> (How do you feel when you haven't managed to get your work done as you like it?) A bit frustrated. Everybody likes to have everything done and sit down. My mother's standards are the same in a way. I was brought up to it . . . *it's drilled into you, like a religion.* ...
>   (Do you remember helping your mother round the house when you were a child?) As soon as we could reach the sink. If I went to play with a friend it was always one or two sisters by the hand to mind them. I'm very used to it. *It's brought up in me.* Bank holidays the beds used to be torn to pieces and the floor was practically pulled up . . . and all my friends used to be off playing and on picnics, and we had to stay at home and clean. When I worked and I used to come home, my friends used to go home and put their rolling pins [hair curlers] in, but I used to come home to a pile of ironing – 'give your mother a rest'.

Portraits of traditional Irish life provide background material here. These describe a highly sex-segregated division of labour, with the accent on the domesticity of women. Conrad Arensberg in his study *The Irish Countryman* quotes one farmer's words:

> If it wasn't for the woman the farmer wouldn't last, and when he is getting a wife for one of his sons, he should look to a house where there has been an industrious and intelligent woman, *because she has taught her daughters how to work and that is what is needed.*[18] (Italics added)

The deliberate induction of girls into the domestic role is, in these traditional Irish communities, an important part of their gender role socialization. According to Alexander J. Humphreys in *New Dubliners* there is a tendency for the same pattern to be carried over into urban life. Humphreys describes the expectations parents in Dublin families have for their children's adult roles:

> The question of marriage does not enter to any important extent into these considerations of the training and education of the boys. But it has the central place in the training and education of the girls, for the role of housewife and mother is the desirable and likely life career for them.[19]

The familial training in the tradition of feminine domesticity is bolstered by an ideology which conceives of male domesticity as *unnatural*:

> With the exception of minor repairs around the house . . . servicing the family is exclusively the wife's job until her daughters are old enough to help her . . . husbands prevalently scorn housework and fear being ridiculed as a 'molly' if they be discovered at it . . . A woman with three sons and no daughters commented 'It is taken for granted that the boys won't do household chores . . . so that, if you happen to have daughters, you have help; if you don't happen to have daughters, you do the work alone.'[20]

Humphreys detects a tendency for urban couples to share more interests and activities than is conventional in rural communities. He also comments that to the wife's role has been assimilated the function of financial manager, but that this has effectively strengthened the system of sex-segregation (though it may give a superficial impression of companionship to the marriage).[21]

In the English urban setting in which the six Irish women in the present sample were living, a pattern of segregated roles – with the wife as financial manager – manifested itself. A tendency for the women's domesticity to be maintained through a constant integration in kin networks is also observable. Five of the six women have relations in England. Faith Abraham is typical of these five: she has, as her most frequent visitors, two unmarried sisters who also live in London. At weekends and whenever they are not working, they visit her. Apart from that, 'I might see the lady next door for something, but otherwise I don't bother to go visiting'. By this she means that she never goes inside other people's houses – for a cup of tea while the children play, for instance. 'People' is used to refer to non-relatives, relatives always being referred to by name. This use of terms is reminiscent of the traditional Irish usage: 'friend' meaning 'relative'.[22]

Material from the present research, together with studies by others, can then be taken to suggest that the traditional upbringing of the Irish girl generally encapsulates a more pronounced emphasis on domesticity than does that of her English-born counterpart, although the upbringing of some working-class English women, as evidenced by some of the interviews in the present sample, may be very similar. If we see feminine domesticity on a spectrum, then the traditional Irish pattern represents one end of the spectrum, together with some of the most domesticated English examples. At the other end would be a pattern in which the girl's non-domestic abilities are encouraged, and where her participation in her mother's household duties is not a prominent part of her upbringing.

Before we leave the topic of childhood socialization and self-concept, a few subsidiary findings should be mentioned. Apart from the greater domesticity of the working-class woman's self-concept, and the middle-class woman's ability to describe her personality, two other social class differences are revealed by the Ten Statements Test. These are (1) the tendency for middle-class women to mention one, or both, of wife and mother roles without mentioning the housewife role (more middle-class than working-class housewives overall referred to the wife role); and (2) the tendency for middle-class women to see themselves in terms of other non-domestic roles, or in terms of political,

Table 7.6 Role and group responses to the Ten Statements Test and social class

Social class	Wife role	Mother role	Mother and/ or wife, not housewife	Mother and/ or wife and housewife	Other roles	Political, religious or ethnic group
	No.(rate)	No.(rate)	No.(rate)	No.(rate)	No.(rate)	No.(rate)
Working class	5 (.25)	17 (.85)	3 (.15)	13 (.65)	3 (.15)	1 (.05)
Middle class	9 (.45)	18 (.90)	9 (.45)	6 (.30)	4 (.20)	4 (.20)

religious, or other types of affiliation. (Table 7.6 gives the figures.) The first of these tendencies points to a slightly greater differentiation between the three family roles in the middle-class group: working-class women are more likely to subsume the roles of wife or mother under the heading 'housewife'. For four middle-class women the *only* mention of a domestic role in the test is a reference to the maternal one.

Overall the incidence of non-domestic role statements as a percentage of all responses to the Ten Statements Test is low – four per cent of the total. This, taken together with the material obtained from the interviews on women's socialization for domesticity, and on their identification with the housewife role, is strong evidence for the importance of domesticity to the forty young housewives in the research sample. Although these women are at a stage in the life cycle in which the emphasis on domesticity is probably at its peak, it is difficult to see how their basic commitment to the housewife role is likely to be eroded in any substantive way by future experiences or life-styles. Social class differences in housewives' statements of self-concepts, which suggest different capacities for self-conceptualization in the two groups, contrast with social class *similarities* in identification with the domestic role; and it is the durability of this latter factor which presents the greatest obstacle to change. A fundamental challenge to the traditional equation between femininity and domesticity is hardly possible so long as the roots of domesticity remain firmly embedded in female personality and self-image.

A final query concerns the importance of identification for work satisfaction patterns. Table 7.7 shows a discernible (but

Table 7.7 Work satisfaction and identification with the housewife role

Identification with the housewife role	Work satisfaction		Total No.(%)
	Satisfied No.(%)	Dissatisfied No.(%)	
High	9(43)	12(57)	21(100)
Medium/low	3(16)	16(84)	19(100)
Total	12(30)	28(70)	40(100)

$x^2 = 3.49$; d.f. $= 1$; $p < .10$

not statistically significant) relationship between the two factors. This lack of a clear relationship is predictable. The – predominantly dissatisfying – experience of doing housework mediates between socialization for domesticity and the achievement of housework satisfaction; too many other variables enter the picture for a high level of domestic role-identification to guarantee an outcome of work satisfaction. Although the factor of job identification has been little studied in the case of employed workers, such studies as have been done do support this finding. High identification with an occupation in the case of the industrial or office worker has been found to be related to general job interest; it also appears to reduce the incidence of job-associated stress.[23] But preparation for a job, through an early identification with it, does not seem to provide a magic solution to the problem of the discontented worker.

8 Marriage and the Division of Labour

Most housewives are married women. On a national scale, one British survey of women's work came up with a figure of ninety-two per cent for the proportion of housewives who are married. (A further six per cent were divorced or widowed.)[1] Legal definitions current in our culture tie the status of 'wife' to the role of unpaid domestic worker. The husband is legally entitled to unpaid domestic service from his wife, and this is a right that courts of law uphold. National insurance and social security systems are based on the presumption that married women are financially dependent housewives,[2] and income tax regulations take the same view; for example, because 'wife' means 'house-wife', neither partner in a marriage can claim against tax the cost of paying a housekeeper.[3] These legal constraints are, of course, supported by other economic, social and psychological pressures which weight the balance firmly in favour of the equation 'wife equals housewife'.

This cheerless picture of inequality is contradicted by a number of studies of marriage published over the last ten years or so. Ronald Fletcher's *The Family and Marriage* (1962) and *Husbands and Wives* by Robert Blood and Donald Wolfe (1960) are two of the earlier works in this genre; Michael Young and Peter Willmott's *The Symmetrical Family* (1973) is one of the most recent to appear. In general these books stress the *equality* of husband and wife in marriage today, compared with the situation in the nineteenth or early twentieth century. They attach a great deal of importance to the legal emancipation of women and to the growth in the proportion of married women employed outside the home – now nearly half, as opposed to a

135

fifth in the early 1950s. The area of the division of labour in the home has received rather less attention by comparison, but the general consensus of opinion is that husbands now participate much more than they used to:

the old pattern of male-dominated, female-serviced family life is . . . being replaced by a new and more symmetrical pattern . . . our domestic ideology is quietly modified and a bloodless revolution occurs, unnoticed, in millions of homes . . .[4]

The vision is dramatic. Certainly the logic of the argument is on the side of the vision; it seems that one consequence of women's equality *should* be men's increasing domesticity. The only way to gauge the truth of these claims is to look at the facts. This chapter examines data on marriage obtained from the forty women interviewed. The first section concentrates on describing the findings themselves, and on analysing their inter-connections with other conclusions already outlined in previous chapters – those relating to the housewife's approach to her work. The second section examines the beliefs about feminine and masculine roles described by the women, as a crucial factor in understanding marital role-patterns. It also looks at the values about men and women's domestic roles which underlie socio-logical research on marriage. This is a particular case of the generalized tendency I discussed in Chapter 1 – the tendency of sociologists to reiterate values about male and female roles current in the wider society, rather than being detached from them. Social science – at least in its popularized version – has played a large part in spreading the view that modern marriage is an egalitarian relationship. If this conclusion is based on false premises, then the weakness in the argument must be exposed.

1 BEHAVIOUR

(a) The Division of Labour in the Home

Interviews were conducted only with the housewives and not with their husbands, so that information on the husband's role comes from the women. It might be objected that women cannot be relied on to report their husband's domestic role accurately; dissatisfied wives might, for example, underestimate the extent to which their husbands help in the home. A careful study of this problem by Michael Rutter and George Brown concludes that the tendency for such bias to occur is insignificant, provided that the questions asked are aimed at the actual performance of specific tasks over a particular time period.[5] The series of questions dealing with marriage in the present survey followed this precept.

Husbands were assessed as 'high', 'medium' or 'low' on their participation in both housework and child-care. The criterion used was how much of a share the husband took in the total amount of domestic work and child-care done. Like the other ratings used in the research, these are *relative* assessments – a husband who has a 'high' level of participation simply does more domestic work/child-care than the men assessed as 'medium' among the husbands of the forty women; these assessments compare the men with each other, rather than with any absolute standard as to what constitutes 'high', 'medium' or 'low' levels of participation. The figures resulting from the assessments are shown in Tables 8.1 and 8.2.

Table 8.1 Husband's participation in housework and social class

| Social class | Husband's participation in housework | | | |
	High No.(%)	Medium No.(%)	Low No.(%)	Total No.(%)
Working class	2(10)	1(5)	17(85)	20(100)
Middle class	4(20)	9(45)	7(35)	20(100)
Total	6(15)	10(25)	24(60)	40(100)

$x^2 = 11.233$; d.f. $= 2$; $p < .01$

Table 8.2 Husband's participation in child-care and social class

| Social class | Husband's participation in child-care | | | |
	High No.(%)	Medium No.(%)	Low No.(%)	Total No.(%)
Working class	2(10)	8(40)	10(50)	20(100)
Middle class	8(40)	4(20)	8(40)	20(100)
Total	10(25)	12(30)	18(45)	40(100)

$x^2 = 5.155$; d.f. $= 2$; $p < .10$

Three main conclusions can be drawn from these tables:
(1) *Only a minority of husbands give the kind of help that asser-tions of equality in modern marriage imply.* Fifteen per cent have a high level of participation in housework and twenty-five per cent in child-care. (2) Patterns of husbands' participation are class-differentiated. (3) There is a greater tendency for men to take part in child-care than in housework.

Jeremy Abbatt is one of the minority whose participation in housework and child-care is described by his wife as substantial (it is classed in the tables as 'high'). He has recently started his own business selling pre-packaged foods; his wife used to be an audio typist before she had a baby. She says:

I help with his work – typing, adding up, that sort of thing, and he helps me with mine. He's a good cook, and he thinks nothing of coming in at the end of the day and cooking a meal. He cooked three meals last week. Or if I was hoovering one room when he came in, he'd help me do the other one. He regularly cleans the windows, empties the rubbish and dries up the dishes. He helps me to get the housework done, because he likes us to sit down together in the evenings. He presses his own suits and trousers as well.

We look after the baby together when he's home. He bathes him in the evening. I dress him, and he gives him his bottle and puts him down.

(Does he ever change a dirty nappy?) He doesn't mind dirty nappies – he's never objected. At the weekend he always gets him up in the morning so I can have a lie in.

This description gives the impression of a shared domestic life. No rigid rules about who should do what dictate the pattern of domestic task behaviour. By comparison, the picture painted by Eleanor Driscoll of *her* husband's behaviour is an inflexibly segregated one (his participation is assessed as 'low' in both domestic areas). She says he never does any housework, shopping or cooking. She adds:

He used to be a head chef and at one time he used to cook the dinner on Saturday. But he's a sod like his father and he doesn't like women to dominate him. He says 'I'm a working man, I come home from work, and I'm tired'.

Meals have to be ready at set times in the Driscoll household, and the kettle has to be on the point of boiling when Larry Dris-coll comes home at 6.20 every evening. A question about whether he does the washing up was greeted with derision: 'You're joking!' Of his relationship with the children – two of his from a previous marriage aged twelve and fourteen, and two younger ones of two and three years – Eleanor Driscoll says:

> He won't look after his children. He loves children – he thinks the world of them ... but he won't look after them ... I wanted to go to a funeral the other day, and he wouldn't let me. 'I'm not looking after the children' he said. If I want to go somewhere Mary, the eldest girl, has got to be there. I mean he wouldn't just sit there and look after them, not because he doesn't like children, but because he's got this typical attitude – you're there for looking after them. He will sometimes get them ready for bed. If I ask him to, he won't – he's like his father – 'I'm not being told what to do by a woman!' He never takes them out, he's never changed a nappy. He plays with them, but it depends on what mood he's in. Not when he comes home from work. I say he's good with children. He does think the world of them.

The last comment contrasts with Eleanor Driscoll's earlier complaints, and suggests an image of a 'good' father who plays with children while taking very little routine responsibility for childcare.

Larry Driscoll's behaviour in the domestic area follows what is seemingly a recognized working-class tradition. Half the working-class husbands are low on their participation in both housework *and* child-care. The social class difference is greater in the case of housework than child-care, indicating a generalized preference for involvement in children as against the alternative of more washing up, shopping, cooking, washing or cleaning. For fifteen of the forty husbands there is, in fact, a discrepancy between their participation in the two areas. This means that a man's performance of housework tasks cannot be predicted from his record in child-care, and vice versa.

This important discrepancy between the two areas of help is illustrated particularly clearly in the case of Robert Bevan, the manager of a small office in a local authority services department. Apart from a son of sixteen from his first marriage there are two younger boys of six and two. Robert Bevan helps a great deal with these children, and both he and his wife take it for granted that he should do so. He regularly gets the two year old up in the morning, dresses him, supervises his play when he is at home, and he puts both children to bed in the evenings. While his wife was being asked questions about child-care, Robert Bevan happened to come into the room for a few minutes. He asked the two year old if he would like to go to the lavatory. The child said 'yes' and was taken there by the father, who came back and reported no success. 'It's a great problem, that' he commented, and then proceeded to launch into a monologue on the problems of toilet training this child. He did not appear to be unusually obsessed with the subject but merely seemed to be emotionally involved in it in a fashion more characteristic of mothers in our society.

Contrasted with this involvement in child-care is a lack of willingness to share household tasks. His wife says he does 'just little things', which turns out to mean clearing the table after the main meal and making a pot of tea at intervals during the day (he comes home from work for lunch). He does no cleaning, shopping, washing or washing up. He was assessed as high on participation in child-care and as low on participation in housework.

The figures given in Tables 8.1 and 8.2 show an overall level of masculine domesticity which is generally lower than that found by other researchers. One reason for this may be the type of interview question used; the area is a delicate one and a valid methodology is all-important. For example, John and Elizabeth Newson found, for their sample of four year olds in Nottingham, that fifty-one per cent of fathers had a high level of participation in child-care and nine per cent a low level.[6] (These figures compare with twenty-five and forty-five per cent for the present sample.) The Newsons do not say on what basis husband's participation was assessed (although from the interview schedule it is clear that the assessments were made at the time of the interview by the person conducting it). The only questions asked were very general ones, for example, 'How much does your husband have to do with... ?' Such questions may get at feelings and values about the father's role, but they are unlikely to provide a precise account of the quantity of child-care done. The Newsons do, however, find that middle-class fathers help more than working-class fathers; this parallels the direction of the present finding.[7]

Comparable data on housework participation are difficult to find. Hannah Gavron in *The Captive Wife* concludes on the basis of information obtained from ninety-eight London housewives that twenty-one per cent of the middle-class and fifty-four per cent of the working-class couples 'simply shared the housework between them'.[8] Again, one has to bear in mind the way in which this conclusion was arrived at. Gavron asked only one direct question on this topic: 'Does your husband help with the housework? (a) If yes, *would* he do: (1) cleaning, (2) washing, (3) ironing, (4) washing up, (5) shopping; (b) if no, why not?'[9] This is not a question about what husbands *actually* do, but about what they might be *prepared* to do.

Blood and Wolfe's American study of *Husbands and Wives* suggests that 'high income' husbands do less work around the house than 'low income' ones.[10] Attention is drawn by this finding to the fact that there are at least two classes of factors which determine the level of male domesticity: career or job patterns, and beliefs about gender roles. When the husband has a demanding and time-consuming career it is simply not possible for him to help a great deal with housework, even if he would like to do so. (It would, of course, be reasonable to ask why a man in this situation chose this kind of career if he really wanted to share child-rearing and housework with his wife.) Within the present sample of forty husbands those with demanding managerial-type (high income) jobs in the middle-class group did tend to be low on help with housework, but there were not many who fell into this category. James Hollister was one. Described by his wife as a 'finance manager' his training is as a chartered accountant, and his job gives him accountancy responsibility for a group of companies. When asked what her husband's working hours were, Angela Hollister said:

> Well, it's usually eight to six, but it varies. Some days it's midnight or later – if he has to entertain a client. He does that once or twice a week. And he also has to do a lot of travelling, and he's often away a couple of nights at a time.

James Hollister sometimes works on Saturdays and may occasionally be away for the weekend. His participation in housework and child-care is low:

> He doesn't do anything regularly, but he'll do anything occasionally. Well, in theory he will: in practice he doesn't usually do anything at all. But he's not one of these people who say 'it's your job, get on with it'.

(b) Marriage Generally

The division of labour is only one area of the marriage relationship. Other areas also have the potential to influence the housewife's definition of, and satisfaction with, her work. Decision-making, financial arrangements, the patterning of leisure activities and social relationships – all these may directly impinge on the housewife's work situation. Her autonomy as a worker is simply vulnerable to dilution through the marriage relationship.

One way to conceptualize marital role-relationships is in terms of a general distinction between 'segregated' and 'joint' roles. Elizabeth Bott, in her study of twenty London families, was the first to describe these concepts.[11] In the families composing her sample she identified two syndromes, one more typically working class than middle class, which she termed a 'segregated conjugal role-relationship' and its converse, more typically middle class, which she called a 'joint conjugal role-relationship'. In the former, husband and wife have precisely defined and differentiated roles. Their division of labour separates male and female tasks; they also have different leisure interests and activities. In a joint role marriage, on the other hand, there is a minimum of task-differentiation. Interests, activities and decision-making are likely to be shared.

Since the division of labour in the present research was assessed on its own, a second, separate classification was made of marital relationships in the two areas of leisure activities and decision-making.[12] The women were asked questions about financial and other decisions relating to home and children and questions about what they and their husbands did in the evenings and at weekends. The distinction between segregated and joint roles appears to describe a definite dimension of the marriage relationship as revealed by answers to these questions. Husbands and wives who share in one area also share in the other, and the same symmetry holds when the accent is on separation. Some examples will serve to put flesh on the bare bones of these generalizations.

Elizabeth and David Gould have a joint role marriage. They live in a new three-bedroom house on a private housing estate, and have one child aged four months. David Gould is a retail chemist and runs his own shop. Elizabeth was asked what they did in the evenings and if she ever went out on her own:

Never. We do everything together. We share all our friends –
his sister's my best friend! We have the same social circle. We
go out at least once a week, sometimes twice – to clubs, friends,
to the cinema, or out for a meal. We do the same things now as
we did before we got married.

As for money:

> He gives me a housekeeping allowance. It's not always the
> same amount. If I run out because I've bought a new dress or
> something, he gives me more. He's not fussy.
> (Who decides how much you should have?) He used just to
> give me a certain amount and I said to my sister-in-law 'do you
> think that's enough?' and my brother said 'that's what I'm going
> to give Hilary'.
> (Do you have an allowance for yourself separate from the
> housekeeping?) No. I've got a bank account with nothing in it!
> Otherwise we have a joint account.
> (Is it important to you to have money you know is your
> own?) I've got no need of it really. I don't feel I'm ever short
> of money.

The baby was planned and wanted by both of them. Their house
is held in joint names and they chose it together. The atmosphere
of jointness is summed up by Elizabeth Gould's answer to a
question about what would happen if she wanted something new
for the house: 'I'd ask him if *we* wanted it' she said.

A very different air of separation is conveyed by Marilyn
Thornton's description of her marriage. Bill Thornton is a
plasterer and his wife does part-time office cleaning. They have
children aged nine, seven and five years and twins aged eighteen
months.

> (What do you do in the evenings?) He goes to the pub. I go
> to see Mother on Thursday evenings – I might go the the pub
> with him on a Saturday or Sunday evening sometimes.
> (What do you do at the weekends?) He goes to football in the
> morning and the pub in the afternoon and evening. I wish he'd
> stay in on a Sunday morning. I don't mind the evenings so
> much.
> (Do you have a housekeeping allowance?) He gives me most
> of his money – he keeps some. I never know how much, but
> he's normally good. If he's had a good week, he takes some
> and says 'you can have £5 extra this week'. But I think he must
> keep about £15 for himself, for petrol and for drink.
> (Who pays the bills?) I get a bulk of money to pay out and
> do the shopping. I pay everything. My husband don't do no

paying out at all. I have to do it. He just won't do it. But I do
mind because sometimes we'll have a row and he'll say to me
'I don't know what you do with all the money' – but as soon as
I say to him 'well, you have the money, just give me the housekeeping' he doesn't want to know. They don't realize the pay-
out – how much things cost nowadays. I pay the rent, the meters,
the insurances, the loan club and my husband's stamps. I save
for tax. *I* have a bank account, not him.
   (Who decided to live here?) I did. I just went back and told
him I'd got a house.
   (If you wanted to buy something new for the house . . . ?) I
might just put it to him first, but I get my own way and it's
bought.

In this marriage financial arrangement is part of the wife's role.
It is interesting to note that this pattern holds for thirteen of the
twenty working-class marriages. The typical arrangement is for
the husband to hand over most of his wage packet to his wife,
keeping 'pocket money' for himself. This state of affairs is not
necessarily a satisfactory one, and may be deeply resented by the
wife: Jill Duffy's husband, for example, has recently got an
evening job working as a drummer in a pub band:

   I'm the worrier about the bills, not him. Since he's been on
   them drums, it's an awful trouble to me because he's not gaining, he's losing. He spends it all on drink. That's no good to
   me. He gives me nearly all his money, but he still spends a lot
   on himself. And then he says 'what did you do with the money
   – there's nothing to show for it?' Men don't understand.

This bitterness seems reasonable. Jill Duffy's financial responsibility extends to the payment of her husband's driving fines, and
these have amounted to £114 over a two year period.
   Sometimes the wife does not know what the husband earns;
five of the twenty working-class women in fact did not know the
exact size of their husbands' wage packets. A 'good' husband is
seen as one who hands over the money regularly, and who does
not keep the whole of any 'extra' he earns for himself.
   Far from being a 'shared' or 'joint' area, the management of
money in these households is firmly located as a component of
the wife's role, and may thus be interpreted as a sign of segregation. In middle-class marriages the 'good' husband is a different
stereotype: he will pay all the bills promptly and without complaint, but will be prepared to discuss any aspect of money

affairs with his wife. Only two middle-class women act as financial managers. Vera Rundle chose to do this because she was a book-keeper before marriage and she gets satisfaction out of balancing the household books. Juliet Warren's reason for taking charge of the money is 'simply because Tom hasn't got the head for it.'

In the sample generally a 'joint' marriage is more likely among the middle-class women, and a 'segregated' relationship is found most often in the working-class group. The figures are shown in Table 8.3.

Table 8.3 Social class and segregation/jointness of marital role-relationship

Marital role-relationship	Working class No.(%)	Social class Middle class No.(%)	Total No.(%)
Segregated	15(75)	2(10)	17(43)
Joint	5(25)	18(90)	23(58)
Total	20(100)	20(100)	40(100)

$x^2 = 17.294$; d.f.$= 1$; $p < .001$

A social class difference of this kind was found by Bott and is reported in numerous studies of family life, both in Britain and in America.[13]

In Bott's original concepts of segregation and jointness these dimensions are held to extend to the marriage relationship generally. That is, a marked division of labour in the home is supposedly accompanied by segregated patterns of decision-making and leisure, and jointness, where it exists, is also a generalized dimension. The use of two different measures in the analysis of the present survey material – husband's participation in domestic work and child-care on the one hand, and segregation/jointness of leisure and decision-making on the other – created an opportunity to test this assumption of uniform segregation/jointness.

The results (Table 8.4) show eleven cases where the assumption does not hold for the housework area and fifteen where child-care is involved. In other words marriages characterized by jointness in leisure activities and decision-making are not necessarily those where husbands help a lot with housework and child-care; in a segregated marriage the husband may, conversely, participate

Table 8.4   Husband's participation in housework and child-care and segregation/jointness of marital role-relationship*

	Husband's participation in: Housework			Child-care		
Marital role-relationship	High/medium No.(%)	Low No.(%)	Total No.(%)	High/medium No.(%)	Low No.(%)	Total No.(%)
Segregated	2(12)	15(88)	17(100)	7(41)	10(59)	17(100)
Joint	14(61)	9(39)	23(100)	15(65)	8(35)	23(100)
Total	16(40)	24(60)	40(100)	22(55)	18(45)	40(100)

Degree of association between participation in housework and segregation/jointness (allowing for maximum possible agreement given the marginal totals) 0.35; degree of association between participation in child-care and segregation/jointness (allowing for the maximum possible agreement given the marginal totals) 0.23.
*Assessed on decision-making and leisure activities.

domestically to a considerable extent. This is an interesting and crucial finding. It highlights the importance of taking into account the domestic task area where assertions of equality in marriage are concerned. Modern marriage *may* be characterized by an equality of status and 'mutuality' between husband and wife, but inequality on the domestic task level is not automatically banished. It remains; there are still two marriages – 'his' and 'hers'.[14] Not only is the level of masculine participation in domestic tasks generally low in the present sample, but an atmosphere of shared roles outside the housework/child-care sphere in some cases gives quite a false impression of sharing within it.

Most of these cases of discrepancy between segregation/jointness and husbands' domestic help do, in fact, involve joint roles.[15] Among these the marriage which shows the biggest split between shared decision-making and shared leisure on the one hand, and segregation of domestic roles on the other, is that of the Rundles.

Phillip Rundle is a journalist on a local newspaper. Vera Rundle, an ex-bookkeeper, now devotes herself full time to the care of her home and two children, aged six and two. Both husband and wife are active Christians, and before a move from the Midlands they ran a church boys' club together. On Sundays they always go to church: during the week they have an evening when they always go out – to see friends or to the cinema. Otherwise they watch television. All the financial affairs are handled by Vera. Decisions are taken together: where to live, which household items to buy, what to name the children. Problems of child-rearing and child discipline are worked out together: '*We* feel you shouldn't tell children not to do things without giving them an explanation'. But as far as housework goes, Phillip Rundle is strictly non-participatory. He helps wash up on Sundays and 'he might fetch a loaf of bread under protest' but that is as much as he is prepared to do. He will 'mind' the children while she shops on Saturdays, but otherwise the children are completely her domain. Though she gives the impression that the marriage is emotionally and psychologically a very close one, she describes a pattern of rigid segregation between the roles of husband and wife in the home.

Elizabeth Bott's method of assessing segregation/jointness – on the three areas of division of labour, decision-making and leisure together – of course did not allow discrepancies of the kind illustrated by the Rundles' marriage to be revealed. In her discussion of the twenty marriages in her sample Bott implies that household tasks and child-care are shared or divided between husband and wife in the same way as decision-making and leisure; she does not raise the question of possible discrepancy.[16] Other researchers have criticized Bott for her assumption that segregation-jointness measures a quality of marriage which is unidimensional. Barbara Harrell-Bond's survey of eighty-five Oxford marriages comes to the conclusion that the pattern of segregation/jointness varies a great deal between four areas – housework, child-care, leisure activities and financial arrangements; in her opinion this shows the importance of different expectations about male and female roles brought to the marriage.[17] An analysis of data on affluent industrial workers by Jennifer Platt produces findings which, in her own words, 'make it highly questionable to regard jointness, at least in the group we studied, as a single dimension'.[18] Couples who gave a 'joint' answer to one question were not especially likely to give a 'joint' answer to another. D. M. Toomey found a similar lack of correlation between answers to questions about domestic task-performance and answers to questions about decision-making and social contacts in his sample of Kent working-class couples.[19]

One likely explanation of these contradictions between Bott's research and other findings relates to what is meant by the division of labour; does this refer to actual behaviour, or to the general attitudes married couples hold towards what each should do in the home? This goes back to a point made earlier: precise questions about which partner performs which tasks, and how often, are liable to receive different answers from questions phrased in a general way which effectively ask what a husband or wife *might* or *would* be prepared to do. A couple who hold the view that marriage is an equal partnership and who are very close to each other in terms of leisure and decision-making are more likely than not to say that the man *would* do almost anything in the home; such a response is simply congruent with the 'companionship' ideal. As D. M. Toomey expresses it somewhat cautiously in relation to his own data:

> It may be that what is especially important in this matter of the jointness of conjugal role-relationships is the general attitudes of each spouse towards the marriage relationship and the feelings of mutuality they have towards one another. These feelings of mutuality are likely to be expressed in a sharing of social contacts as well as in a sharing of decisions and in a general attitude which emphasizes the sharing of tasks in the home.[20]

It could almost amount to a process of double-think. Both husband and wife may believe that the man does more domestically than he actually does; in any case there is likely to be a gap between the general attitude and actual task-performance. Elizabeth Bott in her research appears to place more emphasis on the normative element – what a man would, or should, be prepared to do.[21] This may help to account for her conclusion that segregation/jointness is a general dimension of marriage. The distinction between attitudes and behaviour in this area is clearly of immense importance, since arguments about husband-wife equality in modern marriage are not only arguments about egalitarian *attitudes,* but about changes in behaviour which make new life-styles possible. The significance of married women's increasing employment outside the home must, for example, be seen in the context of women's role in marriage generally; if husbands do not in fact share domestic work equally with their wives then all that has happened is that women have acquired a new[22] work role – employment – in addition to their traditional domestic one. In the present study, only a minority of husbands participate domestically at the level implied by the term 'equality', and the lack of congruence between the patterning of the division of labour and other areas of marriage suggests that a large pocket of domestic 'oppression' may be concealed in what could otherwise be described as 'egalitarian' marriages.

(c) Connections

Before we move on to a more detailed discussion of the determinants of domestic role behaviour in marriage, one important question has to be asked of the data on marriage presented so far. Is the husband's behaviour in the home, or the type of marriage the housewife has, in any way connected with her attitudes to, or satisfaction with, housework?

So far as housework satisfaction is concerned the organization of marriage has little explanatory value. Work satisfaction patterns are not notably affected one way or the other by segregation or jointness.[23] There is no tendency for work satisfaction to be any greater among women whose husbands help substantially with housework or child-care. On the other hand there *are* some relationships with other areas of satisfaction. Satisfaction with marriage[24] is higher among women who report a high or medium level of help with housework from their husbands; of the sixteen women who receive this kind of help, fifteen (ninety-four per cent) are satisfied with marriage, compared with twelve (fifty per cent) of the twenty-four whose husbands give a low level of help $(p < .005)$.

As was noted earlier (page 136) such a finding cannot simply be dismissed on the grounds that the dissatisfied women attribute to their husbands a low level of help and satisfied women attribute a high level. The focus on specifically factual questions about the division of labour makes it extremely unlikely that this is the explanation. The alternative explanation – that women's satisfaction (or dissatisfaction) with the amount of help husbands give is *in fact* a main component of marital satisfaction/dissatisfaction – is supported by what the women say. A woman's opinion of her husband's domesticity is intimately connected with her feelings about the quality of her marriage:

(Does your husband help occasionally or regularly with the housework?) Not now, which grieves me. He did when I was working. I had it out with him – 'we're both working, so we'll both do the housework'. He used to have the vegetables peeled

for dinner, he hoovered... But now he wouldn't touch the flat. It's his attitude, that I'm at home to do it... it gets me a bit niggly sometimes. But he says: 'Well, I'm going out to work and you don't help me in my job' – which is right in a way.
(Would you like him to help?) I don't know whether I would. I'd like him to offer, and I'd probably refuse, but it's just the thought...

(Policeman's wife)

(Does your husband help...?) Oh no, no. Never! He wouldn't lift a hand for you... we have a lot of rows about it. I think he should do things without being asked. My sister's husband's good. He baths the children and everything for her, he puts the babies to bed.

(Wife of a driver's mate)

When this housewife, Janet Gallagher, had her fourth child, her husband was so averse to looking after the three they already had – not to mention doing the housework – that her sister came from another part of London to look after them, bringing her own *five* children with her.

The housewife's resentment of her husband's non-domesticity is common: a corollary is that domesticated husbands are highly valued. A question aimed at the housewife's views about sex equality – 'Do you think there are any ways in which women are treated unfairly in this country at the moment?' – produced the following specific answer from Helen Crane, an ex-secretary and a toolmaker's wife:

I suppose because I'm placed like I am I don't feel that any other woman's worse off... I mean I have a friend and I think her husband treats her despicably – he's not a bit like Peter, he won't help in the house. But when we were all working the help I used to get from Peter and the help she'd get – they just didn't compare. I suppose if I was badly off, I'd be campaigning for equal this and better that.

For Helen Crane, the help she can count on from her husband is a very important feature of their marriage. She raised the topic again, in answer to a question about the women's liberation movement:

(Have you heard of the women's liberation movement?) Yes. I'm afraid I don't take much notice. They're all a bit ridiculous as far as I'm concerned. If husbands and wives can't agree on their own domestic state – because this is what it starts off at – don't give your husband his dinner – leave him with the kids –

I think it's ridiculous. But then, I suppose, *if I had a husband who was different, I might feel stronger* . . .

Not surprisingly the importance of men helping in the home is also carried over into the women's feelings about child-care. Fourteen of the sixteen women (eighty-eight per cent) whose husbands had a high or medium level of participation in housework were assessed as satisfied with child-care.[25] The figure for the group with low participation husbands was thirteen out of twenty-four (fifty-four per cent) (p<.05). This finding draws attention to the problem of what the Rapoports term 'overload'.[26] A housewife-mother who has little help with housework is less able to enjoy child-rearing: children become a source of frustration for the mother in her role as housewife. A willing husband lightens the burden of domesticity and paves the way for a more relaxed approach to the tasks of child-care.[27]

A third connection links the type of marriage a woman has with her general satisfaction – the extent to which she feels content with her life as it is in all its aspects.[28] There is a clear difference between the satisfaction of segregated and joint role wives. Whereas thirteen out of seventeen (seventy-seven per cent) of the women with segregated marriages are dissatisfied generally, only seven out of twenty-three (thirty per cent) of those with joint marriages are (p<.005). For women whose marriages are characterized by shared interests and activities the emotional rewards thus gained probably help to counterbalance the dissatisfactions of housewifery. To compensate for *her* agreed assumption of the housewife role are the achievements of *his* career role. In addition, although housewifery retains its service functions, these are overlaid with an aura of choice and with some degree of commitment to the idea of marriage as an egalitarian relationship. Women with segregated marriages lack these compensations. They are thrown back more on their resources of relationships with others. In traditional working-class communities the existence of the female domestic group provides a strong support for such women, but in conditions where the old patterns of community life are broken up, this prop is removed. It is easy to see how dissatisfaction could result.

A final connection is predictable from an earlier one. If there are some joint marriages in which masculine domesticity is low, is the woman's domesticity high in these cases? In Table 8.5 the

relationship between the women's identification with the housewife role and the segregation/jointness of their marriages is in
the interesting direction of higher domesticity among women in
joint role marriages.

**Table 8.5 Segregation/jointness of the marital role-relationship
and housewife's identification with the housewife role**

	Marital role relationship		
Identification	Segregated No.(%)	Joint No.(%)	Total No.(%)
High	7(33)	14(67)	21(100)
Medium/low	10(53)	9(47)	19(100)
Total	17(43)	23(58)	40(100)

Not significant at 5% level.

The direction of this association makes sense; in joint marriages
where the husband is employed and the wife's principal occupation is that of mother, a high level of feminine domesticity is a
logical corollary. This is particularly so in those marriages in
which the husband's job is especially time-consuming and
generally demanding. In their study *Managers and Their Wives*
J. M. and R. E. Pahl describe many marriages in which husband
and wife share decision-making and social relationships while
remaining separate in the domestic task area. They say

> For the women in this study . . . the roles of wife and home-
> maker were of overwhelming importance . . . A striking result
> of the questions designed to evaluate different roles was the
> relative unimportance to the women of a job or career for
> themselves.[29]

The Pahls point out that if a wife fails to play the supportive
domestic role, the man may be handicapped in the demanding
world of industrial management. Feminine domesticity is a necessary condition here. The pressures exerted on the organization of
roles in the home by the husband's involvement in his career are
also pressures acting to confirm a woman's identification with
housewifery: this identification, laid down in childhood, is reinforced rather than eroded. Although the Pahls are talking about
middle-class marriage the observation would surely hold true of
joint role working-class marriages in which aspects of the

husband's job are similarly demanding. (Five of the fourteen high identification joint role marriages shown in Table 8.5 are working-class marriages.) Jobs with long hours would fall into this category. Indeed, the working-class women who did show this combination had husbands whose daily work-absences from the home were greater than the average for the working-class group as a whole.

2 BELIEFS AND ATTITUDES

In this section I discuss the beliefs about male and female roles held by two different groups of people. The women in my sample compose the first group. The second group is made up of a number of sociological researchers who have dealt with the subject of marital role-patterns. This conjunction may seem rather odd. The rationale behind it is simply that ideas about the 'proper' behaviour of men and women in the home as perceived by these housewives seem to be important organizers of domestic role behaviour in marriage; but the perspectives of researchers *documenting* this behaviour have often been coloured by similar evaluations. The subjective element in their approach to the topic has helped to shape the conclusions that have been drawn.

(a) Housewives

I begin with the housewives themselves. As was observed in the previous section there are a significant number of marriages in which a general air of egalitarianism does not extend into the area of husbands' housework and child-rearing behaviour. In part, this is to be explained by reference to the important place the job or career still occupies in men's lives. But another source of inequality in the home was referred to by most of the forty women. Even where there are individual preferences on the part of men towards greater domestic involvement these may remain unfulfilled through the belief that 'a husband's place is not in the home' – to parody an old saying. In the same way women who might like to participate less in domestic affairs have to face the pressures of the norm that women 'belong' in the domain of housework and child-care.

Two questions threw particular light on the function of gender role norms as organizers of marriage behaviour. The first question – 'Does (or did) your husband change the baby's dirty nappy?' – was a deliberately provocative one. It was planned as a question which would hopefully 'get at' the boundaries of the father's role in child-care.[30] The answers suggest that it had precisely this effect. Here are three typical replies:

No! He absolutely refuses. He says 'no thank you, goodbye, I'm going out!' If I'm changing a nappy, he runs out of the room, it makes him sick. He thinks it's my duty.

(Retail chemist's wife)

He might do it under protest, but I think he tends to think that's not what he *should* do.

(Radio producer's wife)

You're joking! He says 'I'm not doing that – it's a woman's job.'

(Shop manager's wife)

The first two of these answers come from women assessed as middle class on the basis of their husbands' job: the third is from a working-class woman. The social class difference in husbands' co-operation with this task is not very great, as Table 8.6 demonstrates. Slightly more middle-class than working-class men are prepared to change a dirty nappy.

Table 8.6   Answers to question 'Does (did) your husband change the baby's dirty nappy?' by social class

	Answer to question		
Social class	No/occasionally/ under protest No.(%)	Yes No.(%)	Total No.(%)
Working class	17(85)	3(15)	20(100)
Middle class	13(65)	7(35)	20(100)
Total	30(75)	10(25)	40(100)

$x^2 = 2.133$; d.f.$=1$; p$<.20$

Taken together with the responses given to other questions about the father's role, these answers build up a picture of the 'good' father. The physical side of child-rearing is a mother's responsibility. Fathers are there to play with children: 'He's a very good father. He plays with them and he takes them out for walks', as one woman phrased it. The father is expected to take the children off the mother's hands occasionally at weekends, to be generally interested in their well-being, and to take over in times of crisis, like illness or the birth of another baby. This distinction between the hard/unpleasant work aspect of child-rearing and the 'pleasant' side is made explicitly by a policeman's wife:

> (Does your husband change the baby's dirty nappy?) I've asked him a couple of times when I've been busy and he's done it, but he's not too keen...He likes just to play with him – *he doesn't like any of the work involved.*

One husband refuses to change his baby's nappies because she is a girl. Another refuses because the child is a boy ('he's frightened of damaging something' said his wife). Fear is also cited as a reason for not bathing or feeding a baby, and for not holding it longer than a few minutes. Pram-pushing is another delicate subject.[31] Contrary to the widespread belief that fathers are now to be seen pushing prams as much as mothers there are still some who shirk this responsibility:

> I wouldn't let him take the baby out – I don't mind when they turn two or three. I wouldn't like to ask him to push a pram – he wouldn't push a pram, oh God no!
>
> (Painter and decorator's wife)

Even Dawn Abbatt meets resistance on the topic of pram-pushing from her husband, who is otherwise highly domesticated (see page 138):

> Now he will not take him out in a pram...he'll carry him – he says he'll wait till he's in a pushchair. I don't know why, he won't tell me.

A second question women were asked on the subject of gender role beliefs concerned a reversed roles marriage: 'What would you think of a marriage in which the wife went out to work and the husband stayed at home to look after the children?' The answers to this show the existence of a firm belief in the 'natural' domesticity of women, and a corresponding belief that domesticity in men is 'unnatural'. Thirty out of the forty women rejected the possibility of a reversed roles marriage for its transgression of gender role norms. (The remaining ten said it depended on the couple as to whether or not such a marriage was appropriate; none of the women directly approved of this arrangement.) The replies given by Olive Brennan, a factory hand's wife, and Vera Rundle, a journalist's wife, are typical:

(Reversed roles marriage?) Oh, that's ridiculous – it's up to the woman to look after the kids and do the housework. It wouldn't be my idea of a man. I think a man should go out to work and a woman should look after the house.

I don't agree with men doing housework – I don't think it's a man's job ... I certainly wouldn't like to see my husband cleaning a room up. I don't think it's mannish for a man to stay at home. I like a man to be a man.

The 'unmanly' man is a 'henpecked' husband:

I think men should do their share as well, I think they should help.
(Reversed roles marriage?) Oh no, I wouldn't think nothing of that – I'd say he was a henpecked husband. They should help, but not take over.
(Dustman's wife)

I don't like to see a man henpecked – doing all the housework – and forever seeing him dusting and polishing and washing up and everything – but it's nice to have it done now and then.
(Warehouse foreman's wife)

The allegation of unmanliness goes deeper than this, however; an unmanly man is not a man at all:

I don't mind if they [husbands] do their share, but not too much. They should help – but not all the time. Like there's a chappy here who goes out on a Sunday with a pinafore on him – I don't like that, I don't think they should broadcast it, it's not genuine.
(Painter and decorator's wife)

This seems to be a veiled reference to homosexuality. Other women use the words 'effeminate' or 'sissy', or, in the case of Irish women, the word 'molly'.

Against the image of the real man is that of the real wife, described by Eleanor Driscoll in this commentary on her husband's previous marriage:

His first wife was a *typical* wife – she was a *real* wife – she'd have his slippers there, she'd have a cup of tea in his hand. I get very annoyed at times to think why the hell should I have to compete with her? He doesn't say, she was this, she was that, but she was such a *typical good wife*. He often expects me to... I mean, I think blinking heck, we're not under Hitler's reign.

He's like his father. His mother wiped his father's backside practically – she'd walk miles to bring his drink home, take his shoes off. No one would eat till he came home.

A real wife is 'typical' and 'good'. She is the subservient female, dedicated to the satisfaction of her husband's needs. These stereotypes are very influential. Even the women whose first reactions to the reversed roles question were liberal ones later made it clear that they too would prejudge the issue. A university graduate says:

Fair enough, if that's what he [the husband] wants. But I think he'd be asking for it in some respects if people thought he was odd. I wouldn't – well, I suppose I would in a way. I wouldn't query his reasons for doing it, but I think it would make his life miserable because people would think he's peculiar...

More specific reasons are given by some women as to why men are unable to take over the housewife role. Most common are the (supposedly) greater domestic efficiency of women, and the inability of women to earn as much as men. Both are seen as invincible barriers. No one suggested that the domestic incompetence of men might be a result of insufficient experience, or that the problem of financial inequity could be remedied by a concerted attempt on the part of women to change the situation. (It should be remembered that the interviews took place in 1971, before 'women's lib' began to make regular appearances in the media; some of these women might answer differently today.)

But the belief in feminine domesticity is ultimately reduced to beliefs about motherhood. The mother-child relationship is a 'natural' unit. Women have a maternal instinct and are hence closer to children than men ever could be: children need their mothers more than their fathers.[32] This was the view of the sole university graduate in the sample, Joanna Giles, whose opinion on the reversed roles question was quoted above. About the parental aspect of this she said:

The only thing is, I think women are better at bringing up children than men. (Why?) I think it's an instinctive thing

really, due to the fact that they've given birth to the child and they're more anxious and worried about it; therefore they're more likely to spot if there's anything wrong . . .
There's an advertisement in our local newsagent that says 'student doctor available for babysitting'. Well, I suppose the fact that he's a doctor would be an advantage, but the fact that he's a man would mean I would never employ him because I don't think a man is quite as aware of what a child means as a woman, and I think it's a physical thing – it's not anything you could learn, or only a few men could learn.

The idea that men are not, and cannot be, 'maternal' is more than an idiosyncratic one. Helen Crane, the mother of an eight-month-old baby, described an incident that occurred one afternoon when her husband was taking care of the baby:

He took him down to the Broadway, just carrying him – without a pushchair or anything – and he sat down for a rest on the way. He heard two women say 'that's unusual, you don't often see a man out with a baby like that', and he said 'it's my baby! Why *shouldn't* I take him out?'

Such opinions paint a rather reactionary picture of male and female roles. This picture contrasts starkly with the impression of marital equality which comes from other sources. In part the explanation may lie in the fact that during some periods in the marital cycle there is more equality than at others. When women go out to work men may help more: this is confirmed by various British and American studies of marriage and women's employment patterns. Lois Hoffman, an American specialist on women's employment and its effect on the family, reports that the tendency for men to help more when wives work outside the home holds true whether or not the couple profess egalitarian views about marriage.[33] Women in the present sample of forty back up this conclusion that increased male domesticity is a response to the fact of female employment:

He was very good when I was working. He did an equal share. I said 'you're going to do this and this and this' and he said 'alright'.

(Toolmaker's wife)

He just doesn't want to help in the house, and he doesn't enjoy doing it. He feels I'm at home all day and so I should do it, and I do feel he's right. If I was working, that would be different – he did help a bit more then.

(Journalist's wife)

As presented in these and other interviews the temporary rise in male domesticity during the period of dual-employment does not signify a basic egalitarian philosophy. There is a discontinuity between the division of labour in a marriage before there are children and the division of labour between husband and wife where the woman is not employed. When the wife ceases to work outside the home, the willingness of the man to help declines and the division of labour reverts to a more traditional pattern. The couple's basic beliefs about male and female roles have not altered.

A striking aspect of these interviews was that none of the women questioned the assignment to women of the primary duty to look after home and children. This was reflected in the language they used. Housework is talked about as 'my work' ('I can't sit down till I've finished *my* work'); the interior decor of the home is spoken of as the housewife's own ('I clean *my* bedroom on a Monday'; 'I wash *my* basin every day'). The home is the woman's domain. When these housewives discuss their husbands' performance of domestic tasks, they always use the word 'help': 'he *helps* me with the washing up in the evening'; 'On Sunday he *helps* me put the children to bed'. Husbands are housewives' aids. The *responsibility* for seeing that the tasks are completed rests with the housewife, not her husband; shared or interchangeable task-performance is one thing, but shared or interchangeable responsibility is quite another.[34]

Even in joint role marriages where the man's level of participation in domestic affairs is high, a dimension of one-sided responsibility persists. Sarah Maddison, whose marriage is a joint one and whose husband has a high level of domestic participation, illustrates this in her interview. At both ends of the day the husband is a key part of the domestic routine:

We get up at half past seven. I wash and dress and put on my makeup – I have to do that before I come downstairs. At eight my husband starts breakfast – I lay the table the night before.
He comes in from work at 5.30 and takes over the kids. We both put them all to bed about a quarter past six.

This is how she describes her husband's housework behaviour:

He's marvellous. He's a very good cook. Sometimes he'll say

'I'll see to the meal tonight' and when he does he always shows me up because it always turns out terribly exotic. He makes an awful mess, mind you, which I have to clear up. He can do the ironing, though he doesn't do it often. He makes a hot drink for me before we go to bed – little things like that, you know. This is all due to the fact that he shared a flat with three young men when they'd finished at university and I'd strongly recommend it. It makes life much easier for their future wives.

It is also linked with his job as a food technologist:

(Are there any things your husband is particularly fussy about in the house?) He likes things that we eat and we use for eating to be clean – I suppose it's his line: he sees a lot of dangers that the ordinary housewife doesn't. When Sally was on a bottle I used to put it in Milton, but he used to scrub it out, boil it and it used to drive me crackers . . . I'm particular about ironing, so he's got no cause to fuss there. Odd little things can irritate him – such as I can put off defrosting the fridge.

The management of financial affairs, decision-making, and leisure activities in the Maddisons' marriage are all characterized by an intimacy between husband and wife. They take it in turns to go to the children's school for parent-teacher meetings and so forth. In the evenings they mostly watch television, but go out together once or twice a week. At weekends the whole family goes out together, usually swimming, and they all go to church together. But throughout her account of their life together Sarah Maddison makes it clear that the children and the house are her responsibility. He 'helps' her with them. He is more active domestically than most men: instead of merely complaining about the possible lack of hygiene in bottle-feeding, he takes action and sterilizes the bottle himself. But if *she* puts off defrosting the fridge, *he* gets irritated. When *he* cooks, *she* clears up the mess. There is no equal allocation of responsibilities. Only a sharing of some duties.

This question of responsibility is a critical one. As long as the blame is laid on the woman's head for an empty larder or a dirty house it is not meaningful to talk about marriage as a 'joint' or 'equal' partnership. The same holds of parenthood. So long as mothers not fathers are judged by their children's appearances and behaviour (and in dual career families it is the mother's responsibility to find substitute child-care) symmetry remains a myth.

(b) Sociologists

Turning to sociological researchers' own values about the place of men and women in marriage, it is immediately clear that the unequal responsibility factor is concealed or ignored in much existing research. For example, behind Elizabeth Bott's distinction between joint and segregated roles lies the statement (made early in her book, in the first chapter dealing with the research findings) that

> Among the research couples there were some general resemblances in the type of organization characteristically followed in a particular type of activity... Thus in all families there was a basic division of labour, by which the husband was primarily responsible for supporting the family financially and the wife was primarily responsible for housework and child-care; each partner made his own differentiated but complementary contribution to the welfare of the family as a whole.[35]

Bott makes this point when discussing variations in types of organization among couples in her sample. She is clearly observing that, while they vary in the way that some tasks are allocated, these couples all share the same basic division of labour according to which the husband brings home the money and the wife looks after home and children. This is tantamount to saying that 'jointness' in task- and role-organization measures only the extent of variation on the theme of the basic division of labour which 'must' be common to all families.

Jennifer Platt makes an observation along similar lines when she discusses the criteria used in the 'affluent worker' study to distinguish between 'joint' and 'not-joint' marital activities. ('Not-joint' means the same as 'segregated' except that it includes some cases where a decision was made or a task done by a third person.) Platt says her procedure was to

> regard all cases where an activity was done by both husband and wife together, or by either equally, as joint; and to regard all cases as joint where the husband did what would conventionally be regarded as woman's work (e.g. washing up, putting the children to bed).[36]

In classifying as joint all cases in which the husband does 'woman's work', Platt is effectively saying that segregation/jointness measures only one kind of sharing or non-sharing in marriage – the extent to which couples adhere to, or deviate from, traditional distinctions between male and female roles. The same criticism applies to the assessment of segregation/jointness in other areas. For instance, a wife's ability to drive the marital car is taken by Platt as a sign of 'jointness' (whereas, of course, the significance of the husband's ability to drive the car merits no comment at all).

The only questions about household tasks used in Platt's survey were 'Who washes up?', 'Who does the main shopping?', 'Who takes the children out?' and 'Who puts the children to bed?' These are highly selective questions, leaving out, as they do, cleaning, daily shopping, washing, ironing, cooking and the routine care of children. Perhaps it is assumed that these are all feminine tasks, just as the image of washing up and putting children to bed is assumed to be a feminine one. But if so, why were the latter, and not the former, chosen as appropriate questions? A number of studies (including the present one) make it clear that of *all* domestic tasks, putting children to bed, taking children out, washing up, and doing the main shopping are the ones most likely to be engaged in by men.[37] It seems that these tasks tend to be selected precisely because a high level of male participation here is more acceptable than it is in other areas. The possibility is raised that what the researcher has in mind is yet another image – not the image of what a 'traditional' marriage is, but the image of what a 'joint' marriage 'ought' to be.

A third study of marriage mentioned earlier in this chapter was carried out by D. M. Toomey on data obtained from a sample of Kent couples. Toomey's method of assessing the relative roles of husband and wife in the division of labour was to ask the women questions about whether they ever did what counted traditionally as 'men's' tasks ('painting inside the house, wall papering, lighter work in the garden'). The men's questions concerned 'women's work' ('cleaning the house, washing up, laundry, cooking, ironing, looking after the children').[38] Toomey's classification of answers is even more heavily biased by an idea about 'proper' gender role behaviour than is his choice of questions. Thus he counts as joint a wife's response to the effect that she 'very often' or 'often' papers the walls. For the husband's responses about women's tasks:

> The following replies were classed as 'joint': 'Very often' or 'often' for cleaning the house and washing up, 'very often' 'often' or 'sometimes' for ironing and cooking, 'very often', 'often', 'sometimes' or 'rarely' for doing the laundry and 'very often' for looking after the children.[39]

A husband who rarely looks after the children is not making a joint response. But a husband who rarely does the laundry *is* doing so. It is difficult not to conclude from this that it is Toomey's opinion that men ought to look after their children, whereas they ought not to do the laundry. This evaluative approach, as in other studies, extends beyond the domestic work sphere. Husband and wife were asked if the wife knew the husband's weekly earnings (an affirmative reply being classed as a joint response); the couple were not asked if the husband knew the wife's earnings. This raises the interesting question of how a reversal of gender roles would have been assessed. In so far as traditional marital roles were maintained in this situation (although assigned to the opposite gender) the assessment would logically be one of a segregated role-relationship; yet, since this arrangement would allocate 'women's' work to the man, and 'men's' work to the woman, some might classify the marriage as a joint one.

In such studies as these by Bott, Platt and Toomey, an assumption of gender role differences appears as a kind of baseline from which questions are asked and assessments made. The use of such a baseline is an obvious source of bias in the collection of data and the analysis of research findings. However, none of these researchers attempts to generalize their conclusions into broad assertions of egalitarianism in modern marriage. In *The Symmetrical Family* Michael Young and Peter Willmott do precisely this.

Young and Willmott say of the men in their London sample:

> Husbands also do a lot of work in the home, including many jobs which are not at all traditional men's ones ... There is now no sort of work in the home strictly reserved for 'the wives', even clothes-washing and bed-making, still ordinarily thought of as women's jobs, were frequently mentioned by husbands as things they did as well. The extent of the sharing is probably still increasing.[40]

Symmetry in the home is one sign of a more general symmetry in modern marriage, according to Young and Willmott: the move is towards four jobs in marriage, one each inside and outside the home. On what information is the statement about men's domesticity based? The 113-question interview schedule contains *one* question on the division of labour. This was 'Do you/does your husband help at least once a week with any household jobs like washing up, making beds (helping with the children), ironing, cooking or cleaning?'[41] Answers were coded as follows: None = 0, washing up = 1, making beds = 2, help with children = 3, ironing = 4, cooking = 5, cleaning = 6. The code appears to be partly based on the researchers' view of what is socially acceptable: washing up, being acceptable, gets a low code, cleaning, being more unusual, a high one. A tabulation of answers in the sample as a whole shows that fifteen per cent of the men do no domestic work at all. A further thirteen per cent only do washing up, while seventy-two per cent do what is vaguely and euphemistically termed 'other tasks'.[42] The seventy-two per cent sounds impressive, but when one considers how it was arrived at it immediately becomes less so. A man who helps with the children once a week would be included in this percentage; so would (presumably) a husband who ironed his own trousers on a Saturday afternoon. The degree of task-sharing shown by the answers to even this one poorly worded question hardly holds up a convincing image of male domestication. And, of course, as Young and Willmott themselves comment, however much a man may help, the responsibility remains with his wife. Such a division between the spheres of men and women in marriage seems far from symmetrical. There is a long way to go before equality even appears on the horizon.

Such, then, is the message of this chapter. In only a small number of marriages is the husband notably domesticated, and even where this happens, a fundamental separation remains: home and children are the woman's primary responsibility. Doubt is cast on the view that marriage is an egalitarian relationship. The important question is: what is meant by equality? Psychological intimacy between husband and wife, an intermingling of their social worlds, and a more equitable distribution of power in marriage are undoubtedly areas in which marriage in general has changed. But the importance of women's enduring role as housewives and as the main rearers of children continues. Inequality in this area is often overlooked, and sociologists surveying marriage are no exception to the general rule. They bring to their data their own values about the place of men and women in the home, values which repeat the popular theme of gender differences.

9 Children

One unusual aspect of housework as a job is that it is combined with another job: child-rearer. The majority of housewives have children, and virtually all mothers are housewives. Throughout the previous chapters children have put in brief appearances in the guise of factors affecting the way housewives do their work. Children are mentioned as influencing the enjoyment of particular work tasks, for instance, and they appear to make a long working week more likely. They are also cited as a general source of frustration for the housewife as houseworker – her work is interrupted by the constant need to look after children. Satisfaction with housework is more likely when a woman's husband takes over some of the child-care burden; when this happens, the strain of combining the two roles is lessened. Since the object of the research was to find out about housework attitudes and satisfaction, the main focus of the interviews was not on women's feelings about child-care or their definitions of the maternal role. However, a small amount of material was collected in the course of the interviews on the subject of children, and this chapter is devoted to a brief discussion of it.

The child-care/housework combination, as previous chapters have implied, poses certain problems. But the contradiction is not simply that children are messy creatures who untidy the tidy house, and demand to be fed and played with while a meal is being cooked or a room cleaned. The two roles are, in principle, more fundamentally opposed. The servicing function is basic to housework; children are people. Child-care is 'productive'; housework is not.[1] Housework has short-term and repetitive goals; the house is cleaned today and again tomorrow, and so on, for five, ten, fifteen, twenty years ahead. Motherhood has a single long-term goal, which can be described as the mother's

166

own eventual unemployment. A 'successful' mother brings up her children to do without her.

It was a criterion used in selecting the present sample that all the women interviewed should have at least one pre-school child. Altogether, the forty women are responsible for seventy-nine children, although three of these are children of a husband's previous marriage. The twenty working-class wives have forty-seven children, and the twenty middle-class women have thirty-two; this difference is partly accounted for by the earlier age of marriage among working-class women. Since none of the housewives was older than thirty at the time of interview, the number of children they have probably does not represent completed family size. Only fifteen of the forty say they intend to have no more children (four of these have been sterilized).

Following through the theme of children as a variable in the housewife's work environment, control of fertility could be seen as a technique of controlling the conditions of work. Answers given by the women to a question[2] about whether children were planned or not show that a substantial number were not planned, and that these children are more likely to be working class than middle class. Thirty-two of the seventy-nine children were unplanned, and twenty-eight of these thirty-two were born to working-class women:

> I didn't want the last one – I already had three. Actually I didn't plan any of them, they just happened. When he was born and he was a boy, well, it was alright then. But if I had another I'd definitely do away with it.
> (Wife of a driver's mate)

> If I'd known then what I know now, I wouldn't have had any of them.
> (Painter and decorator's wife)

This last comment refers to ignorance about contraception – still, according to other surveys, widespread.[3] But less tangible barriers to fertility control also operate. As Rainwater and Weinstein observe in *And the Poor Get Children*:

> The ideas of family planning and planned parenthood embody a particular world view, a particular way of looking at the world and at oneself . . . A sense of stability and trust in the future . . . is one precondition for effective planning.[4]

Working-class women tend to see the future as less predictable than their middle-class counterparts, and also to believe less in the notion of personal control over one's future. This social class distinction is, of course, a generalization; there are some cases in which it does not apply. But overall, it is supported by the present interviews. The middle-class women were inclined to be more specific about the complex psychological decisions, motivations and reactions surrounding the conception of children:

> After we'd been married about two and a half years, my husband said we really should have a baby. I wasn't too keen at first, but we'd always planned to have three children in six years and we had to start sometime! Then, after the third girl, we said we should have four in eight years, but I chickened out on the last one. Four children really would be a handful.
>
> (Publisher's wife)

Middle-class women also, on the whole, convey a greater sense of determination about the future. Mary Byron was the only woman among the forty who did not really intend to become a mother:

> No I didn't plan her, we didn't really want any children. We certainly don't want any more. I think if I hadn't had Emma, I wouldn't have had a baby – I think as you get older you get selfish – children tie you down.

She is adamant in her refusal to be pressured into having a second child:

> Tony says we won't have any more. Number one reason it keeps me tied to the home too much. When people say to me 'when are you having the next one, then?' he says to them 'Mary's not standing behind a kitchen sink for the rest of her life!'

A more precise concept than social class here is the segregation/jointness dimension of marriage. Rainwater and Weinstein show in their study that contraception is more likely to be practised effectively where husband and wife share interests and activities. Table 9.1 shows the relationship in this sample between type of marriage and the incidence of planned/unplanned children. Eighty per cent of the children born in joint role marriages were planned and sixty-five per cent born in segregated role marriages were unplanned.

Table 9.1   Type of marriage and incidence of planned/unplanned children

Type of marriage	Planned No.(%)	Children Unplanned No.(%)	Total No.(%)
Joint	31(80)	8(21)	39(100)
Segregated	13(35)	24(65)	37(100)
Total	44(61)	32(39)	76(100)

Total does not add up to 79 – the total number of children cared for by these housewives – since three of the children are children of husbands' previous marriages.
$x^2 = 14.06$; d.f. $= 1$; $p < .001$

In the case of joint role marriages the woman is likely to discuss the subject of children using the pronoun 'we', but if her marriage is a segregated one, 'I' is more often used:

> My husband wanted more children. *I* was quite content with two. People kept telling me 'you've got one of each, you don't need any more'. But *I* think I should think of my husband first, and *I* thought 'well, if *I'm* going to have them, I'm going to have them when I'm young.' So *I* decided on number three, and I discovered I was pregnant anyway.
>
> (Car patrolman's wife)

> *We* wanted all the children, but I can't have any more – I've been sterilized, for medical reasons because I had a lot of difficulties with the last one. But *we* don't want any more children anyway.
>
> (Food technologist's wife)

No clear relationship emerges between the factor of planned/unplanned children and satisfaction with housework. In so far as children do represent a part of the work environment over which women have potential control, the effectiveness or otherwise of this control does not appear to be reflected in different degrees of satisfaction/dissatisfaction with housework. There is, however, a small (non-significant) relationship between *number* of children and housework satisfaction, with the trend in the direction of increased satisfaction with increased family size:

Table 9.2   Housework satisfaction and number of children

| Number of children | Housework satisfaction | | Total |
	Satisfied No.(%)	Dissatisfied No.(%)	No.(%)
One	2(13)	14(88)	16(100)
Two	4(33)	8(67)	12(100)
Three or more	6(50)	6(50)	12(100)
Total	12(30)	28(70)	40(100)

$x^2 = 3.68$; d.f.$= 2$; p$<$.20

This relationship is not in the direction that common sense suggests it should be; one might predict more frustration and therefore more dissatisfaction among women with the largest families. However, housewives' comments suggest two partial explanations. First, with additions to the family the pressures of being a 'perfect' housewife and a mother at the same time mount up to a point at which some relaxation of housework standards is the only viable outcome. As Sarah Maddison, a middle-class mother of three children, said:

> As long as I'm not interrupted I like housework. Once the children came along then housework became a real chore simply because you couldn't get on in peace, and even when you got it nice the children messed it up, so I got so I said 'to hell with this' and I got more slap happy than I'd ever been before.

The trend towards a relaxation of housework standards is not in itself an adequate explanation for the higher satisfaction of the group with more than one child, since out of the twelve women with three or more children, half are *dissatisfied* with housework. The second explanation is that a particularly dissatisfied group of women are those with only one child: of fourteen in this category, only two are satisfied with housework.[5] Being a mother for the first time appears to induce a discontent with routine housekeeping chores. Mothers spontaneously make the comparison between the experience of caring for one child and the experience of housework. From the mother of an eight-month-old baby:

> (Do you find housework monotonous on the whole?) Yes, especially with him around. There are so many things you

could be doing if you didn't have rotten old washing and ironing.

(Toolmaker's wife)

Susan Golding, an engineering manager's wife, has a four-month-old baby:

> I would like to get away from the housework but not from the baby. I would only be too happy to hand over all the daily chores to someone else, so I could spend *all* my time with her!

These comments are evidence of a clear separation in the housewife's mind between the two roles of mother and house-wife. Not all women make this separation. Indeed, one of the most impressive aspects of many women's attitudes to child-care is precisely the *lack* of differentiation between the two roles. This is shown most clearly in the following remarks, made by Sandra Bishop, a painter and decorator's wife:

> (Do you like looking after the child?) Yes. The only thing is with her nappies. I get so disappointed if they don't look so white when I do them by hand. I think to myself 'don't they look awful?' I used to boil them at his Mum's on the stove, but I can't do it here, I've got an electric one – I started boiling them in one of me saucepans, but it looked so awful I stopped... I'm trying to train her now, and I get disappointed when she keeps messing . . . sometimes she does it beside the pot when the pot's right there, and I don't like that. (This child is eighteen months old.)

The two roles are merged. For Sandra Bishop 'looking after the child' means the work involved in keeping the child and the child's clothes clean. The single word 'yes' expresses her enjoy-ment of child-care and what follows is a monologue on the problems of keeping nappies white.

A main consequence of this undifferentiated approach to housewifery and motherhood is, thus, a pronounced stress on the servicing aspects of the maternal role: child-care and house-work become synonyms. The synonimity implies a strong emotional investment in the child's cleanliness and tidiness, and 'perfectionist' standards applied to the home tend to be carried over to the child. Another sign of this syndrome is an emphasis on the consumer function. Janet Gallagher, a working-class woman married to a driver's mate and the mother of four children, said, when asked whether she liked looking after her children,

> I buy them something nearly every week. This week I bought them a couple of pairs of pyjamas and a couple of covers and some shoes...

This theme was expounded in more detail, and the items bought for the children were listed with a tremendous air of pride. A number of other women also eagerly described the clothes they had bought, or were intending to buy, for their children, without saying very much about the many other facets of child-care.

This similarity of approach to the two roles – housework and motherhood – was, in the present sample, found most often among the working-class women. Comparable findings emerge from an American study of working-class motherhood, Rainwater, Coleman and Handel's *Workingman's Wife*. The following passage from this study makes some additional points about the working-class mother's approach to child-care:

> A great deal of what the working-class wife holds dear is located in her children. This is a central attitude, even though children are also a source of frustration. In talking of their children, these women... felt 'tied down' by their children, they considered them a 'terrific nuisance and bother,' yet they were exaggeratedly concerned over their physical well-being and happiness, and called them the 'most prized possession in our house'... The working-class woman looks for gratification from her children in the present rather than the future. She tends to regard the child as something that should give her pleasure even as she cares for it... A child is for her, in one of its major aspects, a passive object to be hugged close, or to deck out in appealing clothes, or to be enjoyed for its antics.[6]

In part the equation between housewife and mother roles can be considered as a simple response to the situation in which women find themselves. The two jobs are carried out simultaneously, and there is a general lack of differentiation in social attitudes to women: 'housewife' means woman, wife and mother, and the separate components are rarely spelled out. The occupational description sanctioned by society for a woman who is at home looking after children is not 'mother' but 'housewife'. However the confusion between housewife and mother is also tied in with other facets of the – more typically – working-class orientation to children. Working-class women less often mention interest in the child as a unique individual (which does not of course mean that in practice the child is not treated as an individual). A greater importance is attached to the child's *public* appearance and behaviour. Both these characteristics appear in the interview with Carol West, a warehouse foreman's wife:

> (Do you like looking after the child?) What, the child? Sometimes. Sometimes he drives me up the wall. He's got terrible bad language at the moment and that really annoys me, but he's better with me when we're on our own. He's awful when we go out. He's rude, and he just runs away from me all the time... I'm Roman Catholic and I'd like to take the child to church with me, but I'm frightened to go to church with him because he swears so much.
>
> (Do you ever feel as though you're on your own too much...?) It doesn't worry me, being on my own. I've got the dog. I find that company – lots of people wouldn't – a dog and a cat. I mean you just talk to them as though they were human.

There is no mention of the child as 'company' here.

In the middle-class group, by contrast, there are many references to the pleasure in children as personalities that develop before one's eyes, as active and independent people in the making, rather than as passive objects to be decorated or controlled. Catherine Prince, a journalist's wife, typifies this attitude when she says, in answer to the question 'Do you like looking after the child?'

> Yes, I like it. I'd rather be at home with the child than at work – or doing anything else I could think of ... I expected to find it rewarding, but not quite as much as it is... Just the whole thing of seeing a person developing and somebody learning right from nothing to do things and *be* – and the amount of influence you have on this for good or for bad.

Such an approach is only possible where child-care is clearly seen as different from housework. A characteristic middle-class tendency to differentiate these roles is found by Michael Fogarty and his co-authors in *Sex, Career and Family*. Analysing answers to a question about preferences in handling different household tasks they conclude:

> The most striking element to emerge from these clusterings is the detachment of the child-care item from the cleaning cluster [of activities]. This would suggest that while the cleaning and mending items are chores that most of the wives would prefer to delegate ... the child-care area is separate.[7]

While in practice their sample of graduate women often associated child-care with the least enjoyed housework activities – budgeting, washing and cleaning – in theory there was a detachment of the child-care category from all other tasks. The practical difficulties of making this separation are described by Juliet Warren, a middle-class housewife in the present sample:

> When I was working, I used to come back here and get a tremendous kick out of doing housework. But now I'm doing it every day, it really is the biggest bore of my life. I suppose it's partly because I can't do anything uninterrupted and I still can't get used to that. It takes a lot of effort.
> I used to read all the literature available about having a baby, and really there is a tremendous halo of enjoyment – no one ever tells you about the hard work – no one tells you how shattering it is to be doing it all the time, seven days a week ... it's not all a super enviable state. It sounds awful, because one has a child and she's super and beautiful and I wouldn't be without her either – to suddenly change from working – I'm thirty now – to suddenly find yourself doing housework all the time ...

As Juliet Warren observes, it may take a lot of effort to get housework done and concentrate also on the rewarding aspects of child-rearing. The child may be 'super' and 'beautiful' but she is also the cause of the housewife's internal disarray, the quality of which is only matched by the external chaos of the home she cannot find enough (uninterrupted) time to clean. Another factor is the 'myth' of motherhood, absorbed from her ante-natal reading, which Juliet Warren finds contrasts so strongly with the reality of the situation she is in. She does not deny that motherhood has its rewards; what she is saying is that it has considerable deprivations too, and that the social glorification of motherhood in our society acts to conceal them.

Satisfaction with child-care is definitely lower among working-class women, as Table 9.3 indicates.

Table 9.3   Satisfaction with child-care and social class

| Social class | Satisfaction with child-care | | Total |
	Satisfied No.(%)	Dissatisfied No.(%)	No.(%)
Working class	10(50)	10(50)	20(100)
Middle class	17(85)	3(15)	20(100)
Total	27(68)	13(33)	40(100)

p<.025

'Satisfaction' in this context means the degree of emotional reward reported by the women in relation to child-care, rather than the somewhat different dimension of the importance attached to 'being' a mother. Some of the greater dissatisfaction among working-class women may be related to the greater number of unplanned children they have, although the relationship between the two variables (satisfaction with child-care and planned/ unplanned children) is not significant at the five per cent level.[8]

Behind this general concept of 'satisfaction' with child-care lie more subtle differences to do with *ambivalent* feelings about children and the demands of the maternal role. A parallel question to the question 'Do you like housework?' was asked of child-care: 'Do you like looking after the child/children?' In its phrasing this question is hardly conventional: it allows a negative answer in an area where social attitudes condone only positive ones.[9] In fact none of the forty women said 'no' to this question; the lack of negative response may simply be a sign that negative attitudes towards the mother-child relationship are not socially acceptable. Through the strong pressure to identify with the maternal role the expression of dislike towards child-rearing activities may be experienced as self-threatening. Where the social image of motherhood invests the mother-child relationship with an aura of mutual contentment, women grow up expecting that they will enjoy their child-care activities. An equation between the adult feminine role and the maternal role rules out the possibility that children and child-care tasks will be overtly rejected.

Although none of the forty women initially declared a dislike of child-care, a considerable number did go on to express ambivalent feelings towards it.[10] Table 9.4 shows total responses

to the 'Do you like looking after the child/children?' question
in the sample as a whole.

**Table 9.4　Answers* to question 'Do you like looking after the
child/children?' and social class**

Social class	Answers			
	Like very much/like No.(%)	Don't mind No.(%)	Sometimes/ ambivalent No.(%)	Total No.(%)
Working class	4(20)	1(5)	15(75)	20(100)
Middle class	14(70)	3(15)	3(15)	20(100)
Total	18(45)	4(10)	18(45)	40(100)

*Includes initial answers and later ones.
$x^2 = 14.556$; d.f. $= 2$; p$<$.001

Three-quarters of the working-class women express ambivalence,
while about the same proportion of the middle-class group are
definitely positive in their answers. Here are some examples of
ambivalent statements:

> (Do you like looking after the children?) I do. But I can't
> stand a lot of whining, this sort of thing, and I haven't got a
> lot of patience. I wish I had.
>
> (Shop manager's wife)

> I do, yes. I prefer to look after them myself than go to work.
> If I didn't have them I'd be at work. (Is there anything you
> particularly enjoy about looking after the children?) Not really,
> I suppose I've got used to everything. I have to do it. It's not
> that I don't enjoy it, but you get fed up at times ... with doing
> the same things. Sometimes I have to wash the lino twice a day
> because of the children.
>
> (Factory hand's wife)

June Doyle also 'likes' looking after her children:

> If I hadn't had him [the third child] I would have put her in
> a nursery, I think. When he turns three, he's off. When I was
> carrying him, I held on to her, she was company for me. She
> used to come in and out of the hospital with me. But I won't
> hold on to him. It's definitely not fair on the child, because
> you're inclined to get short-tempered with them. When you
> think about it, when you've got a quiet moment, you realize
> they're only being natural ... They're irritating. I give him [the

baby] a belt sometimes, and I'm sorry after.

June Doyle's attempt to adjust to a situation which she finds difficult is evident from a later remark:

> Except for going out to work, I haven't been anywhere in five years. (Do you mind that?) I've gotten adjusted to it. I've gotten in such a state now I wouldn't leave them. I wouldn't mind – so long as the ironing's done, you get in such a state you just watch television and do the ironing...

At this point she becomes incoherent and it is not clear what she is trying to say. These comments certainly reflect on the conditions of maternity in modern industrial societies: the isolation, and the constant, unrelieved responsibility which mothers have for their children. But June Doyle's comments are also deeply ambivalent. Are children her most important source of emotional reward and satisfaction? Or are they simply a burden? Are they both at the same time? How does she reconcile these different feelings?

A core quality is the high value placed on closeness to one's children, combined with an inarticulate resentment of the tie this imposes. Jill Duffy, another working-class mother, answers the question 'Do you like looking after the children?' indirectly, saying: 'I bring them everywhere with me. Nobody else has them except at night'. By this she means that she is a 'good' mother, because she refuses to be separated from her children in their waking hours. But there is also a note of self-persuasion: 'I must be a good mother (I must like my children) if I'm with them all the time'. Later in the interview, when asked 'If you could have the last ten years over again, would you do anything differently?' she said:

> I'd never get married and I'd never have children. They just drive you round the bend at times. You don't get a minute away from them, really. You're all for the children, never for yourself.

Other evidence of her ambivalence is contained in answers to two further questions:

> (When you feel really happy, what sort of thing makes you feel like that?) When the children aren't annoying me. When they don't get me down and I get me things done, and I get out.

And

(What would you say are the best things about being a house-wife?) You've got your children.

Sally Jordan, a dustman's wife, is more honest with herself than Jill Duffy:

(Do you like looking after the children?) Well, I won't say I dislike it, but as I said before, my patience is gradually wearing down.

This comment she followed directly with:

I breastfed the first child [now aged nine] for seven months because it was always drummed into me that a mother's milk is better for the baby. But I didn't feed the second – I didn't have enough time.

One wants to know why the question 'Do you like looking after the children?' provokes this particular response. Sally Jordan is impatient with her children – that she recognizes. But she is also concerned, like Jill Duffy, to be accepted as a 'good' mother – hence the reference to breastfeeding, and the assertion that 'not enough time' was the factor that prevented her from feeding the second child herself.

A related characteristic of these women's attitudes to children is an apparent inability to express strongly positive feeling. Joy in child-rearing, the emotional reward children give, love for children – none of these is mentioned directly. The impression is one of a rather *uncommitted* attitude to children, an attitude at odds with the motherhood ideals transmitted by many modern social agencies:

I don't mind looking after the children, they're not too bad.
(Car patrolman's wife)

I don't mind looking after the children, but they get you down when you're stuck with them all week.
(Plasterer's wife)

There is a *theoretical* importance attached to children:

(What would you say are the best things about being a house-wife?) I think children makes a home really. I see people who are married and don't have children who are quite miserable.

But, in practice,

> (What would you say are the worst things about being a house-
> wife?) Looking after the children.
> (Wife of a driver's mate)

These social class differences are, of course, not absolute. There
are women in the middle-class group who are 'working-class-like'
and some 'working-class' women have more in common with the
majority of the middle-class women on the dimension of attitudes
to child-care. As the Newsons comment:

> If we knew enough about it, the way in which parents bring
> up their children might well provide a safer guide to social
> categorization than can the father's occupation alone.[11]

It must also be emphasized that in the discussion of social class
differences above no impression that the working-class women are
'deficient' as mothers is intended. The involvement in material/
technical aspects of child-care which some of these women mani-
fest can, as I said earlier, be interpreted as a response to the
situation in which women find themselves. In this sense it is a
logical outcome of the modern definition of women as 'servicers'.
In the housekeeping role the servicing function is far more
central than the productive or creative one. In the roles of wife
and mother also, the image of women as servicers of men's and
children's needs is prominent: women 'service' the labour force
by catering to the physical needs of men (workers) and by raising
children (the next generation of workers) so that the men are free
from child-socialization and free *to* work outside the home.

The place of children in the housewife's life can be described,
and differences between women, discussed. Value judgements can
also be made. My own conclusions are that these interviews
document well the dissatisfying social context in which the role of
mother is carried out today. Social isolation and constant responsibility bring about discontent. Competition with the demands of
housewifery means that to the mother as houseworker the child
is sometimes seen as an obstacle to job satisfaction; for the child,
the need to juxtapose its demands with those of housework cannot
but be experienced as frustrating. Although, as the last chapter
showed, men do something to remedy this difficulty by involving
themselves in child-care, the trend could be seen as a retrogres-
sive one from the women's point of view. Playing with children,

taking them out, and putting them to bed, are the child-care activities that men prefer. There is, apparently, a strong feeling *against* involvement in the work-like, routine, less pleasant aspects of bringing up children. This kind of enlargement in the father's role is an unfortunate development for women, who stand to gain little from it but temporary peace to do household chores ('he plays with the children every evening so I can get the washing up done'). At the same time, they lose some of the rewards parenthood offers. Satisfaction with housework may be increased, but only at the expense of satisfaction with child-care.

10 Conclusions

The survey of housework presented and discussed in previous chapters goes some way towards remedying the predominantly male orientation of sociology which was charted at the beginning of the book. One of the many yawning gaps caused by an underlying concern with male interests and activities within the discipline can begin to be, if not filled, then at least bridged. But the survey also has a wider relevance. Issues concerning the situation of women today are now publicly, and even popularly, discussed. The assignment to women of domestic activities both inside and outside the home, and women's own seeming predilection for domesticity, are structural features of their general situation in industrialized societies at the present time. Therefore any research which examines women's feelings and attitudes about housework can be expected to have something to say about both the 'oppression' and the 'liberation' of women.

1 THE RESEARCH FINDINGS: A SUMMARY

Before moving on to this latter question, I want first of all to summarize some of the main findings of the research. This will serve the dual function of recapitulating the important findings, and also of drawing together themes relevant to the discussion of housewives and women's liberation which occupies the last part of the chapter. The first group of findings comes under the heading of *feelings about housework*.

(a) Feelings about Housework

The principal aim of the study was to conceptualize housework as work, rather than simply as an aspect of the feminine role in marriage. In this way it differs from previous sociological surveys of family life or women's domestic situation. The concept of 'satisfaction with housework', analogous with the notion of job satisfaction in the employment sphere, follows from the housework-as-work perspective.

1 The major finding here is that dissatisfaction with housework predominates. Seventy per cent of the women interviewed came out as 'dissatisfied' in an overall assessment of feelings expressed about housework during the course of a long depth interview. This figure lays to rest the idea that only a tiny minority of women are discontented housewives.

2 Monotony is a common experience. Three-quarters of the sample report it, and eighty per cent of these are dissatisfied with housework. Fragmentation – a characteristic of work related to monotony – is also experienced by the majority of housewives, but is not associated with work dissatisfaction. The reason for this lack of connection appears to be the expectation that housework must necessarily be fragmented work; women are not made dissatisfied by an outcome they predict. Excessive pace in work, a second characteristic of work often associated with monotony in studies of industrial workers' attitudes, is reported by half the sample. Like fragmentation, it is unrelated to work satisfaction patterns. All three of these experiences – monotony, fragmentation and excessive pace – show a higher incidence among housewives than among factory workers. In this respect housewives have more in common with assembly line workers than with factory workers engaged in more skilled and less repetitive work.

3 Loneliness is a frequent complaint. Most of the women who are dissatisfied with housework report a low level of social interaction with others. This parallels the finding from industrial sociology that the opportunity to engage in social relationships with other workers is one of the most prized aspects of any job.

4 Autonomy is the most highly valued dimension of the housewife role. 'Being one's own boss' – a phrase used by nearly half the sample – and exercising control over the pace of work is a

facet of housewifery which contrasts favourably with employment work.

5 Housework is the most disliked aspect of 'being a housewife'.

6 Another disadvantage is the low status of the housewife role: the low social prestige and trivialization of housework implied by the phrase 'just a housewife'. A perception of low status is related to housework dissatisfaction – more of those who complain about their status are dissatisfied than satisfied.

7 Attitudes towards the separate tasks that make up housework show considerable variation between tasks, although not between women. The most liked tasks are (in order) cooking, shopping, washing, cleaning, washing up and ironing. The consistency between different women's answers follows from the fact that particular work conditions or contexts are experienced as more satisfying than others. For example, the opportunity to talk to other people while working, having enough time in which to complete tasks, and possessing the right environment or tools of work, are conditions which promote a positive attitude to housework activities. While the *heterogeneity* of housework duties is emphasized in these findings, so also is the *similarity* of the experiences women cite as leading to enjoyment of these duties.

8 Housewives have a long working week. The average in this sample is seventy-seven hours, with a range from forty-eight (the only housewife employed full time at the time of interview) to 105.

9 An important dimension of work behaviour is the felt need to specify standards and routines to which the housewife must adhere in the course of work performance. This process has a number of origins and functions. First, it appears to be a means of creating unity out of a collection of heterogeneous work tasks. Secondly, it is a way of expressing the feeling of personal responsibility for housework. Thirdly, it establishes a means of obtaining reward in housework – satisfaction can be gained daily from successful adherence to these standards and routines. An incidental function is that of job enlargement. There is a relationship between the extent of standards- and routine-specification and the number of hours worked; the majority of those housewives with a 'high' specification work seventy or more hours a week.

With the provision of these job definitions women relinquish, to a considerable extent, the experience of autonomy. For a day-to-day control over work rhythms is substituted a psychological need to follow certain rules. These become 'objectified' i.e. are felt as, in some sense, *external* to the housewife as worker.

10 The relationship between the specification of standards and routines and work satisfaction patterns is in the direction of more satisfaction in the high specification group. This draws attention to the importance of self-reward; by attaining the standards and repeating the routines they set themselves, women may be able to gain a measure of psychological satisfaction. The corollary to this is that a failure to achieve one's pre-set goals may bring about substantial dissatisfaction.

11 Experiences connected with women's performance of jobs outside the home have some bearing on their satisfaction with work in the home. All the women who held high status jobs in the past (such as computer programmer, manicurist, fashion model) are dissatisfied with housework. This phenomenon can be described as a case of incongruency between the housewife's separate statuses: the high status of one's previous job contrasts with the low status of being a housewife, and the resulting stress pushes the balance in favour of present dissatisfaction.

The factor of satisfaction with employment work is also important. Dissatisfaction with housework is higher among those who report work satisfaction in a previous job; in the women's comments housework is unfavourably compared with employment work which, whatever the particular nature of the work, offers company, social recognition and financial reward.

(b) Orientation to the Housewife Role

A second group of findings is very closely connected to the first group, but is separated by a conceptual distinction which at first sight appears trivial. In fact this distinction is of fundamental importance, both to an analysis of the housewife's situation, and to the wider question of how the research interconnects with the women's liberation issue.

The concept of *feelings about housework* relates to women's approaches and responses to the daily experience of doing housework. By contrast, the concept of women's *orientation to the housewife role* describes the relationship between the notion of 'being a housewife' and the psychological identity of women. While the former is a question of job satisfaction in the home, the latter refers to the whole construction of psychological femininity and its 'fit' in a social world predicated on gender differences. The sense of self as a housewife (or not) is a deeply rooted facet of self-identity as feminine; the equation of femininity with house-wifery is basic to the institution of family life and to the gender divisions which obtain in the paid work world (the existence of low paid women's jobs being a structural feature of this world).

The discontinuity between the two concepts – feelings about housework and orientation to the housewife role – is, of course, only partial; the two have a degree of overlap. Nevertheless, a differentiation between factors that could be subsumed under the heading of one concept rather than the other was an important feature of the way the research developed. Four conclusions in particular can be identified as relating to orientation to the house-wife role.

1 The extent to which housewives are personally identified with the housewife role shapes their whole orientation to it. The majority of the women in the sample have a high or medium identification; a low identification is uncommon. A high personal identification with the role of housewife means that the performance of house-work is felt to be one's personal responsibility.

2 The level of identification with the housewife role is related to the way housework is done. Those women with a high identifi-cation were likely to have a high specification of standards and routines.

3 In the shaping of domestic role identification in women, the function of the mother as role model is all-important. Mothers are frequently mentioned as influences over women's own house-work behaviour; there may not be direct imitation of the mother's way of doing housework, but both imitation and rebellion are essentially aspects of the same identification process.

4 Paralleling the importance of an underlying identification with the housewife role are declared beliefs in favour of 'natural' feminine domesticity, and opposed to a similar degree of domes-ticity in men. Women locate their orientation to the housewife role within the context of a general view of feminine and mas-culine roles, according to which the place of each sex is clearly and differently defined. This definition of appropriate gender role behaviour thus covers not only the equation of femaleness with

housewifery, but also the patterning of the division of labour
between the housewife and her husband.

The distinction between feelings about housework and orientation
to the housewife role has manifold implications. In the first place,
it enables us to explain certain apparent disagreements on the
subject of women's satisfaction or dissatisfaction with domesticity
which abound in popular discussion, and which may also be found
in academic research. Secondly, this distinction offers a unified
understanding of both social class *differences* and *similarities* in
housework attitudes/satisfactions. These two particular advantages
of distinguishing between the two concepts can be illustrated by
taking the prototype of a common conversation today – one which
contains the two alternative propositions that women are 'happy'
and 'unhappy' as housewives:

A   I don't understand why everyone talks as though all housewives have a miserable time. Lots of women like being
housewives.

B   It's ridiculous to pretend that anyone actually *likes* cleaning floors and washing dishes – how can they? Housework
is awful work. It's lonely and boring. There's nothing to
show for it – it's all got to be done the next day. You don't
get paid for it, either.

A   That may be your view, but the plain fact is that most
women want to get married and become housewives. They
don't complain about it – it's very important to them to
look after their homes and their children, and they don't
really have any other ambition. It's only a small minority
of militant women who put your point of view. You're
degrading the housewife. There's nothing wrong with being
a housewife and liking it. Running a home is more satisfying than doing a dreary office or factory job.

B   But being a housewife is the only option open to many
women. It's because there's no alternative that they say
they like being housewives – that they like housework. If
things were different they might declare their real feelings . . .

Participant A in this conversation is talking about women's
relationship to the housewife role, whereas participant B is focusing on feelings about housework. A is not saying that women like
housework – only that they like being housewives. Similarly, B
is saying women dislike housework, but is not arguing that women

dislike being housewives. The disagreement is spurious. It is caused by a failure to see that the values of the two factors – feelings about the work, and approach to the role – may not coincide. A woman may be positively oriented to the housewife role but dislike housework; or she may be negatively disposed towards housewifery – not feeling herself to be a housewife – but at the same time enjoy doing housework.

A similar concentration on one or other of the two factors helps to explain why some studies of women's domestic situation emphasize satisfaction, while others highlight dissatisfaction. For example, Mirra Komarovsky's *Blue Collar Marriage* and Lee Rainwater, Richard Coleman and Gerald Handel's *Workingman's Wife* both offer portraits of the working-class woman's life in America, but their conclusions on the whole disagree; Komarovsky stresses the women's satisfaction with housewifery and Rainwater and his colleagues draw attention to the frustrations and dissatisfactions of housework. While Komarovsky focuses on feelings about the role as such, the other study asks questions specifically about daily routine and about feelings towards household tasks. The working-class woman in this study 'characterizes her daily life as "busy", "crowded", "a mess", "humdrum", "dull, just dull" . . . They see themselves as "hard working" women'[1] whereas Komarovsky's subjects 'accept housewifery'.[2] This sharp contrast in the tone of the two conclusions stems from the different approaches adopted. The authors of *Workingman's Wife* turn the spotlight on feelings about housework; in *Blue Collar Marriage* Komarovsky is concerned with the acceptance/non-acceptance of the housewife role.

(c)   Social Class

How is an explanation of social class differences aided by the distinction between orientation to the housewife role and feelings about housework?

Some clear differences between working-class and middle-class women did emerge in the interviews; there were also ways in which the two groups were similar. The incidence of dissatisfaction with housework, attitudes to work tasks, the specification of standards and routines, and identification with the housewife role are some of the most important dimensions on which no class difference is manifested. On the other hand considerable class differences were shown in answers to the question 'Do you like housework?' and in responses to a 'test' of self-attitudes given half way through the interview. Broadly speaking, these two components of the interview show working-class women as much more closely involved with the housewife role and with domestic interests and activities generally. 'Like' or 'don't mind' answers to the 'Do you like housework?' question, which were provided chiefly by the working-class housewives in the sample, were interpreted (pages 66–8) as statements symbolizing an attachment to the norm of feminine satisfaction with housework – this norm being more characteristic of working-class than middle-class communities, and adherence to it being facilitated by the more typically 'working-class' mode of language use.

The conjunction of these differences and similarities between the classes can be summed up by saying that, while similar feelings about housework are shared by working-class and middle-class housewives, their orientation to the housewife role tends to differ. The working-class orientation is, on the whole, more positive: there is a strong motivation to declare a personal identi-' fication with domesticity, and this, in turn, leads to a search for satisfaction in housework. Correspondingly, the middle-class tendency is towards a disengagement from the housewife role on a verbal and cognitive level (despite an underlying childhood identification with the mother-housewife): instead of a striving after satisfaction with housework there tends to be a recognition of housework dissatisfaction. It is important to note, however, that neither outcome is guaranteed. A woman who wants to be satisfied as a housewife may find that this orientation cannot over-ride the routine daily dissatisfactions of doing housework. Similarly, the recognition of housework dissatisfaction as a possibility (or even probability) may enable some satisfaction to be felt.

It is on the dimension of work attitudes and feelings that the identity of experience between working-class and middle-class women is most in evidence. This, on its own, constitutes a main finding of the study. The incidence of dissatisfaction with housework among the two class groups is the same. If one substitutes the women's education for the social class categorization based (chiefly) on husband's occupation, there is still no differentiation: housewives with an early-completed education are no more likely than those whose education was more prolonged to be satisfied with housework.[3] A finding from industrial sociology was cited in Chapter 4 to support this conclusion. In his study of Detroit automobile workers Arthur Kornhauser shows that occupational differences in 'mental health' (broadly equivalent to 'satisfaction') persist apart from the influence of education. The proportion of workers having good mental health consistently decreases with level of skill required by the job for each of three educational categories separately.[4] In other words the level of skill obtaining in a job, rather than the worker's educational background, is the factor associated with differences in mental health. Applied to the case of the housewife, one could suggest that it is the nature of housework as a job that makes dissatisfaction with it likely. This influence may be stronger than the effect of education or any experience related to social class membership. Such a conclusion requires some revision of the conventional sociological assumption that the unhappy housewife is a purely middle-class phenomenon. Together with other findings it may also be taken as evidence against the appropriateness of the usual approach which assigns women to one social class or another on the basis of their husband's occupation. In some cases the lines drawn may be spurious ones, i.e. there may be no significant differences between women which parallel the class division; the class boundaries thus constructed may actually divert attention from meaningful contrasts which do exist.

2 HOUSEWIVES AND LIBERATION

Whereas the first chapter of this book was addressed to the problem of sexism in sociology, this last section is devoted to the more general question of women's position in society at large. In particular it is concerned with the problem of the kind of awareness housewives have, or might be encouraged to have, of their situation as women. Do they think of themselves as an oppressed group? Does the women's liberation movement appeal to them? In what ways has organized feminism made its ideology and strategies relevant to the housewife? What kinds of tactic are most appropriate to the 'liberation' of housewives – that is, to the goal of fostering among women an understanding of the social and economic forces that mould their role in society, and of the ways in which this role is potentially open to change? Although only the question about future tactics is 'political' in the narrow sense, all such questions are 'political' in that they arise out of a particular set of values – feminist values. In other words these questions are only intelligible and important if the situation of women *is* different from that of men; if women *are* discriminated against; if gender divisions are *cultural* in origin, and if it is regarded as *desirable* that changes in women's position should be brought about. I take these conditionals as axiomatic; the case for them is argued elsewhere.[5]

Feminist values, as was pointed out in Chapter 1, may seem to coexist unhappily with the value-free stance of sociology; they are, however, simply *different* from (and hence immediately more visible than) the usual male-oriented values which inform the sociologist's perspective.[6] The overworked analogy between sex and class (or ethnic group) inequality does, as usual, drive the point home. Studies of unequal resource- or opportunity-distribution between different social classes almost invariably contain some discussion of how the inequalities could be remedied.[7] In part this is a question of raising awareness among the disadvantaged – of communicating facts and increasing aspirations. These practical issues are essentially the same for gender inequality as they are for inequalities related to class or ethnicity.

When the housewives in the present research sample were asked for their opinions on the women's liberation movement, the attitude revealed was a predominantly negative one. This is perhaps not surprising, since the interviews were carried out in early 1971 when public opinion was much less alert to the women's liberation issue than it is today. Eight of the forty women simply had not heard of the women's liberation movement, and many of the rest referred jokingly to the image portrayed by the mass media – of militant women angrily burning their bras. A few simply said that they knew about the movement, but were not personally interested in it. Of those who mentioned particular topics in this context, most cited equal pay (four disagreeing with it) or other dimensions of job discrimination against women. Two women offered coherent descriptions of more basic ways in which women are trained for second-class citizenship. One gave an account of the processes involved in socializing little girls for domesticity – an account apparently derived from her own observations as the mother of a female child and as a wife in a particularly unhappy and unequal marriage; the other, who described herself as 'a bit of a Pankhurst', talked about the 'degrading' way in which men look at women, the indignities of the Miss World contest, and how 'even in hospital [having a baby], you're talked to as though you're rubbish'.

Apart from these, most of the comments on the women's liberation theme were extremely conservative ones. A preference for retaining differences between men and women and preserving the traditional privileges of femininity were stressed, as in this answer from an ex-secretary married to a supermarket manager:

> (Have you heard of the women's liberation movement?) Yes, I have. I agree with some of their ideas, but I think they're going a bit too far. I don't think women were made to be completely equal. Most of us like to be feminine, and feel that someone is going to give up a seat on the bus for us!

A desire to maintain the status quo in marriage is in keeping with this generally conservative attitude towards gender differences. There is, apparently, no feeling that the customary feminine responsibility for home and family should be shed, or divided between husband and wife. Answers to the 'women's liberation' question may contradict what has been said earlier in the interview: this can be seen clearly in the interview with Marilyn Thornton, a plasterer's wife. About the women's movement, she said:

> I think it's ridiculous. Well, I always think it's a man's place to be head of any family, and what they're trying to do is put the woman up above the man, and it'll never work. It's degrading to the man, isn't it? I mean the way it stands at the moment, a woman's not degraded by being the level she is – I mean, I don't feel degraded because my husband goes out and earns a higher wage than what I do.

These remarks need to be set against the picture of the Thornton's marriage which comes out earlier in the interview. According to Marilyn Thornton, her husband is a rather shadowy figure in the marriage. She controls the monetary situation, pays all the bills and puts any residue in a bank account which is in her name only. He has no idea what happens to his wage packet once he has handed it over to her, and he refuses to take any financial responsibility. All decisions to do with where they live, which items are bought for the house, where they go on holiday and so forth, are made by her. She chose the names of the five children, although, in one case where he objected, she did change the name to one he found acceptable.

Marilyn Thornton jokes about being 'the boss' and says she likes it and that all her friends are the same. Clearly she is happy about an arrangement which gives her a marked degree of control over decisions to do with the house. To all intents and purposes she *is* the boss. In the comment quoted above, she implicitly denies this, saying that 'it's a man's place to be head of any family'.

In some cases inconsistencies between views stated at different points in the interview take the form of expressions of discontent which are then denied in answer to the women's liberation question. For example, a warehouse foreman's wife complained at length about her husband's freedom and predilection for spending a great deal of time and money in the pub, ending with the rhetorical question 'it's not right, is it?' She then went on to answer the women's liberation question with this remark:

> Yes, I have heard about it. I think it's daft. We're liberated enough really.

Complaints about the greater freedom of men in marriage become assertions to the effect that women's greater restriction to the home is 'only natural'. Objections to the husband's lack of participation in housework and child-care are transformed into arguments that women like being housewives. Such responses to the idea which is implicit in the question about women's liberation – that some women are seeking to change the customary pattern of women's lives – suggest considerable anxiety about the meaning and effect of gender role change. A general failure to connect with the ideas of the women's liberation movement is also indicated.

The level of concern shown by members of the women's movement with the psychological and economic position of the housewife has varied a good deal over the years since the movement first acquired an autonomous character. This variation seems to be bound up with fluctuations in class-consciousness within the movement, through an underlying tendency to identify 'the house-wife' as 'working class'.[8] Being at different times differently aware of the predominantly middle-class nature of its membership, the movement has assigned to the housewife different degrees of political importance in the total feminist struggle. At the present time there is an increasing vogue for seeing housewives at the centre of women's revolutionary potential.[9] In one sense this is obviously an accurate perception. As was pointed out at the beginning of this book the term 'housewife' can be, and is, applied to the majority of the female population. Therefore (by definition) a mass revolt of women must involve housewives as the largest single group.

On the other hand the revolutionary potential of the house-wife seems immediately to be less than that of other women. Difficulties of reaching and organizing housewives politically make them less accessible than employed women workers. A more fundamental obstacle is the tendency among housewives towards a strong psychological identification with traditional definitions of femininity. This identification is not *necessarily* greater among housewives than other groups. However, the 'fit' between socializ-ation for domesticity, adult performance of the housewife role and the other social arrangements in which housewives are often implicated (marriage and motherhood) makes for a particularly complete encapsulation within the world of traditional femininity.[10] The more closed the system, the fewer the possibilities of seeing beyond it. A mystification of the housewife's discontent closes one potential escape valve. Systematic social mechanisms for the concealment of dissatisfaction do not exist in the same way for other feminine roles. Among the practical-minded, a part-time job, further education or voluntary social/community work are the magic (but inadequate) panaceas offered to the unhappy housewife. Dissatisfaction or 'depression' among housewives is a recognized medical phenomenon; the 'cure' is thus medical, not social-structural (revolutionary).[11] Popular gender role psychology explains the complaining housewife as a 'nagging wife', an 'irritable mother' or simply as an 'hysterical woman'. The con-ventional psychoanalytical explanation is a little more profound, and hence a little more dangerous. An unsatisfied housewife is an unsatisfied wife and a maladjusted mother; the moral is that, once the wife and mother components are corrected, housework dissatisfaction will right itself.[12]

The attribution of the housewife's discontent to sources external to the housework situation serves to reinforce the identification of women with the home. It is difficult to break out of this trap. How far have the strategies of organized feminism to date helped women to escape this identification? Most of the women interviewed for this study had the idea that feminists are not interested in housewives – that they 'look down' on them, and consider the occupation inferior to a job or career outside the home. Jane Ellis's answer to the question about women's liberation conveys this point, and it is worth quoting for another reason: in her criticism of the television programme that she mentions she is reproducing one of the most common social diagnoses of housework dissatisfaction – that it is due to some personal deficiency in the woman herself:

(Have you heard of the women's liberation movement?) Yes, I have heard of it: what I don't like is their attitude that there's something wrong with being a housewife. What annoys me is that I'm happy as a housewife and a mother, but I'm sure that a lot of people are. They think it's wrong that you should be happy – they think you're a bit slow, or not intelligent enough – and that annoys me, I think it's wrong. You don't have to be an idiot to be a mother or a housewife.

I was watching a programme the other day that annoyed me intensely. There was a girl of my age, and she had three children and you saw her doing the washing, and you heard another woman talking, saying how dreadful it is to be a housewife. Quite honestly I thought, well for a start lady, you can clean your cooker – she was just sitting with her head in her hands, smoking a cigarette, utterly cheesed off, and the kids were running around screaming at her, and of course they were driving her mad. Now this annoys me, because there's no need for that – there's no need to have that attitude. Well, her children *will* scream if she sits there like that – they sense it. I'm sure she never goes anywhere, but you have to *make* the effort to make friends and to do things. This was what annoyed me, she was just sitting there feeling sorry for herself; no one asked her to have three children and be a housewife.

Jane Ellis's soliloquy expresses very well an opinion about contemporary feminists that one hears over and over again. This misapprehension seems to have something to do with the way feminists have communicated feminism to women outside the movement (although distorted reporting by the media must take part of the blame). As a feminist myself I am cautious about making a statement to the effect that 'the movement' has done this or that; I am simply offering a personal diagnosis of the situation. The diagnosis is based partly on what the housewives I interviewed had to say.

The commitment of the majority of women to conventional housewife, wife and mother roles cannot simply be seen as a consequence of their location within certain social and economic structures.[13] The centrality of traditional notions of womanhood to the psychology of women is denied by this explanation. The oppression of women is not something that can be thrown off like a raincoat when the weather changes: it is an internal malignancy that has to be painfully dug out and destroyed. Total liberation from the constraints of a divisively feminine upbringing in a decidedly sexist culture implies such an unrealistically optimistic view of the human capacity to change that it is probably never possible. We can excavate and eliminate the main source of the disease, but various hidden tributaries remain. A major – perhaps *the* major – tool of feminist revolt is a comprehensive understanding of the way in which women 'internalize their own oppression'. The logic is that structures which oppress women cannot be altered unless there is a prior awareness among women of the need for change. This awareness includes a knowledge of the resistance to change which flows from women themselves. The strategy of raising awareness is most needed in the case of the housewife, and it is precisely the failure to develop it which has negated or reduced the appeal of the movement in this area.

The raising of women's consciousness within the context of a small, supportive all-female group is at the same time the ideology and the organization of the women's movement.[14] Such a structure might seem peculiarly suited to the personal discovery by housewives of their own internalized constraints towards domestication. However, a major difficulty is that entry into this structure demands prior agreement with two other ideological axioms of women's liberation: the need to exclude men from the consciousness-raising process, and the goal of 'sisterhood' – that is, the forging of a new kind of non-competitive relationship between women.[15] Many women do not find these ideas easily acceptable.

Even within the consciousness-raising group more attention may be devoted to the subjects of sexuality and motherhood than to housework. Adherence to the media stereotype of the perfect housewife may be collectively ridiculed, but ridicule is trivialization; what is needed is a serious attempt to uncover and dissect the personal need to *be* a housewife which is at the heart of the female predicament.

Because the consciousness-raising group only reaches those who are already, in some sense, 'converted', it is necessary to find other routes of access to the sympathies of the majority of housewives. Organizing housewives around the demand 'wages for housework' has been suggested.[16] The arguments seem to be that women *should* be paid for housework, and that if they receive a wage they would then be in a position to take further political action to improve their situation. This seems to be false reasoning; a demand for wages is a move to affirm, rather than reject, the identification of women with housewifery. It is difficult to see how such a move would increase awareness of the many interconnected ways in which women are led to accept a secondary status.

A more appropriate tactic would be a direct attempt to raise women's awareness about the origins of the felt need to do housework and of the compulsion to do it in accordance with certain standards. In carrying out the research interviews I was constantly struck by the eagerness with which women talked to me about housework, and by the relief and pleasure they showed when they realized, after our first few exchanges on the doorstep, that I was interested in their feelings about housework – an area of immediate and practical concern to them. It became clear to me that, in talking about the reasons why they did housework in a certain way, many women became aware (perhaps for the first time) of the connections between their own behaviour and their upbringing. An approach to consciousness-raising couched in these terms would have the advantage of focusing on a daily concern rather than a theoretical problem. The topic of housework is a foundation that can be built upon. A thorough comprehension of gender differences, their origins and implications, can develop out of the realization of the socially imposed tie between femininity and domesticity – a realization which is, at the same time, an awareness of how women are led to acquiesce in their own subordination.

The 'deconditioned' housewife is thus a potential revolutionary.

This question of how relevant women's liberation has appeared to the majority of women is closely bound up with another difficulty: the lack of any general theoretical understanding of the development of femininity in a sexist society. Labels such as 'oppression' or 'subjection' are not able to convey a sense of the many complex processes involved in the emergence of femininity. The way forward leads, at first, backwards along the path biological females take to 'become' women. A new interest among feminists in Freudian theory stems from the realization that Freud provided a description of the psychological structures which fit women for a subjugated status in society; a feminist re-analysis of Freud has potentially a great deal to offer.[17] Freud dealt primarily with sexuality, not with domesticity. Thus systematic account needs also to be taken in this new theoretical enterprise of the development of domesticity in women. If women are to sever the bonds which tie them to the home, we must learn how these bonds are constituted. The relationship between a childhood identification with the feminine stereotype and a replication of traditional 'houseproud housewife' behaviour, demonstrated in Chapter 6, is critical here; so is the incorporation of the label 'housewife' into the self-image, which was discussed in Chapter 7. Both connect with the portrait of traditional marital roles given in Chapter 8. Whilst it can be said that the husbands of the women in the study were not reported as wanting to remedy this unequal division of labour, it is also apparent that no stimulus towards major change was discernible in the women themselves.

The systematic correction of sexism in our society is an operation which has to proceed on many different levels simultaneously. Theoretical analysis constitutes one level; another level consists of the practical measures which must be taken towards institutional equality; yet a third is concerned with the erosion of biases against women in social attitudes. To argue that a greater emphasis should be put on the need for women to amend their own gender-divisive notions of 'woman's place' is not to deny the appropriateness of action on other levels. But, beyond these kinds of action, it remains true that one major limit to the possibility of change is the capacity to envisage it.

Appendix I
Sample Selection and
Measurement Techniques

This appendix contains more detailed information about methodological aspects of the housework study than is given in the text. It covers two areas: (1) methods of selecting the forty housewives interviewed; and (2) procedures used to assess 'satisfaction' and other areas of women's responses. These assessments play a key part in the analysis of the research findings.

1 SAMPLE SELECTION

For the purposes of developing an interview schedule, ten pilot interviews were carried out some weeks before the main survey interviewing (which took place between January and March 1971). The ten respondents for the pilot interviews (five 'working class', five 'middle class' on the basis of husband's occupation) were chosen simply by knocking on doors in two areas: one working class, one middle class.

The main sample of forty women was selected from the practice lists of two general practitioners in London – one in a predominantly working-class, one in a predominantly middle-class, area. The names of potential respondents were selected from the practice lists on an alphabetical basis. Two names were selected for each letter of the alphabet – the first two names occurring of married female patients born between 1940 and 1950, with at least one child under five. These criteria were used in order to obtain a relatively homogeneous sample of young housewife-mothers. Seventy-one names were yielded by this method. Each doctor was then asked whether any physical or mental illness in his view justified the exclusion of patients from the research sample. They were also asked to indicate the ethnic group of the patients chosen, and West Indian, West African and Indian patients were then withdrawn from the sample list; those remaining were all either Irish-born or British-born women. Again, the purpose of controlling ethnic group was to increase the homogeneity of the sample. (The argument for homogeneity is given in Chapter 2.)

After excluding individuals on the basis of ethnic group, the sample size was reduced to sixty-five. The procedure then used was to call at the address given on the medical card, using the doctor's name as an introduction,[1] stating the aim of the research ('to find out what housewives think about housework') and inviting co-operation. Names were taken in alphabetical order, one from each letter in both class lists until a total of forty interviews had been obtained. The sample of forty was equally divided into working-class and middle-class groups, using the main criterion of husband's occupation (see Chapter 2). A fairly high proportion of patients in the working-class area had moved since the address on the medical card had been given; in most cases the new address was not available, but when it was, and when it was within the same local area, the potential respondent was followed up.

In sixteen cases out of the total forty, the woman agreed to be interviewed straight away. In the remaining cases an appointment was made for some future time. In no case in which a woman

Table 1   Size of sample drawn and reasons for failures to interview.

	Number
Sample drawn	65
Moved, unable to trace	16
Failed to contact	7
Contacted, not interviewed:	
(i) refused	0
(ii) offered appointment too far ahead	2
Sample interviewed	40

was contacted was there any refusal to co-operate, although in two cases the appointment offered was so far ahead (due to a sick husband and a holiday respectively) that it seemed better to substitute another respondent. Table 1 gives a summary of data relating to sample size and reasons for failure to interview. In each of the seven 'failed to contact' cases the address was visited five times,[2] over a period of a few days and at different times of the day.

The interviews were completed in one session using a tape recorder, and lasted between one and a quarter and three and a half hours, with an average of about two hours. The interview schedule is reproduced in Appendix II.

2 MEASUREMENT TECHNIQUES

A number of ratings of satisfaction and other aspects of the housewife's work situation were based on the interview responses. Levels of satisfaction with housework, child-care, marriage, employment work and life generally were assessed separately from each other. In addition an assessment was made of each woman's level of identification with the housewife role, and of the degree to which she specified standards and routines for housework activity. The marital relationship was rated as 'segregated' or 'joint' on the two areas of decision-making and leisure activities, and, lastly, an assessment was made of the husband's level of participation (as reported by his wife) in housework and child-care tasks.

One possible procedure in making ratings of this kind is to ask respondents themselves to make the assessments – for example, to place themselves on a 'scale' of satisfaction ('highly satisfied', 'satisfied', 'unsatisfied' and so forth). Although this approach has the merit of requiring no interpretation on the part of the researcher, it also has the disadvantage that different respondents may use different yardsticks in making their assessments, and the researcher has no way of judging these. A strategy similar to self-report is the use of 'standardized' questions to obtain ratings of satisfaction or some other attitudinal/behavioural dimension. Undermining the utility of both self-report and standardized

question-answer procedures is the problem of 'conventionalization' – the tendency of people to choose the socially desirable
response – which results in a reporting distortion of the
phenomenon under study.[3] Thus, for example, people tend to say
they are satisfied with marriage when asked a direct question
about marital satisfaction, since this response has a higher social
acceptability than one stating dissatisfaction. Because of the draw-
backs associated with these methods, the ratings for the research
were all undertaken by the interviewer-researcher.

(a) Satisfaction Ratings

In view of the tendency of people to respond positively when asked
for a direct report of their satisfaction, the question 'Are you
satisfied/dissatisfied with work/marriage/child-care?' was not
asked in the present survey. Instead a number of questions were
asked to elicit responses on which assessments of satisfaction/
dissatisfaction could be made.
(1) For *satisfaction with housework*, the particular questions were:
(i) 'Do you like housework?' This is clearly a focused question, but
it was employed for two reasons: first, because the more neutral
question 'What do you feel about housework?' was greeted with
some confusion in the pilot interviews. For working-class housewives it appeared to lack intelligibility, and middle-class women
tended to answer it by making general statements about their
domestic role-orientation (e.g. 'I don't mind being a housewife
really'). The second reason for using this question was that it
proved immensely useful as a 'way in' to the whole area of housework attitudes; its simplicity enabled some rapport to be established between interviewer and respondent.
(ii) A second approach was to ask about attitudes to particular
work tasks. Thus, questions were asked about six basic household activities: cleaning, shopping, cooking, washing up, washing and ironing.
(iii) A third group of questions related to the experiences of
monotony, fragmentation, excessive pace, social isolation and
'captivity' in housework. These questions formed part of the
attempt to understand the housewife's experience of housework,
but they were also asked to achieve some degree of comparability
with other studies.

(iv) Two last questions, asked in the final section of the interview, invited the housewife to compare her present work satisfaction with alternatives experienced by her in other roles, or alternatives which she might conceive of as potentially open to her. (Where these more general questions provoked responses which gave information about other areas of satisfaction – employment work, for instance – responses were taken into account in the assessment of other areas of satisfaction.)

(2) The attempt to assess *satisfaction with marriage* presented a different problem: that of how to obtain enough material in the course of one interview to cover this assessment, as well as those relating to housework, child-care and employment work. This was not only a technical problem of time and length, but also a problem of how the whole research project, and the interview in particular, was presented to the respondent. Initially, respondents were told that the study was of housewives' attitudes to housework. It was felt that detailed questions about intimate aspects of the marital relationship would be perceived by respondents as contradicting the stated aim of the research and of going beyond the interviewer's brief. The pilot interviews confirmed that the housewife tended to pick up as discrepant any attempt to ask detailed questions about the personal relationship between herself and her husband.

For these reasons there were no questions dealing explicitly with the topic of satisfaction with marriage. Questions about the division of labour in the household, about leisure activities, social relationships and decision-making were readily accepted and did not appear to involve these complications. These groups of questions were included in order to make an assessment of the 'jointness/segregation' dimension in marital role-relationships (see below), but they also provided an opportunity for the women to talk about their marriages generally.

It is probable that lower validity attaches to the assessment of marital satisfaction than to the assessment of other satisfactions, simply because this area was not explicitly covered in the interview. In some cases, much more information about the quality of the marriage was given than asked for, but such spontaneously offered information was likely to be focused on the expression of negative rather than positive feeling. The validity of the assessment the marriage was given than was asked for, but such spontaneously greater in cases of dissatisfaction than in cases of satisfaction, this latter being somewhat of a deduction based on the absence of evidence to the contrary.

(3) Unlike satisfaction with marriage, *satisfaction with child-care* was an assessment based on responses to specific questions dealing with child-care. There were questions on child-care and child-care tasks which followed those on housework, and were designed to get at the area of feelings about child-care activities. Responses to questions in the final section of the interview which invited a comparison between housework and other work were sometimes answered in terms of satisfaction or dissatisfaction with child-care. For instance, a number of housewives said 'the children' or 'the baby' was the 'best thing' about being a housewife. This indicates a positive attitude towards children and some satisfaction, at least, with child-care activities. Mention of positive satisfaction seemed as likely to occur as mention of dissatisfaction. Indeed, there appeared to be a certain amount of reluctance in some cases to admit dissatisfaction openly; this is discussed in the text (see Chapter 9).

(4) A specific section in the interview schedule dealt with the topic of attitudes to employment work; on the basis of answers to these questions an assessment of *satisfaction with employment work* was made. The questions covered the housewife's employment work history, the advantages and disadvantages of each job she had held, and reasons for choosing these jobs and changing from one to another. In all cases except two employment work satisfaction was assessed in relation to the housewife's main previous job. The two exceptions were Pauline Cutts, the one housewife who was employed full time, and Sally Jordan, who held a five-morning-a-week job at a local factory.

(5) The remaining area of satisfaction – that with *life in general* – was assessed using relevant responses from any point in the interview. Although no particular reliance was placed on answers to specific questions, all the questions in the last section of the schedule were oriented towards the production of relevant material. The interviews themselves suggest that general satisfaction at this stage of the life cycle – young motherhood – is more critically dependent on the acceptance/rejection of domesticity than the other dimensions of satisfaction. What seemed to be important was the value to the individual of 'being' a housewife/

wife/mother. Thus the concepts of satisfaction with marriage, child-care and work are all more intimately bound up with the day-to-day rewards and deprivations of role-performance than is satisfaction with life in general.

In addition to the inclusion of groups of questions covering these areas of satisfaction, two further provisos influenced the assessment of satisfaction. Firstly, relevant spontaneous comments made at any point in the interview were included in the responses on which the assessments of satisfaction were based. As Brown and Rutter observe:

> In the course of a lengthy interview, respondents quite commonly spontaneously express negative feeling which they have denied in response to a direct question; or fail to express positive feeling which may have been expected from their answers to direct questions.[4]

A second proviso was that the assessments of satisfaction should take into account two kinds of subjective material – the 'verbal' and the 'vocal'.[5] On the one hand there are self-reports of feelings ('I get very irritated shut up in the house all day') and on the other there are feelings expressed in non-verbal aspects of speech such as tone, pitch and rhythm. There may be times during an interview when the verbal meaning of what the respondent says is reinforced by the vocal aspects of speech, but there may also be occasions when the two are discordant. In these instances the vocal dimension may offer an essential clue to the respondent's actual feelings. In the assessments of satisfaction for the present survey it was found particularly important to take into account the quality of the feelings housewives expressed spontaneously, i.e. unprompted by direct questions. There was often a discrepancy between these spontaneously offered feelings and those stated in response to direct interview questions.

The criteria used to assess what constitutes 'satisfaction' and 'dissatisfaction' were those which Kornhauser has described as 'simple, commonly accepted ideas' about what these conditions represent in terms of people's expressed attitudes and feelings.[6] The meaning and justification of such an approach, as Kornhauser says,

> rest largely upon the 'face validity' of the indexes – that is, upon the apparent reasonableness of the response material as

indicative of what is ordinarily believed to characterize mental health [satisfaction/dissatisfaction] in our culture.[7]

A further test of 'common-sense' measures is their 'relational fertility' – the extent to which their relationships with other variables appear to be meaningful.[8]

Housewives who, in these interviews, made statements of unhappiness or generally negative feeling in relation to housework, employment work, marriage, child-care or life generally were assessed as 'dissatisfied' or as 'very dissatisfied' if such statements dominated their overall interview response in each of these areas. Those who showed evidence of predominantly positive feeling were rated as 'satisfied' or as 'very satisfied'. The scale adopted for each area of satisfaction was a four-point one: 'very satisfied', 'satisfied', 'dissatisfied', 'very dissatisfied': it thus covers the two distinct dimensions of negative and positive feeling. The scale is collapsed into a two-point one – satisfied/dissatisfied – in the analysis of findings.

The use of a bipolar scale instead of unipolar scales needs some explanation. It has been shown that, generally speaking, the separate assessment of positive and negative feeling is a more reliable procedure than the use of scales which combine the two.[9] This is because inconsistent or ambivalent feelings may be expressed in the interview situation; in relation to the same object, event or person there may be a contradiction between feelings stated at one point in the interview and those expressed at another. The use of unipolar scales ensures that all feeling is recorded. It dispenses with the difficult task of weighting the positive comments against the negative ones, and is an important tool in minimizing the chances of the 'halo effect' – the tendency for raters to record more consistently than is warranted by the data their generalized impressions of the respondent.

The pilot interviews for the present survey were approached with the advisability of unipolar scales in mind. It was thought likely, for instance, that housewives would express ambivalent feelings in relation to housework, and that it would therefore be necessary to record positive and negative dimensions of feeling separately. In practice, however, such ambivalence was not found on any significant level. This does not mean that no negative feeling was expressed by a housewife assessed as satisfied, or that 'dissatisfied' housewives expressed no positive feeling. However, it does mean that these combinations did not, in the researcher's opinion, warrant the label of 'ambivalence', nor was it felt that the use of a scale covering both positive and negative feeling would result in substantial loss of validity. Bipolar scales were therefore used. Given this choice an appropriate procedure would have been to use several raters to minimize the possibility of halo effect. This proved difficult to arrange for various technical reasons, but one procedure was adopted which, it is hoped, goes some way towards the reduction of halo effect. The procedure used involved rating by satisfaction area rather than by respondent. Thus, a work satisfaction rating was made for housewives numbered one to forty, then a marriage satisfaction rating for housewives numbered one to forty, and so on. No name was recorded on the tape itself, and no name was included on the interview response schedule at this stage.

Very careful attention was paid to the problem of 'contamination' between separate ratings: this applies not only to the assessments of satisfaction but to the ratings made in other areas. Different interview material was, of course, used for each assessment area. This is clearly necessary if the relationship between the different ratings are to have any substantive meaning. For example, it does not make sense to look at possible relationships between satisfaction with marriage and husband's level of participation in the division of labour if both have been assessed using the same data: any relationship would be spurious. (This does not mean that information about marital satisfaction conveyed by the respondent's *tone of voice* in the course of describing her husband's division of labour cannot be counted towards the assessment of marital satisfaction: such information is of a different order from the data about which tasks the husband does in the home.)

(b) Other Ratings

Many of the above remarks also apply to the non-satisfaction ratings made on the interview material. The attempt to reduce halo effect, to avoid overlap between different ratings, and to take account of spontaneous remarks made by respondents holds equally for these other ratings. The particular questions/interview areas used to make this general group of ratings were as follows:

(i) *Identification with the housewife role* was assessed using material from Sections F ('Domestic Role Identity'), G ('Attitudes to the Domestic Role') and I ('Sources of Role Identity') of the interview schedule. The women were categorized as 'high', 'medium' or 'low' on this dimension.

(ii) The rating of *specification of standards and routines* was based on Sections C ('Domestic Work Routine'), D ('Attitudes to Work Tasks') and E ('Specification of Standards and Routines'), and on any other relevant comments. There were three categories: 'high', 'medium' and 'low'.

(iii) The *segregation/jointness dimension of marriage* was assessed on the basis of the women's descriptions of leisure activities and decision-making in marriage. These descriptions were obtained in Sections J1 and J2 of the interview, which covered various aspects of marriage relating to the housewife's work. Each marriage was assessed as 'segregated' or 'joint'.

(iv) Another aspect of marriage – *the husband's level of participation in housework and child-care* – was assessed separately, on the basis of answers which gave information about the husband's level of help. Ratings were made of the husband's participation as 'high', 'medium' or 'low' in the two areas of housework and child-care separately.

Some examples of the satisfaction and other ratings made are given in the text (for example, pages 63–4 on housework satisfaction, pages 101–3 on standards and routines, pages 117–8 on identification, pages 138–9 on the division of labour, pages 149–50 on marriage satisfaction). For the curious reader who wishes to pursue the matter further, detailed examples of each rating are cited in full elsewhere.[10]

Appendix II
Interview Schedule

A BACKGROUND DATA

1 Name, address and age of respondent
2 Number, sex and ages of children
3 Children at playgroup/childminder/nursery school/primary school? Which child and for how many hours each day?
4 Occupation of husband
5 Hours of husband's work-absence from home
6 Present occupation of wife, if any (any *paid* work whether done at home or outside home)
7 Hours of wife's paid work-absence from home
8 Who looks after the children while wife is out at work?
9 Wife's education
    (a) Education to 15
    (b) Education to 15 + 1–2 years training/further education
    (c) Education to 16, O Level + 1–2 years training/ further education *or* school till 17–18
    (d) School till 18 + 1–2 years training/further education
    (e) School till 18 + university
    (f) School till 18 + university + extra training/further education

B DOMESTIC WORK CONDITIONS

1 Number in household (for whom housewife cooks)
2 Type of home

    (a) House
    (b) Flat
    (c) Rooms
    (d) Furnished
    (e) Unfurnished
    (f) Rented, council
    (g) Rented, other
    (h) Owned

3 Amenities
    (a) Separate kitchen
    (b) Inside lavatory
    (c) Bath
    (d) Running hot and cold water
    (e) Garden/play area
    (f) Within five minutes' walk of shops
    (g) Within five minutes' walk of launderette
    (h) Within ten minutes' walk of school/playgroup/nursery
    (i) Separate bedrooms for parents and children
    (j) Television
    (k) Telephone

(A score was obtained for the possession of amenities. (a) to (j) scored 1, (k) scored $\frac{1}{2}$. A shared kitchen scored $\frac{1}{2}$; so did an outside lavatory and running cold water only. Maximum score is 10$\frac{1}{2}$.)

4 Household aids
    (a) Washing machine (type?)
    (b) Mechanical drier (type?)
    (c) Vacuum cleaner
    (d) Refrigerator
    (e) Separate freezer
    (f) Dishwasher
    (g) Central heating
    (h) Car/use of car
    (i) Other
    (j) Paid domestic help
    (k) Use of commercial services (e.g. laundry)

(A score was obtained for the possession of aids. (a) to (d), (g) and (j) above scored 1; (e) (f) (h) (i) and (k) scored $\frac{1}{2}$. Garden plus inside drying space scored $\frac{1}{2}$. Maximum score is 8$\frac{1}{2}$.)

C DOMESTIC WORK ROUTINE

Now, can I ask you about what you do on an ordinary day? What
about yesterday? Was yesterday out of the ordinary in any way?
Could you please tell me everything you did, beginning with when
you woke up?
Could you tell me what happens during the rest of the week?
And at the weekend?

D ATTITUDES TO WORK TASKS

I'd like to ask you now about all the things you do as a housewife.
Do you like housework?
(a) Household tasks
     1 Cleaning (tidying, dusting, polishing, vacuuming)
     2 Household shopping
     3 Cooking
     4 Washing up
     5 Washing
     6 Ironing
     7 Mending
     8 Buying/making clothes
     9 Buying/making house durables
(b) Children
     1 Physical care of children: getting up and dressing, put-
       ting to bed, nappy changing, other
     2 Feeding children
     3 General supervision of children
     4 Playing with children
     5 Buying/making/mending children's clothes
     6 Buying/making children's toys
     7 Taking children out
Then ask:
 1 Do you find housework monotonous on the whole?
 2 Do you find you can think about other things while you're
    working?

3 Do you find you have too much to get through during the day?

4 Do you ever feel as though you're on your own too much in the daytime? (n.b. 'on your own' means *with* the children)

5 Do you feel you have enough time to yourself?

6 Would you like more time/some time away from the housework and the children? If yes, what would you do with it?

E SPECIFICATION OF STANDARDS AND ROUTINES

1 Would you say you have particular ways of doing things (standards) you regularly keep to in housework?

2 Is it important to you to keep to these standards?

3 Why do you think it's important/not important?

4 What sort of things (if any) would make you drop/lower your standards?

5 How do you feel when you've got the house as you like it?

6 How do you feel when you haven't managed to get your work done as you like it?

7 What do you think are the most important things a housewife should do?

8 On a day when you've got too much to do, which things do you put first?

9 Would you say you have a fixed routine you keep to in doing your housework? (Compared to other people you know?)

10 Have you always had a routine? Why do you think you have one?

11 Is it important to you to keep to your routine?
Why do you think it's important?
How do you feel when you have to change it?

12 What sorts of things (if any) make you change your routine?

F DOMESTIC ROLE IDENTITY

Ten Statements Test

Could you please write on this card ten answers to the question 'Who am I?' (addressed to yourself). Try to give the answers as

though you were answering the question to yourself, not to some-
body else. Just write down what occurs to you: don't stop to
think about it. (A maximum of fifteen minutes was allowed for
this test.)

G ATTITUDES TO THE DOMESTIC ROLE

Probe on results of Ten Statements Test
(E.g. You have written in second place 'I am a mother'. How
important do you think this is to you?)

H ATTITUDES TO PAID WORK AND PAID WORK ROLES

1   What sort of job did you do before you got married? Length
    of time? (And for other jobs, if more than one?)

(The following questions to be asked in relation to main previous
job – the one held for the longest period; if no such job, then
last job held.)
2   Why did you choose that?
3   Did you enjoy it?
4   What did you enjoy about it?
5   Was there anything about it you didn't like?
6   Why did you stop working?
7   How did you feel about stopping?
8   Have you ever felt you would like to be back at work? If
    yes, why haven't you gone back to work?
9   Would you like to work now? If yes, why don't you?
10 Do you think you will go back to work eventually? If yes,
    when? If no, why not?

(If working outside the home now)
11 Have you always worked since you got married? If yes, has
    it been difficult in any way? Why have you continued to
    work?
    If no, why did you give it up? Why did you start working
    again?

12 Why do you work now?
13 Do you enjoy your work?
14 What do you enjoy about it?
15 Is there anything you don't like about it?

(All respondents)
16 What do you feel in general about mothers working?
17 Does your husband agree with you?

I SOURCES OF ROLE IDENTITY

(a) Female Role Model
Establish who brought respondent up: mother, stepmother, grandmother, etc.
(Assuming mother):
1 Did your mother work outside the home when you were a
   child? If yes, do you know why she worked?
2 Does your mother work now? If yes, what does she do?
   Do you know why she works? If no, why not? Do you feel
   she's happy with the situation?
3 Do you think your mother was happy as a housewife when
   you were young?
4 What sort of housewife is your mother?
(b) Identification with Female Role Model
1 Do you remember helping your mother round the house when
   you were a child? At what age do you think you started to
   do that? Did she ask you to? What did you feel about it?
   Did your brothers/sisters help too? If no/not much: what
   did you feel about this?
2 What would you say were your mother's main interests when
   you were young?
   Do you remember having any particular feelings about this?
3 When you were older – say 13 or 14 – do you remember
   whether you wanted to be like your mother?
   For instance, did you want to get married and have children?
   Did you expect to work when you were married?
   Did you want to train for any career?
(c) Parental Expectations

With reference to end of full-time education:
1 What did your mother want you to do? Was it her idea you should leave school at – ? What did she want you to do next?
2 And how about your father? Did he agree with your mother on this?
3 Whose advice did you follow, and why?
4 (Employment) Did your mother/father approve of that job? If yes, why? If no, why not?
5 Was you mother/father pleased when you got married? If yes, why? If no, why not?
6 Was your mother/father pleased when you had children? (When – was born?) If yes, why? If no, why not?
(d) Present Relationship with Mother
1 How do you get on with your mother at the moment?
2 How often do you see her? (Speak to her on the telephone?)

J1 THE MARITAL RELATIONSHIP: ORGANIZATION OF ACTIVITIES

(a) Household tasks
Does your husband help occasionally or regularly with the housework?
Specify, and ask how many times last week: —
1 Cleaning house
2 Household shopping
3 Cooking
4 Washing up
5 Washing
6 Ironing
(b) Children
Does he help occasionally or regularly with the children?
Specify, and ask how many times last week: —
1 Physical care of children: getting up and dressing; putting to bed; nappy changing; other
2 Feeding children
3 General supervision of children
4 Playing with children
5 Taking children out

6 Getting up at night
(c)   Leisure Activities
1 What do you do in the evenings?
   (i)   together
   (ii) wife separately
   (iii) husband separately
2 How often do you go out and where?
   (i)   together
   (ii) wife separately
   (iii) husband separately
3 What do you do at weekends?
   (i)   together
   (ii) wife separately
   (iii) husband separately

J2 THE MARITAL RELATIONSHIP: CONTROL OVER DOMESTIC WORK CONDITIONS

(a)   Financial
1 Do you know how much your husband earns?
2 How do you divide it? (i) Do you take it all and give your husband pocket money? (ii) Does your husband give you a fixed allowance? (iii) Do you share it, according to how much each of you needs from week to week?
If (i) who decides how much *he* should have?
If (ii) who decides how much *you* should have? What do you do when you need a rise in your housekeeping? Are you usually successful in getting it?
If (iii) do you quarrel over how much each of you should have?
3 Do you have an allowance for yourself separate from the housekeeping?
If yes, who decides how much? Do you tell your husband (have to tell your husband) what you spend it on?
If no, do you mind? How do you decide how much of the housekeeping to spend on yourself? (Tights, cosmetics, etc.)
4 Who pays the bills? Rates? Electricity? Rent? Gas?
If two or more children:

5   Do you add the family allowance to the housekeeping, or do you keep it for something in particular?

6   What is the housekeeping meant to cover?
    (i)   Food
    (ii) Rent
    (iii) Fuel
    (iv) Clothes and shoes (entire family)
    (v)   Other expenses connected with children (school meals, playgroup fees, etc)
    (vi) Entertainment

If outside job:

7   Is the money you earn your own so far as your husband is concerned? Can *you* decide what to do with it?
    If yes, has he always taken this view?
    If no, do you mind?

8   What do you usually spend your wages on?

9   How much do you earn?

10 Is it important to you to have some money you know is your own/you have earned?
    If yes, why?
    If no, why not?

If no outside job:

11 What do you do for money when you want to buy your husband a present?

12 Does it bother you at all, having to ask him for money?
    If yes, why?
    If no, why not?

13 Would you like to have some money of your own (i.e. by working?

(b)   The House

1   If house owned (mortgaged): do you own it together, or is it in your husband's name only?

2   Who decided to live here? (Buy/rent this particular flat/rooms/house?)
    (i)   Husband
    (ii) Wife
    (iii) Both
    (iv) Circumstances

3   Do you like this house/flat/rooms?
    If not, why not: have *you* tried to do anything about it?

4 Do you find it suitable for children?
If no, what is wrong with it?

5 Would you like to move? Does your husband agree with you?
If yes, what stops you? If you want to move and he doesn't, whose decision is final?

6 If you wanted to buy something for the house – say a washing machine – would you (i) ask your husband to buy it/save for it for you; (ii) buy it/save for it yourself; (iii) buy it/save for it together?

7 If you said you needed something for the house, would he argue with you, or would he trust your opinion?

8 If you need to call a plumber or builder, do you or your husband do so?

9 Who decides what sort of meals you have?
    (i) Do you like the same sort of food anyway?
    (ii) Do you cook the food he likes?
    (iii) Do you cook the food you like?
    (iv) Do you cook a mixture of the things you both like?
If (ii) why? What happens if you don't?
If (iii) does he mind?

10 Are there any things he is particularly fussy about in the house (e.g. tidiness upon arrival home, well-ironed shirts)?
If yes, do you feel he has a right to be fussy?
Do you make a special attempt to do these things for him?
Do you feel it's your (a wife's) duty?

(c) *The Children*

1 Did you decide to have children, or did they just happen?
If decided, who decided, and did the other agree?

2 Are you happy with the number of children you have?
Does your husband agree with you?
If no, why not?

3 Who chose the children's names?

4 Who decided where the child/children should go to school and when? (Or playgroup or nursery, and why in these cases?)

5 Who sees the child's teacher/headmistress/headmaster?

6 Does your husband feel strongly about how the children should be brought up? (e.g. good manners, religion, discipline?)
If yes, do you agree with him?

If no, do you feel that he appreciates what you are doing for them?

7 Do you feel that overall you have enough say in things to do with the house and the children?
If no, why not, in what respects and what are the consequences of this for you?

K GENERAL SATISFACTION

1 Do you ever feel there is anything else you would rather be doing now – apart from being a housewife and mother, that is?
If yes, what?

2 If you could have the last ten years over again, would you do anything differently?

3 When you feel really happy these days, what sort of thing is it that makes you feel like that?

4 And when you feel really down/fed up, what sort of thing is it that makes you feel like that?

5 Would you describe yourself as generally satisfied, or unsatisfied with life – or neither, particularly?

6 If you compare your life now with what it was like before you became a housewife and a mother, would you say you are happier now, less happy, or about the same?

7 What would you say are the best things about being a housewife?
And the worst?

8 Before you became a housewife, did you have any ideas about what it would be like? What were they? Were they right?

9 Did you expect, for instance, to enjoy housework? Having children? Looking after children? Looking after your husband?

10 When you fill in a form, and you write 'occupation housewife', what do you feel about that?

11 Do you think that women work as hard, harder, or not so hard as their husbands?

12 Do you think that women get a better or worse deal in

marriage than men?

13 Do you believe that women are generally inferior to men?
   If yes, how?
   If no, are they the same or superior? How are they different?

14 Do you agree with men doing housework and looking after
   children?

15 What would you think of a marriage in which the wife went
   out to work, and the husband stayed at home to look after
   the children?

16 Do you envy your husband ever?
   How, when, and why?

17 Do you think there are any ways in which women are treated
   unfairly in this country at the moment? (e.g. pay, tax,
   national insurance?)

18 Have you heard of the women's liberation movement?
   If yes, what do you think of it?

Notes

CHAPTER 1

1 P. B. Bart 'Sexism in Social Science: From the Gilded Cage to the Iron Cage, or, the Perils of Pauline' *Journal of Marriage and the Family* (1971) **33**, p. 735
2 See Ann Oakley *Sex, Gender and Society* London: Maurice Temple Smith (1972)
3 Anna Coote and Tess Gill *Women's Rights: A Practical Guide* Harmondsworth: Penguin Books (1974)
4 See the analysis in Ann Oakley *Woman's Work* New York: Pantheon (1974) Chapter 4 'The Situation of Women'
5 Thus sociology is racist as well as sexist. See J. A. Ladner (ed.) *The Death of White Sociology* New York: Random House (1973)
6 C. Wright Mills *The Sociological Imagination* New York: Oxford University Press (1959) p. 21
7 For example, A. Myrdal and V. Klein *Women's Two Roles* London: Routledge and Kegan Paul (1956)
8 For example, Sheila Rowbotham 'Women's Liberation and the New Politics' in M. Wandor (ed.) *The Body Politic* London: Stage I (1973)
9 See S. Firestone *The Dialectic of Sex* London: Paladin (1972); Oakley *op. cit.* 1974, Chapter 9 'Breaking the Circle'; also, on gender roles, A. Rossi 'Equality between the Sexes: An Immodest Proposal' in R. J. Lifton (ed.) *The Woman in America* Boston: Houghton Mifflin (1956)
10 F. Heidensohn 'The Deviance of Women' *British Journal of Sociology* (1968) **19**, p. 171
11 Much functionalist analysis of deviance commits this error. The view argued is that, while male deviance can be interpreted in terms of the centrality to men of the occupational/financial syndrome, female deviance characteristically involves the violation of sexual mores because sexual relationships with men are a key component of the adult feminine role. See A. Cohen *Delinquent Boys* London: Routledge and Kegan Paul (1955)
12 An instance is the interpretation proposed by G. H. Grosser 'Juvenile Delinquency and Contemporary American Sex Roles' (unpublished Ph.D. thesis, Harvard, 1951)
13 In Britain the 1972 figures for people found guilty of offences were 1,661,300 males and 164,900 females. Central Statistical Office

Annual Abstract of Statistics 1973 London: HMSO Table 74

14 P. Sainsbury 'Suicide, Delinquency and the Ecology of London' in W. G. Carson and P. Wiles (eds.) *Crime and Delinquency in Britain: Sociological Readings* London: Martin Robertson (1971) p. 73

15 J. Davies and N. Goodman *Girl Offenders Aged 17 to 20 Years* Home Office Research Studies No. 14 London: HMSO (1972) p. 1, p. 3

16 The category of violent female crime is increasing. See Davies and Goodman *op. cit.* p. 6

17 B. Wootton *Social Science and Social Pathology* London: Allen and Unwin (1959) p. 318

18 T. C. N. Gibbens and J. Prince *Shoplifting* Institute for Study and Treatment of Delinquency (1962)

19 M. Gold 'Undetected Delinquent Behaviour' in M. E. Wolfgang, L. Savitz and N. Johnston (eds.) *The Sociology of Crime and Delinquency* New York: John Wiley (1970)

20 D. A. Ward and G. C. Kassebaum *Women's Prison: Sex and Social Structure* London: Weidenfeld and Nicholson (1966); R. Giallombardo *Society of Women* London: John Wiley (1966)

21 See, for example, J. A. Bryan 'Apprenticeships in Prostitution' *Social Problems* (1965) **12**, pp. 287–97, and N. R. Jackman, R. O'Toole and G. Grieg 'The Self-Image of the Prostitute' *Sociological Quarterly* (1963) **4**, pp. 150–61.

22 J. Cowie, V. Cowie and E. Slater *Delinquency in Girls* London: Heniemann (1968)

23 Moreover females are still excluded from research samples on the grounds that there are too few of them. See J. W. B. Douglas, J. M. Ross, W. A. Hammond and D. G. Mulligan 'Delinquency and Social Class' in Carson and Wiles (eds.) *op. cit.*

24 See D. Downes *The Delinquent Solution* London: Routledge and Kegan Paul (1966) p. 32

25 *Ibid.* A relevant question here concerns the sex of the person who investigates delinquent or criminal gang-culture. Can a male investigator – and all those who have studied the topic have been men – expect to be accepted by female deviants as a bona fide person to carry out a study of them?

26 Downes *op. cit.* p. 251. Peter Willmott has a chapter on 'Girls, Sex and Marriage' in his *Adolescent Boys of East London* Harmondsworth: Penguin Books (1969)

27 J. P. Ward 'Adolescent Girls: Same or Different'. Paper given at British Sociological Association Annual Conference at Aberdeen, Scotland, April 7th–10th (1974)

28 See the discussion in Cohen *op. cit.*

29 M. Rutter in *Maternal Deprivation Reassessed* Harmondsworth: Penguin Books (1972) discusses the literature on maternal employment and children's 'anti-social' behaviour. See especially p. 61.

30 See Chapter 6

31 O. Pollak *The Criminality of Women* University of Pennsylvania Press (1950)

32 In part, of course, the conceptual and empirical confusions surrounding the place of women in stratification theory are a result of basic confusions and problems within this theory. In this chapter I am not aiming to deal with these general issues.

33   *Statistical Abstract of the United States 1971*, Tables 6, 8 and 44
     US Bureau of the Census (1971)
34   General Register Office (1968) *Sample Census 1966 England and
     Wales* Household Composition Tables, Table I
35   W. B. Watson and E. A. Barth 'Questionable Assumptions in the
     Theory of Social Stratification' *Pacific Sociological Review* (1964)
     7, pp. 10–16
36   General Register Office *op. cit.*
37   E. Haavio-Mannila 'Some Consequences of Women's Emancipation'
     Journal of Marriage and the Family (1969) 31, pp. 123–34
38   Recent amendments to British Inland Revenue procedures have made
     it possible for a husband and wife to be separately assessed, if they
     so wish. However, this makes no difference to the amount of tax
     they have to pay: the basis for the assessment is still the married
     couple as a unit. (Thus, for example, the husband still receives the
     married man's allowance for a wife.)
     A second clause alternatively allows a married woman to have her
     earnings assessed as if she were a single woman. (This is only
     advantageous if the couple pay more than the standard rate of tax.)
     The husband must give his consent to the wife's choice of assess-
     ment on a single woman basis. Information about these procedures
     is, of course, initially conveyed on a tax return guide addressed to
     the husband, the second paragraph of which is entitled 'wife's
     income'.
39   See D. V. Glass (ed.) *Social Mobility in Britain* London: Routledge
     and Kegan Paul (1954) p. 6
40   J. Acker 'Women and Social Stratification: A Case of Intellectual
     Sexism' *American Journal of Sociology* (1973) 78, p. 942
41   It is sometimes argued that since gender is a dichotomy – feminine/
     masculine – it is not meaningful to talk about 'stratification', which
     implies the notion of hierarchy, in this context. However, there is
     no reason why a duality cannot be hierarchical. The two classes –
     capitalists and wage-labourers – of Marxist analysis are obviously
     hierarchically arranged, for example.
     To argue that stratification by gender exists is clearly not to deny
     the existence of other types of stratification.
42   G. E. Lenski *Power and Privilege* New York: McGraw Hill (1966)
     pp. 402–6, is one such reference
43   R. Collins 'A Conflict Theory of Sexual Stratification' in H. P.
     Dreitzel (ed.) *Family, Marriage and the Struggle of the Sexes* Recent
     Sociology No. 4 New York: Macmillan (1972)
44   Oakley *op. cit.* 1972, expands these distinctions
45   Some of Collins' statements are very peculiar, e.g. 'Father-daughter
     incest is by far the most common form of incest, especially if the
     mother is dead or absent' (p. 76). His theory about 'low-technology
     tribal' societies asserts that in such cultures, among other common
     characteristics, 'norms favouring premarital sexual permissiveness
     are found' and that 'superior male force can be used to enforce
     sexual property rights' p. 62). The Greek mountain shepherds
     described by J. K. Campbell in *Honour, Family and Patronage*
     (Oxford: Clarendon Press 1964) provide a counter-example on the
     first point – the premium on female chastity is strong here, as it is
     generally in Mediterranean peasant communities. J. Henry's study

of the Kaingang of Brazil, *Jungle People* (New York: Vintage Books 1964) portrays a low-technology community in which sexual aggressiveness is not the prerogative of the men: it is shared by both sexes.

46 F. Parkin *Class Inequality and Political Order* London: MacGibbon and Kee (1971) pp. 14–5

47 Such questions are, as Ronald Frankenberg pointed out in a recent paper ('Community Life and the Interaction of Production Systems: The Source of Sex Differentiation and the Genesis of Gender', paper given to British Sociological Association Annual Conference, Aberdeen, Scotland, April 7–10 (1974), significantly unasked in community studies where their relevance is especially acute. Frankenberg considers James Littlejohn's study of *Westrigg* (London: Routledge and Kegan Paul 1963) the best in this respect. Littlejohn argues, for example, that the function of *maintaining* the family's status is a central responsibility for the working-class wife (p. 123).

48 See, for example, Jean Gardiner 'Political Economy of Female Labour in Capitalist Society'. Paper given to British Sociological Association Annual Conference, Aberdeen, Scotland, April 7–10 1974
    A paper by Robin Oakley ('Comparative Perspectives on Gender as a Structural Principle') which was delivered at the same conference examines the importance of gender as a structural principle using anthropological data.

49 See Ann Oakley 'The Family, Marriage and Its Relationship to Illness' in D. Tuckett (ed.) *The Sociology of Medicine* London: Tavistock Publications (forthcoming)

50 S. Giner *Sociology* London: Martin Robertson (1972) p. 145

51 P. Worsley 'The Distribution of Power in Industrial Society' in *The Development of Industrial Societies* Sociological Review Monograph No. 8, University of Keele (1964) p. 17

52 E. Katz and P. F. Lazarsfeld *Personal Influence* Glencoe: Free Press (1964) p. 160

53 OED

54 An article by M. Harrington entitled 'Co-operation and Collusion in a Group of Young Housewives' *Sociological Review* (1964) **12**, pp. 255–82 discusses some allied themes.

55 I.e. about different topics and in different social- and work-situations.

56 M. Gluckman 'Gossip and Scandal' *Current Anthropology* (1963) **4**, p. 307. Anthropology also gives more attention than sociology to the notion of informal power. Women are often mentioned in this context; see, for instance, Ian Cunnison's *Baggara Arabs* Oxford: Clarendon Press (1966) pp. 116–18

57 L. Tiger and R. Fox *The Imperial Animal* London: Secker and Warburg (1971) pp. 200–1

58 See some of the passages in C. Hole *A Mirror of Witchcraft* London: Chatto and Windus (1957). One seventeenth-century writer said witches were more likely to be women than men because women are 'more tongue ripe' (p. 30).

59 See Ann Oakley 'Changes in Childbirth' in J. Mitchell and A. Oakley (eds.) *Women and Change* London: Allen Lane (forthcoming)

60 R. Fletcher *The Family and Marriage in Britain* Harmondsworth: Penguin Books (1966)

61 See the contributions in J. N. Edwards (ed.) *The Family and Change* New York: Knopf (1969)

62 H. Gavron *The Captive Wife* Harmondsworth: Penguin Books (1966)

63 See, for example, F. I. Nye and L. W. Hoffman *The Employed Mother in America* Chicago: Rand McNally (1963)

64 A. Cartwright and M. Jefferys 'Married Women Who Work: Their Own and Their Children's Health' *British Journal of Preventive Social Medicine* (1958) **12**, pp. 159–71

65 N. Y. Metherey, F. E. Hunt, M. B. Patton and H. Heye 'The Diets of Preschool Children' *Journal of Home Economics* (1962) **54**, pp. 297–308

66 P. Jephcott *Married Women Working* London: Allen and Unwin (1962) p. 19

67 E. Ginzberg, I. E. Berg, C. A. Brown, J. L. Herma, A. H. Yohalem and S. Gorelick consider this in relation to middle-class women in *Life Styles of Educated Women* New York: Columbia University Press (1966) but there is no parallel analysis for the working-class woman.

68 It is customary in studies of child-rearing to draw the data from mothers only. This is the practice adopted in, e.g., J. and E. Newson *Patterns of Infant Care* Harmondsworth: Penguin Books (1965)

69 Quoted in P. B. Bart *op. cit.* p. 736

70 Central Statistical Office *Annual Abstract of Statistics 1973* London: HMSO Table 139

71 On 'feminine' occupations generally see Oakley *op. cit.*, 1974, Chapter 4. M. Wray has studied women in textiles in *The Woman's Outerwear Industry* London: Duckworth (1957); there are a few historical studies of domestic work, such as J. J. Hecht *The Domestic Servant Class in Eighteenth Century England* London: Routledge and Kegan Paul (1956) and D. Marshall *The English Domestic Servant in History* London: Historical Association Pamphlet (1949); Leonore Davidoff is now systematically studying this area: see *The Best Circles* London: Croom Helm (1973) and 'Mastered for Life: Servant and Wife in Victorian England'. Paper delivered to the Anglo-American Conference on Labour History, April 1973, Rutgers, New Jersey (to be published *Journal of Social History*, June 1974) Teaching, nursing and social work are described as 'semi-professions' in A. Etzioni (ed.) *The Semi-Professions and Their Organization* New York: Free Press (1969)

72 *1971 Advance Census Analysis* London: HMSO (1973)

73 S. R. Parker, R. K. Brown, J. Child and M. A. Smith *The Sociology of Industry* London: Allen and Unwin (1967) p. 117

74 As in Parker *et al. op. cit.*, Chapter 4 'Industry and the Family'.

75 This interpretation is suggested by A. Hunt in *A Survey of Women's Employment* Government Social Survey, London: HMSO (1968) Volume I, p. 181, and by V. Klein in *Working Wives* London: Institute of Personnel Management (1957) p. 24

76 R. Blauner *Alienation and Freedom* University of Chicago Press (1964) p. 81

77 R. Wild and A. B. Hill *Women in the Factory: A Study of Job Satisfaction and Labour Turnover* London: Institute of Personnel Management (1970)

78 J. Bernard 'My Four Revolutions: An Autobiographical History of

the A.S.A.' *American Journal of Sociology* (1973) **78**, pp. 773–91

79   H. Draper 'Marx, Engels and Women's Liberation' *Female Liberation* (1971)

80   A. Mitzman *The Iron Cage: An Historical Interpretation of Max Weber* New York: Knopf (1970) p. 279

81   Quoted by J. and H. Schwendinger 'Sociology's Founding Fathers: Sexists to a Man' *Journal of Marriage and the Family* (1971) **33**, p. 784

82   It might be objected that Comte was hardly sane when he devised this scheme. However the stance taken to women in it is consistent with views expressed elsewhere in his writings.

83   Quoted in S. Lukes *Emile Durkheim: His Life and Work* London: Allen Lane (1973) p. 185

84   H. Becker and H. E. Barnes *Social Thought from Lore to Science* Washington: Harren Press (1952) p. 570

85   I. Berlin *Karl Marx: His Life and Environment* Oxford University Press (1939) pp. 78–9

86   Lukes *op. cit.*, p. 99

87   See Schwendinger and Schwendinger *op. cit.* on the early American sociologists.

88   C. Wright Mills 'The Professional Ideology of Social Pathologists' in I. L. Horowitz (ed.) *Power, Politics and People* New York: Oxford University Press (1967) p. 527

89   The level of awareness is not much higher these days. A 1969 survey of 'Some Trends in the Social Origins of American Sociologists' by N. D. Glenn and D. Weiner in *American Sociologist* 5, pp. 291–302, excludes women from the sample altogether.

90   H. M. Hughes (ed.) *The Status of Women in Sociology 1968–72* American Sociological Association (1973)

91   See Tessa Blackstone and Oliver Fulton *Sex-discrimination among University Teachers: A British–American Comparison* (forthcoming). A motion was accepted at the 1974 Annual Conference of the British Sociological Association to set up a committee with the brief of investigating the position of women in sociology.

92   *Ibid* p. 26

93   J. Plamenatz *Ideology* London: Macmillan (1970) p. 15

94   Two examples are S. Thorsell 'Employer Attitudes to Female Employees' in E. Dahlstrom (ed.) *The Changing Roles of Men and Women* London: Duckworth (1967); C. F. Epstein (on the stereotyping of career women as 'unfeminine') in *Woman's Place: Options and Limits in Professional Careers* University of California Press (1970)

95   F. Herzberg, B. Mausner, R. Peterson and D. Capwell *Job Attitudes: Review of Research and Opinion* Psychological Service of Pittsburgh (1957) p. 14

96   V. Vroom *Work and Motivation* New York: John Wiley (1964) p. 42

97   *Ibid* p. 31

98   Myrdal and Klein do devote some space to a discussion of housework hours and ways of 'rationalizing' housework. Myrdal and Klein *op. cit.* pp. 35–9, pp. 174–7

99   H. Lopata *Occupation Housewife* New York: Oxford University Press (1971) p. 35

226 THE SOCIOLOGY OF HOUSEWORK

100 Gavron *op. cit.* p. 131
101 See C. Erlich 'The Male Sociologist's Burden: the Place of Women in Marriage and Family Texts' *Journal of Marriage and the Family* (1971) 33, pp. 421–30; and J. L. Laws 'A Feminist Review of the Marital Adjustment Literature: the Rape of the Locke' *Journal of Marriage and the Family* (1971) 33, pp. 483–516
102 Oakley *op. cit.* (1974) Chapter 7 'Myths of Woman's Place: I The Division of Labour by Sex'.
103 M. Zelditch 'Role Differentiation in the Nuclear Family: A Comparative Study' in T. Parsons and R. F. Bales *Family, Socialization and Interaction Process* London: Routledge and Kegan Paul (1956) p. 313

CHAPTER 2

1 Audrey Hunt *A Survey of Women's Employment* Government Social Survey London: HMSO (1968) Volume I, p. 5. This definition allows men who are responsible for household duties to be classed as housewives. However, men in this situation are not in *practice* assigned to the category 'housewife' e.g. in income tax regulations, or for national insurance and social security purposes.
2 See, for example, relevant chapters of Michael Fogarty, Rhona Rapoport and Robert N. Rapoport *Sex, Career and Family* London: Allen and Unwin (1971); R. K. Kelsall, Anne Poole, and Annette Kuhn *Graduates: the Sociology of an Elite* London: Methuen (1972)
3 Margaret Stacey *Methods of Social Research* Oxford: Pergamon Press (1969) p. 6
4 C. A. Moser *Survey Methods in Social Investigation* London: Heinemann (1958) p. 73
5 Michael Young and Peter Willmott *The Symmetrical Family* London: Routledge and Kegan Paul (1973) p. 294
6 See George W. Brown 'Some Thoughts on Grounded Theory' *Sociology* (1973) 7, pp. 1–16
7 Johan Galtung *Theory and Methods of Social Research* London: Allen and Unwin (1967) p. 341
8 Elizabeth Bott *Family and Social Network* London: Tavistock Publications (revised edition 1971)
9 J. M. and R. E. Pahl *Managers and Their Wives* London: Allen Lane (1971)
10 Hannah Gavron *The Captive Wife* Harmondsworth: Penguin Books (1966)
11 The Pahls do not set out to generalize: 'we do not spell out precise hypotheses or relate our material to a precise scholarly universe' (*op. cit.* p. 12)
12 Various factors (amount of domestic help employed, possession of cars and so on) do suggest that the middle-class segment of the sample is probably less 'upper' middle-class than the middle-class samples included in some other studies.
13 See Galtung *op. cit.* pp. 372–3
14 Moser *op. cit.* p. 300

15 William J. Goode and Paul K. Hatt *Methods in Social Research*
New York: McGraw Hill (1952) p. 256
16 For the second and third years the rate was £425, but the differential between the 'married woman' rate and the full grant (raised to
£550) was maintained.
17 See pp. 129–32
18 In their *Patterns of Infant Care* Harmondsworth: Penguin Books
(1965) pp. 152–3
19 Hunt *op. cit.* Volume 11, p. 151
20 Lee G. Burchinal and Lloyd L. Lovell 'Relation of Employment
Status of Mothers to Children's Anxiety, Parental Personality and
P.A.R.I. Scores' Unpublished Manuscript No. 1425 *Agricultural and
Home Economics Experiment Station* Ames, Iowa, Iowa State
University (1959)
A study reported by Powell found that mothers of pre-school children who were *full-time housewives* showed a slightly greater
tendency than other mothers to reject the housewife role (Kathryn
Powell 'Family Variables' p. 235, in F. Ivan Nye and Lois W.
Hoffman (eds.) *The Employed Mother in America* Rand McNally
1963).

CHAPTER 3

1 Dorothy Hopper 'But We Must Cultivate Our Gardens' p. 25 in
Beverly Benner Cassara (ed.) *American Women: the Changing Image*
Boston: Beacon Press (1962)
2 Helen Lopata in *Occupation Housewife* New York: Oxford University Press (1971) reports a similar finding (p. 35)
3 Martin Patchen *Participation, Achievement and Involvement on the
Job* Prentice-Hall (1970) p. 234
4 A particularly clear illustration of this is given in Suzanne Gail's
perceptive description of the housewife's work in Ronald Fraser
(ed.) *Work: Twenty Personal Accounts* Harmondsworth: Penguin
Books (1968) p. 141.
5 David Lockwood *The Blackcoated Worker* London: Allen and
Unwin (1958) p. 123
6 Shortly before the interviews took place, an issue of a Sunday newspaper magazine carried an article on the housewife role, portraying
on the front cover a picture of a cabbage. This may have influenced
the incidence of 'cabbage' responses.
7 See Chapter 7
8 Betty Friedan in *The Feminine Mystique* London: Victor Gollancz
(1963) discusses the whole question of images presented to women via
the advertising industry.
9 The Newsons' table (John and Elizabeth Newson *Patterns of Infant
Care* Harmondsworth: Penguin Books, 1965, p. 198) shows class
differences in the ownership of washing machines in a larger sample.
According to their figures, washing machine ownership varies from
seventy-two per cent in classes I and II to twenty-six per cent in
class V.

CHAPTER 4

1 Alva Myrdal and Viola Klein *Women's Two Roles* London: Routledge and Kegan Paul (1956) p. 151–2
2 Colin Rosser and Christopher Harris *The Family and Social Change* London: Routledge and Kegan Paul (1965) p. 208
3 Mirra Komarovsky *Blue Collar Marriage* New York: Vintage Books (1967) p. 55
4 Arthur Kornhauser 'Towards an Assessment of the Mental Health of Factory Workers: A Detroit Study' *Human Organization* (1962) **21**, p. 45
5 Basil Bernstein *Class, Codes and Control: Volume I Theoretical Studies Towards a Sociology of Language* London: Routledge and Kegan Paul (1971)
6 *Ibid.* p. 46
7 *Ibid.* p. 61
8 See Harold Rosen's pamphlet, obtainable from the Falling Wall Press. Bernstein discusses some of these criticisms in the introduction to *Class, Codes and Control.*
9 Rosser and Harris *op. cit;* Komarovsky *op. cit.*
10 John and Elizabeth Newson *Four Years Old in an Urban Community* Harmondsworth: Penguin Books (1970) p. 162 and p. 445
11 Komarovsky *op. cit.* p. 49
12 This concept is formulated and discussed by (among others) Elton F. Jackson 'Status Consistency and Symptoms of Stress' *American Sociological Review* (1962) **27**, pp. 469–80; Gerhard Lenski 'Status Crystallization: A Non-Vertical Dimension of Social Status' *American Sociological Review* (1954) **19**, pp. 405–13; R. J. Pellegrin and F. L. Bates 'Congruity and Incongruity of Status Attributes Within Occupations and Work Positions' *Social Forces* (1959) **38**, pp. 23–8
13 There is some relationship (p<.10) between the status of the husband's job and the housewife's satisfaction with life generally. This would appear to reflect on the importance of the husband's job as a determinant of the couple's life-style.
14 In all cases except two, occupational status (and employment work satisfaction) was assessed in relation to the job the housewife held for the longest period prior to giving up paid work. The two exceptions were Pauline Cutts, a full-time secretary, and Sally Jordan, who held a five-morning-a-week factory job.
15 Nurses, for example, are often said to have the advantage of a worthwhile job (as against the disadvantage of not being paid very much for doing it).

CHAPTER 5

1 For a brief survey of factors associated with job satisfaction see S. R. Parker 'The Subjective Experience of Work' in S. R. Parker, R. K. Brown, J. Child and M. A. Smith *The Sociology of Industry*

London: Allen and Unwin (1967)

2 Peckham Rye Women's Liberation Group, Paper on Housework in *A Woman's Work is Never Done* London: Agitprop (1971)

3 John H. Goldthorpe, David Lockwood, Frank Bechhofer and Jennifer Platt *The Affluent Worker: Industrial Attitudes and Behaviour* Cambridge: University Press (1968) p. 17

4 Twenty-six (ninety-three per cent) of the twenty-eight women dissatisfied with housework said 'yes' to the fragmentation question, compared with ten (eighty-three per cent) of the twelve who were satisfied.

5 See Edwin A. Locke 'What is Job Satisfaction?' *Organizational Behaviour and Human Performance* (1969) 4, pp. 309–36

6 For some women this concept of housework as 'mindless' work appears to be part of the self-concept; when writing about themselves later in the interview they say 'I am a dreamer'.

7 See Chapter 9

8 Jason Ditton 'Absent at Work: Or How to Manage Monotony' *New Society* (21 December 1972) p. 680

9 Thirteen (forty-six per cent) of the twenty-eight work-dissatisfied women say they have too much to do, compared with seven (fifty-eight per cent) of the twelve satisfied housewives.

10 See, for example, Goldthorpe *et al. op. cit;* Martin Patchen *Participation, Achievement and Involvement on the Job* Prentice-Hall (1970)

11 See Chapter 6

12 'Satisfaction with life generally' was assessed particularly on the basis of answers to questions in the last section of the interview. See Appendix I.

13 Patchen *op. cit.* p. 70

14 Hannah Gavron *The Captive Wife* Harmondsworth: Penguin Books (1966)

15 Herbert Gans *The Levittowners* New York: Pantheon (1967) pp. 225–34

16 See, for example, F. Herzberg, B. Mausner and B. B. Snyderman *The Motivation to Work* New York: John Wiley (1959)

17 See Chapter 9

18 Theodore Caplow *The Sociology of Work* University of Minnesota Press (1954) p. 285

19 These studies are:
    Rural
    Maud Wilson 'Use of Time by Oregon Farm Homemakers' *Oregon Experiment Station Bulletin 256* (November 1929); US Bureau of Home Economics survey, cited in Wilson *op. cit.*; May L. Cowles and Ruth P. Dietz 'Time Spent in Homemaking by a selected group of Wisconsin Farm Homemakers' *Journal of Home Economics* (January 1956); Alain Girard and Henri Bastide 'Le Budget-Temps de la Femme Mariée dans la Campagne' *Population* (1959) pp. 253–84
    Urban
    US Bureau of Home Economics survey, reference as above; Bryn Mawr 'Women During the War and After' (1945) cited in Alva Myrdal and Viola Klein *Women's Two Roles* London: Routledge and Kegan Paul (1956) pp. 36–7; Jean Stoetzel 'Une Etude de Budget-Temps de la Femme Mariée dans les Agglomérations

Urbaines' *Population* (1948) pp. 47–62; C. A. Moser 'Social Research: the Diary Method' *Social Service* (1950) **24**, pp. 80–4; Mass Observation Bulletin No. 42 (May/June 1951) *The Housewife's Day*; Alain Girard 'Le Budget-Temps de la Femme Mariée dans les Agglomérations Urbaines' *Population* (1958) pp. 591–618

20 Eighteen of the twenty-eight housewives (sixty-four per cent) who work seventy-one hours or more a week are dissatisfied with work: so are ten of the twelve (eighty-three per cent) whose working week amounts to a total of seventy hours or less.

21 Some were cited in Chapter 3

22 F. Herzberg, B. Mausner, R. Peterson and D. Capwell *Job Attitudes: Review of Research and Opinion* Psychological Service of Pittsburgh (1957) p. 74

23 The figures are as follows: for aids, eight (fifty-seven per cent) of the fourteen women with a score of less than three are dissatisfied, compared with twenty-one (eighty-one per cent) of those who have a score of three or more; for amenities, thirteen (sixty-eight per cent) of the nineteen housewives with a score of less than eight are dissatisfied, as against fifteen (seventy-one per cent) of the twenty-one with a score of eight or more.

24 Herzberg, Mausner and Snyderman *op. cit.* p. 82

25 Arthur Kornhauser *Mental Health of the Industrial Worker* New York: John Wiley (1965) p. 264

CHAPTER 6

1 Material used for this assessment came from Sections C, D and E of the interview schedule. The interviewer's own assessment of the state of the house was also taken into account in some cases. There was an obvious difference between housewives who were interviewed by appointment and those who were interviewed immediately the interviewer first called; those with appointments might be expected to have, in some sense, 'prepared' the house for the interviewer's eyes. Thus, only in cases where the housewife could not have altered her behaviour in this way – where she agreed to be interviewed immediately - was the interviewer's assessment of the state of the house taken into account.

2 There are two theoretically separate issues here. First, there is the *degree* of specification: how precise (or lacking in precision) is the definition and how rigidly (or flexibly) is it followed? Then there is the question of the *kind* of standards and routines set. How 'high' (or 'low') relative to those of the other women are the standards set? How repetitive (or non-repetitive) are the routines? In theory it would be possible for a housewife to have a 'low', i.e. loose, specification of standards and routines which are 'high' and 'repetitive' compared to those of other housewives. Conversely, it could be imagined that there might be a high, i.e. precise, specification of relatively low standards and flexible routines. In practice, however, such combinations were not found in this sample.

All the assessments of standards- and routines-specification made (like the other measures used in the research) do not, necessarily, have absolute validity: they are, strictly speaking, assessments of the forty housewives *in relation to one another.*

3 John Cooper 'The Leyton Obsessional Inventory' *Psychological Medicine* (1970) **1**, pp. 48–64

4 The houseproud housewives were chosen by local authority health visitors who considered them 'unusually houseproud or perfectionist in their approach to housework and child-rearing'. Twenty-one of the sixty normal women were selected as controls for the houseproud group, and the remaining thirty-nine were obtained 'in any way which was convenient, being friends, relatives, acquaintances, colleagues and members of research units in nearby offices' (*Ibid.* p. 54).

5 See Victor H. Vroom *Work and Motivation* New York: John Wiley (1964) p. 132

6 The normal women were not a statistically representative group (see note 4). A representative sample might have modified the results and drawn the scores of houseproud and normal groups closer together.

7 Ten of the normal men were husbands of the control group of normal women, and thirty-one were obtained in the same way as the majority of the normal women.

8 Betty Friedan *The Feminine Mystique* London: Victor Gollancz (1963)

9 *Ibid.* p. 241

CHAPTER 7

1 Ruth Hartley 'A Developmental View of Female Sex Role Identification' in B. J. Biddle and E. J. Thomas (eds.) *Role Theory* New York: John Wiley (1966)

2 See, for example, Tessa Blackstone 'The Education of Girls' in Juliet Mitchell and Ann Oakley (eds.) *Women and Change* (forthcoming); Carole Joffe 'Sex Role Socialization and the Nursery School: As the Twig is Bent' *Journal of Marriage and the Family* (1971) **33**, pp. 467–75; Lenore J. Weitzman, Deborah Eifler, Elizabeth Hokada and Catherine Ross 'Sex Role Socialization in Picture Books for Preschool Children' *American Journal of Sociology* (1972) **77**, pp. 1125–50

3 Hartley *op. cit.* p. 357

4 *Ibid.*

5 'Identification with the housewife role' is used instead of 'identification with the mother', because some women were not brought up by their mothers. One was reared by her grandmother, one by an older sister, and one in an orphanage.

   Identification was assessed on the basis of Sections F, G and I of the interview, and also on the basis of spontaneous comments made throughout the interview.

6 For references to studies which argue social class differences see Chapter 4.

7   Ruth Hartley 'Children's Perceptions of Sex-Role Activity in Child-hood' *Journal of Genetic Psychology* (1964) **105**, pp. 43–5
8   Rhona Rapoport and Robert Rapoport *Dual Career Families* Harmondsworth: Penguin Books (1971)
9   In 1971 just over half the female work-force was concentrated in three industries (out of a possible twenty-four in the Standard Industrial Classification): distributive trades, miscellaneous services (laundries, dry cleaning and so on), and professional/scientific services, which so far as women are concerned means teaching and nursing. Max Hanna 'The Typecast Third' *New Society* (1 February 1973).
      On this theme generally see Ann Oakley *Woman's Work* New York: Pantheon (1974), Chapter 4 'The Situation of Women'
10   Albert Bandura and Aletha C. Huston 'Identification as a Process of Incidental Learning' in Thomas D. Spencer and Norman Kass (eds.) *Perspectives in Child Psychology* New York: McGraw-Hill (1970)
11   *Ibid.* p. 384
12   *Ibid.*
13   Manford H. Kuhn and Thomas S. McPartland 'An Empirical Investi-gation of Self-Attitudes' *American Sociological Review* (1954) **19**, pp. 68–76; Manford H. Kuhn 'Self-Attitudes by Age, Sex and Profes-sional Training' *Sociological Quarterly* (1960) **1**, pp. 40–55; Thomas S. McPartland and John H. Cumming 'Self Conception, Social Class and Mental Health' *Human Organization* (1958) **17**, pp. 24–9
14   Kuhn and McPartland *op. cit.* pp. 72–3
15   Kuhn *op. cit.* pp. 47–8. Kuhn suggests that the salience of sex for women is a consequence of their minority group position in society. Another factor is the greater salience of marriage, and thus of 'pair-bonding' for women – Kuhn found early mentions of their sex by women in the Twenty Statements Test to be most frequent in adolescence and early adulthood.
16   Ernest Q. Campbell 'The Internalization of Moral Norms' *Sociometry* (1964) **27**, p. 392.
17   Basil Bernstein *Class, Codes and Control: Volume I Theoretical Studies Towards a Sociology of Language* London: Routledge and Kegan Paul (1971) p. 153
18   Conrad M. Arensberg *The Irish Countryman* Gloucester, Mass: Peter Smith (1959) p. 53
19   Alexander J. Humphreys *New Dubliners: Urbanization and the Irish Family* London: Routledge and Kegan Paul (1966) p. 126
20   *Ibid.* p. 141
21   See Chapter 8 for more on this point
22   Conrad M. Arensberg and Solon T. Kimball *Family and Community in Ireland* Cambridge, Mass: Harvard University Press (1940) p. 79
23   Martin Patchen *Participation, Achievement and Involvement on the Job* Prentice-Hall (1970) pp. 96–7

CHAPTER 8

1   Audrey Hunt *A Survey of Women's Employment* Government Social Survey London: HMSO (1968) Volume II, p. 3

2   See Dalmar Hoskins and Lenore E. Bixby *Women and Social Security: Law and Policy in Five Countries* United States Department of Health, Education and Welfare (1973)

3   Inland Revenue, income tax notes for guidance, 1973, paragraph 21: 'Housekeeper or person looking after children. *Subject to certain conditions,* an allowance of £75 is given (a) if you are a widower or widow and you have a *female* relative resident with you as a house-keeper: (b) if you are unmarried and you maintain your mother (being a widow or separated from her husband) or some other *female* relative resident with you to look after a brother or sister of yours for whom child allowance is given' (italics added).

4   Leonard Benson *Fatherhood: A Sociological Perspective* New York: Random House (1960) p. 310 and p. 302

5   Michael Rutter and George W. Brown 'The Reliability and Validity of Measures of Family Life and Relationships in Families Containing a Psychiatric Patient' *Social Psychiatry* (1966) **1**, pp. 38–53

6   John and Elizabeth Newson *Four Years Old in an Urban Community* Harmondsworth: Penguin Books (1970), p. 548

7   A class difference is reported for an American sample by Melvin L. Kohn and Eleanor E. Carroll 'Social Class and the Allocation of Parental Responsibilities' *Sociometry* (1960) **23**, pp. 372–92

8   Hannah Gavron *The Captive Wife* Harmondsworth: Penguin Books (1966) p. 91 and p. 93

9   *Ibid.* p. 162

10 Robert O. Blood and Donald M. Wolfe *Husbands and Wives* New York: Free Press (1960) p. 60

11 Elizabeth Bott *Family and Social Network* London: Tavistock Publications (revised edition 1971)

12 Sections J1 and J2 of the interview schedule provided material on which these assessments were made.

13 These studies include the portraits of segregated-role working-class marriages given in the British community studies, for example Norman Dennis, Fernando Henriques and Clifford Slaughter *Coal is Our Life* London: Eyre and Spottiswoode (1956); M. Kerr *The People of Ship Street* London: Routledge and Kegan Paul (1958); and Michael Young and Peter Willmott *Family and Kinship in East London* London: Routledge and Kegan Paul (1957). Two parallel American studies are Mirra Komarovsky *Blue Collar Marriage* New York: Vintage Books (1967), and Lee Rainwater, Richard P. Coleman and Gerald Handel *Workingman's Wife* New York: Oceana Publications (1959)

14 Jessie Bernard's *The Future of Marriage* London: Souvenir Press (1973) develops this idea of two marriages; she has two separate chapters entitled 'The Husband's Marriage' and 'The Wife's Marriage'.

15 In Table 8.4 nine joint role marriages are discrepant (i.e. 'low') in the area of housework participation, and eight for child-care; the cases of discrepancy between segregated role marriages and high/medium levels of domestic participation number two for housework and seven for child-care.

16 Bott *op. cit.* pp. 53–5. She gives no indication in her discussion of methodological procedures as to whether she attached particular importance to any one of the three areas (division of labour, leisure

activities, and decision-making) in her assessments of segregation/
jointness. Almost the only point she makes of relevance to this is
one about the adequacy of the data itself: 'the data on modes of
organization ... were not collected with quantification in mind so
that we did not make exactly the same observations or ask exactly
the same questions of each couple' (*Ibid.* p. 55).

17 Barbara E. Harrell-Bond 'Conjugal Role-Behaviour' *Human Relations*
    (1969) **22**, pp. 77–91
18 Jennifer Platt 'Some Problems in Measuring the Jointness of Con-
    jugal Role-Relationships' *Sociology* (1969) **3**, p. 291
19 D. M. Toomey 'Conjugal Roles and Social Networks in an Urban
    Working Class Sample' *Human Relations* (1971) **24**, pp. 417–31
20 *Ibid.* p. 429
21 Although Bott seems to stress the normative dimension, usage slips
    in the direction of overt behaviour practices in some of her discus-
    sion.
22 The historical tradition of women's productive work outside the
    home (and before industrialization, of course, within it) is a long
    one. The twentieth-century increase in married women's employment
    is a post-second world war development, but it was not until the
    early years of this century that working-class women really 'retired'
    into full-time domesticity.
23 There is a small tendency for work satisfaction to be associated
    with joint roles and for work dissatisfaction to be higher among
    those with segregated roles. (This relationship is not significant at
    the five per cent level.)
24 Marital satisfaction was assessed on the basis of spontaneous com-
    ments made throughout the interview, but particularly on the feel-
    ings expressed about marriage in sections J1 and J2 of the interview.
25 Satisfaction with child-care was assessed on the basis of responses
    given to sections D and G of the interview, and any spontaneous
    comments made were also taken into account.
26 Rhona Rapoport and Robert Rapoport *Dual Career Families*
    Harmondsworth: Penguin Books (1971) p. 286
27 An alternative explanation is, of course, that women who are
    satisfied with child-care put pressure on their husbands to share
    housework.
28 Section K of the interview schedule contained questions focused on
    satisfaction with life generally.
29 J. M. and R. E. Pahl *Managers and Their Wives* London: Allen
    Lane (1971) p. 114 and p. 126
30 The Newsons comment 'Husbands often seemed to be disgusted by
    the job of nappy changing and "drew the line" here for this reason'.
    John and Elizabeth Newson *Patterns of Infant Care in an Urban
    Community* Harmondsworth: Penguin Books (1965) pp. 135–6
31 The significance of pram-pushing as a traditional index of femininity
    is alluded to by Titmuss in a discussion of 'Industrialization and the
    Family' (one of the essays in *Essays on the Welfare State* London:
    Allen and Unwin 1958).
    Titmuss comments on the increased domestication of men in modern
    family life: 'One has only to notice the way in which husbands
    now do the shopping, take the laundry to the launderette (perhaps
    because the wife has been out to work), play with the children, and

unashamedly push prams, to realize that family life in industrialized Britain is changing' (p. 117) (italics added).

32 For a dissection and criticism of beliefs in 'the maternal instinct' see Ann Oakley *Woman's Work* New York: Pantheon (1974) Chapter 8 'Myths of Woman's Place: II Motherhood'

33 Lois W. Hoffman 'Parental Power Relations and the Division of Household Tasks' in F. Ivan Nye and Lois W. Hoffman (eds.) *The Employed Mother in America* Rand McNally (1963)

34 This point is made by Ruth Hartley 'Some Implications of Current Changes in Sex Role Patterns' *Merrill-Palmer Quarterly* (1960) **6**, pp. 153–64, and also by Helen Z. Lopata *Occupation Housewife* New York: Oxford University Press (1971)

35 Bott *op. cit.* p. 54

36 Platt *op. cit.* p. 288

37 See, for example, Blood and Wolfe *op. cit.* p. 51; Hunt *op. cit.* **1**, p. 117; and Newson and Newson *op. cit.* (1965) p. 135

38 Toomey *op. cit.* p. 419

39 *Ibid.*

40 Michael Young and Peter Willmott *The Symmetrical Family* London: Routledge and Kegan Paul (1973) p. 94

41 *Ibid.* p. 331

42 *Ibid.* p. 95

CHAPTER 9

1 For a discussion of the notion of 'productivity' in the housewife's situation see Wally Secombe 'Housework Under Capitalism' *New Left Review* (Jan–Feb 1974)

2 'Did you decide to have children, or did they just happen?'

3 One such study is Jean Morton Williams and Keith Hindell *Abortion and Contraception: A Study of Patients' Attitudes* PEP Broadsheet 536 (March 1972)

4 Lee Rainwater and Carol Jane Weinstein *And the Poor Get Children* Chicago: Quadrangle Books (1960) p. 50, p. 52

5 An overall test of association between child-care satisfaction and housework satisfaction (Yules Q) produces a positive association of 0.25, which is not high.

6 Lee Rainwater, Richard P. Coleman and Gerald Handel *Workingman's Wife* New York: Oceana Publications (1959) pp. 88–9

7 Michael Fogarty, Rhona Rapoport and Robert N. Rapoport *Sex, Career and Family* London: Allen and Unwin (1971) p. 246

8 Eighty-one per cent (seventeen) of the twenty-one housewives with planned families are satisfied with child-care, as against fifty-three per cent (ten) of the nineteen who have one or more unplanned child. Number of children is not the answer to the question of why satisfaction with child-care is lower among working-class women: six of the twelve women with three or more children are dissatisfied with child-care, but six are satisfied.

9 See Lee Comer 'The Myth of Motherhood' Spokesman Pamphlet No. 21 (1972)

10	Those women who showed a high degree of ambivalence were classed as 'dissatisfied'. The use of a bipolar scale (satisfied-dissatisfied), although appropriate in the other areas of satisfaction used in the research, turned out to be less so for child-care: hence the need to take into account answers to the question 'Do you like looking after the child/children?', in which ambivalence is manifested.

11	John and Elizabeth Newson *Patterns of Infant Care in an Urban Community* Harmondsworth: Penguin Books (1965) p. 152

CHAPTER 10

1	Lee Rainwater, Richard P. Coleman and Gerald Handel *Workingman's Wife* New York: Oceana Publications (1959) p. 32 and p. 41

2	Mirra Komarovsky *Blue Collar Marriage* New York: Vintage Books (1967) p. 49

3	It should be noted that the range of differences in length of education among women in the sample was quite restricted. Twenty-seven of the forty left school at sixteen or before, and, of the remaining thirteen, most completed their education at seventeen – only one was a university graduate.

4	Arthur Kornhauser 'Towards an Assessment of the Mental Health of Factory Workers: A Detroit Study' *Human Organization* (1962) **21**, p. 45. The three educational categories are 'grade school', 'some high school' and 'high school graduate'.

5	See Ann Oakley *Sex, Gender and Society* London: Maurice Temple Smith (1972); Ann Oakley *Woman's Work* New York: Pantheon (1974)

6	'Value-neutrality' is thus often simply a cover for patriarchy. (See the example of functionalism cited in Chapter 1.)

7	This is particularly true in the sociology of education. For example Olive Banks in *The Sociology of Education* London: Batsford (1968), has a section called 'Education and the Underprivileged'.

8	So far as a consciousness of oppression/exploitation is concerned, both these groups do, of course, present similar problems.

9	See, for example, Selma James 'Sex, Race and Working-Class Power' *Race Today* (January 1974)

10	This draws attention to the fact that the discussion in this chapter is particularly oriented towards the 'problem' (vis-à-vis women's liberation) of full-time housewives with young children; it is probably equally relevant to older women who are full-time housewives. But the argument also covers any woman who, through self-categorization or social classification, answers to the label 'housewife'.

11	Harriet Holter in *Sex Roles and Social Structure* Oslo: Universitetsforlaget (1970) p. 240, points out that the syndrome 'housewife's disease' is described in the Yearbook of Neurology, Psychiatry and Neurosurgery.

Anti-depressants, tranquillizers and psychotropic drugs generally are handed out in far greater numbers to women than to men by the medical profession. See Michael Balint, John Hunt, Dick Joyce, Marshall Marinker and Jasper Woodcock *Treatment or Diagnosis:*

A Study of Repeat Prescriptions in General Practice London: Tavistock Publications (1970)

12 This type of explanation is not, so far as I know, to be found in Freud's work; it is 'popularized' psychoanalysis. A representative example is Theodore Lidz's *The Person: His Development Throughout the Life Cycle* New York: Basic Books (1968). Lidz says, in a chapter on 'Occupational Choice': 'Most women recognize, even if the colleges they attend do not, that being a good wife, and even more, being a good mother, requires many refined abilities and skills and forms a career in itself. *Dissatisfaction with this limiting career will often arise; this will be discussed in the chapter on marital adjustment*' p. 384 (italics added).

It is interesting to note that the association between housework dissatisfaction and dissatisfaction with marriage in the present sample of forty housewives is low: 0.25 (Yules Q). Looking at possible relationships between different areas of satisfaction in this way, the largest statistical relationship is between housework satisfaction/dissatisfaction and satisfaction/dissatisfaction with life generally (the association is 0.45).

13 In a recent analysis, 'Housework Under Capitalism' *New Left Review* (January–February 1974), Wally Secombe discusses the relationship between housework and the housewife's consciousness. His argument seems to commit precisely this error: of assuming that the commitment to housewifery follows from, rather than precedes, involvement in housework. Secombe says: 'In the absence of a paycheck to justify her toil, the housewife must account for her work in non-economic terms. Hers is a "labour of love performed out of a devotion to her family"... Often, therefore, her alienation from her work must be repressed from consciousness, lest she implode with guilt and feelings of personal inadequacy. The end result of this is that housework takes on the appearance of an arrangement of destiny, a natural female vocation and duty' (p. 20). This is not the *end* result; the housewife *brings to* her situation an already formed belief in housework as a feminine vocation.

14 See 'Organizing Ourselves' and 'The Small Group' in Micheline Wandor (compiler) *The Body Politic: Writings from the Women's Liberation Movement in Britain 1969–72* London: Stage I (1972)

15 These two axioms are interconnected. The politics of woman-woman relationships in a sexually divided society are shaped by competition between women for men. Hatred of other members amounting to self-castigation is a characteristic of minority group status generally: see Helen Hacker 'Women as a Minority Group' *Social Forces* (1951) pp. 60–9. Partly for this reason, and partly because dual-sex political meetings tend to be marked by female deference to male authority, consciousness-raising is impeded by the presence of men. Sexism in male attitudes and behaviour may be uncovered within the consciousness-raising group, but it is best tackled outside it. For an excellent account of sexual politics in housework see Pat Mainardi 'The Politics of Housework' in Robin Morgan (ed.) *Sisterhood is Powerful* New York: Vintage Books (1970)

16 Selma James 'Women, the Unions and Work' pamphlet, Crest Press (1972)

17 See Juliet Mitchell *Psychoanalysis and Feminism* London: Allen
    Lane (1974)

APPENDIX I

1 Hannah Gavron in *The Captive Wife* Harmondsworth: Penguin Books
   (1966) used the same procedure. It is obviously important, when mentioning a doctor's name in this way, to clear up any possible confusion
   in the respondent's mind about why she/he was chosen. For example,
   in the case of a survey about housework, a woman might think she was
   being interviewed because the doctor suggested her name as an example
   of a particularly 'good' or 'bad' housewife. In carrying out the
   present research interviews, I made a point of explaining that the
   names were selected at random.
2 Three visits are usually held to be the minimum acceptable. See
   C. A. Moser *Survey Methods in Social Investigation* London:
   Heinemann (1958) p. 135
3 See Vernon H. Edmonds 'Marital Conventionalization: Definition
   and Measurement' *Journal of Marriage and the Family* (1967) **23**,
   pp. 681–8
4 George W. Brown and Michael Rutter 'The Measurement of Family
   Activities and Relationships' *Human Relations* (1966) **19**, p. 246
5 This distinction is made by W. F. Soskin 'Some Aspects of Communication and Interpretation in Psychotherapy', paper read to American
   Psychological Association, Cleveland, September 1953
6 Arthur Kornhauser 'Towards an Assessment of the Mental Health
   of Factory Workers: A Detroit Study' *Human Organization* (1962)
   21, p. 43
7 *Ibid.* p. 44
8 *Ibid.* p. 30
9 Brown and Rutter *op. cit.*
10 Ann Oakley 'Work Attitudes and Work Satisfaction of Housewives'
   unpublished Ph.D. thesis, University of London, 1974

Index

239

About the Author

Dr. Ann Oakley is Research Officer at Bedford College, University of London. She is the author of *Sex, Gender and Society* (1972) and of *Woman's Work* (1974), is a member of the London Women's Liberation Workshop, and has written many articles about women's roles and situations for various journals and magazines. She is currently working on a study of childbirth in contemporary society.

Women's Studies from Pantheon

The Charlotte Perkins Gilman Reader:
The Yellow Wallpaper and Other Fiction
edited by Ann Lane (1980)
A collection of the work of the nineteenth-century feminist.
0-394-73933-7 $4.95

Herland: *A Lost Feminist Utopian Novel*
by Charlotte Perkins Gilman (1979)
Herland describes a society of women discovered by three male explorers who then must re-examine their assumptions about women and their roles in society. "A pure delight...a serendipitous discovery."
—Susan Brownmiller
0-394-73665-6 $2.95

The Sociology of Housework
by Ann Oakley (1975)
Oakley challenges the conventional trivialization of housework.
0-394-73088-7 $3.95

Subject Women
by Ann Oakley (1981)
A richly documented assessment of where women stand today—
economically, politically, socially, emotionally.
0-394-74904-9 $7.95

We Were There:
The Story of Working Women in America
by Barbara Wertheimer (1977)
A narrative history of women's work from pre-colonial times to the present. "The best single volume of the history of American working-class women."—Herbert Gutman
0-394-73257-X $6.95

Women's Work, Women's Health:
Myths and Realities
by Jeanne M. Stellman (1978)
Lays to rest several historical myths about women's working and childbearing years.
0-394-73452-1 $5.95

Working It Out:
23 Women Writers, Artists, Scientists and Scholars
Talk About Their Lives and Work
edited by Sara Ruddick and Pamela Daniels (1977)
Candid assessments of the rewards and dilemmas of creative work.
0-394-73452-1 $5.95

3